KATE LARKINDALE

Evernight Teen ®

www.evernightteen.com

KATE LARKINDALE

DEDICATION

For the readers

If you've picked up this book, or any of my others, this one's for you.

ACKNOWLEDGEMENTS

The romantic vision of a writer's life sees them sitting alone, banging out words until the book is finished. In reality, it takes a village to get a book from the mind of a writer into the hands of a reader. And this is my chance to thank my village.

Thanks to Jeanne, Suzanne, Dena, and Kim who were early readers of this book and offered so much invaluable feedback. The book is so much better for your suggestions.

My critique group is one of the few places I feel comfortable sharing the weird stories and characters that constantly spin through my head, so thanks always to Breanna and Max for allowing me to spill my raw words on you. You're my safe space.

I'm lucky enough to have published six books with Evernight Teen now, so thanks go to the hardworking team there, especially my editors who get the dubious privilege of tidying up my wonky three-continent grammar.

And finally, a huge thanks to my family for allowing me the time and space to do this thing I love. You're the bomb!

STANDING TOO CLOSE

Kate Larkindale

Copyright © 2025

Chapter One

The bell rings as I empty my locker. After so many years, I'm conditioned and jump, ready to slam it shut and run to class. All around me people rush in every direction, voices raised to be heard over the chatter and banging of locker doors. I should be among them, hurrying to get to bio on the second floor.

But I don't hurry. I don't need to worry about being late to bio or to French or English or any of my classes anymore. As of ten minutes ago, I'm no longer a student at Milton High.

The thought makes me dizzy, and I let my body sag against the lockers. Something swims through my midsection, but I can't tell if it's nerves, excitement, or terror. Probably all three.

"You coming, Blue?"

I turn and find Sacha McLeod looking up at me, her violin slung over one shoulder as always.

"I'll catch up," I tell her, diving back into my locker. I bump my head on the shelf inside, the same way I have at least once a day since school started. Whoever designed these things didn't have guys my size in mind.

"Well, okay," she says. "But hurry. You know how Mr. Farnsworth gets if you're late."

She runs off and I rub the sore spot above my eye while I watch her join a group of kids at the base of the staircase. My head feels light—and not from banging it—my throat thick. I am not going to get emotional. It's my choice to quit.

Well, that's what I keep telling myself. If I don't, I'll rip up the piece of paper the principal signed and take the detention Mr. Farnsworth will no doubt give me for being late.

I shove the last of my things into my backpack and sling it over my shoulder. It's surprisingly light. But why wouldn't it be? I've returned all my textbooks. All I had to clear out of my locker were a handful of dead pens, some stinky gym clothes, and a binder full of papers I'll never look at again.

The halls are empty now and eerily silent. I slam the locker closed, enjoying the way its clang echoes through the corridor. I picture teachers frozen in front of their classes, heads cocked at the noise, kids, straightening in their chairs, eager for whatever is going on outside to take them away from the boredom of conjugating verbs or solving quadratic equations.

"Sorry, peeps," I mutter as I march down the hallway and out the double doors at the far end. "Nothing to see here."

I squint in the bright, morning light. Despite the sun, it's cold and I zip my jacket to my chin, turning the collar up in the hope it might keep my ears warm. The bus stop is outside the school grounds. I only have to make it across the parking lot and I'm out.

I glance back at the hulking brick building. Sage is in there somewhere. Hopefully not in a classroom on this side. Or if he is, I hope he's not looking out the window. I didn't tell him where I was going when we got to school this morning. Didn't tell him about the form in my pocket on which I'd forged Mom's signature. Telling my brothers I've dropped out isn't going to be easy. I'd rather tell them both together, rather than having to go through it twice.

Cringing, I step off the grass verge and onto the parking lot. Wiley won't be so bad. He's too young to understand the seriousness of what I've done. Sage though... Well, Sage will. And he'll know why. I only hope I can keep him from blaming himself.

A car barrels into the parking lot.

"Hey!" I leap out of the way, back onto the verge which is damp and slippery from the morning's frost, now melted. The heel of my work boot hits a bald spot and skids across slick mud. I stumble, falling to one knee as the car pulls up and stops a little past me.

The click clack of heels hurries toward me. "Are you okay?"

I get up, brushing at the mud and grass stains streaking the right leg of my jeans. Great. A meeting with the boss at noon, and now I look like I've been playing football or something. I sigh. "Yeah, I'm fine."

"Blue?" The woman's voice is hoarse but familiar. I look up from my ruined jeans and find myself looking at my English teacher. She's been in and out of school the last few weeks. She looks thin and pale. Something happened. Something terrible. I can't remember exactly what. People whispered about it in the hallways, but like most school gossip, it drifted over me without sticking.

"Hi, Mrs. Applegarth," I say. "No classes this period?"

"I could ask the same thing of you."

I shake my head. "No. I don't have class. I won't ever have a class again."

Saying the words aloud makes them real.

Fuck. I don't ever have to suffer through a boring lecture again. I don't have to do homework again. I don't have to deal with Coach Gary constantly trying to recruit me for his football team.

My throat thickens. Not having to do homework or dodge overzealous football coaches sounds good, but I know as well as anyone doing this will limit my future.

"Blue?" Mrs. Applegarth raises her eyebrows, a curious expression on her face. "Is everything all right?"

I like Mrs. Applegarth. Her class was fun. She never asked us to dissect books or asked dumb questions about why certain characters do the things they do. People do stupid things. It's a fact of life. The same way people hurt the ones they're supposed to care about the most.

"I gotta go," I say. "See you around, Mrs. A."

"Blue." She touches my arm as I step off the grass. "What's wrong? Please tell me."

I shake loose. "Nothing's wrong. I dropped out this morning. Now I have to catch the bus."

"You dropped out?" Mrs. Applegarth gasps. "You? Oh, Blue, why?"

I bite at my lower lip, scraping my teeth across the just-healing split. It's not visible because the worst of the cut was on the inside, but I can feel the scab beneath my teeth.

"Talk to me, Blue." She sounds tired. I look at her and realize she *looks* tired too. Exhausted. She's put makeup on, but it isn't enough to hide the dark rings beneath her swollen, bloodshot eyes.

"Are you okay, Mrs. A?" I ask. She looks like she's been crying all night. "You look…Well…"

I trail off. Probably not a good idea to tell your teacher, even a former teacher, she looks like shit. Especially a teacher like Mrs. Applegarth who always seemed so pulled together.

She gives a bitter, humorless laugh. "Am I okay? No. I'm not. But we're not talking about me. Why would a smart boy like you drop out?"

Way to deflect, lady. She's smooth. I'll give her that. But if she's not answering me, and I'm not answering her, I guess we're at an impasse.

"Smart, huh? So smart you gave me a C on my last paper."

The hint of a smile twitches the corner of her lips. "That's not why you're dropping out. I gave you a C because you're better than that paper. You're too smart to turn in sloppy work like that."

I rub my hand across my forehead. The paper *was* sloppy. I wrote most of it in stolen moments between packing boxes at the warehouse, and finished it between three and five in the morning while trying to keep Mom from choking on her own vomit.

"No. That's not why I'm dropping out." But I'm not going to tell her anything more.

"Can I help?" Mrs. Applegarth takes a step toward me. "If you're having problems at home…"

I shake my head, backing away from her. "I'm fine. I don't need any help. Everything's good."

I hate the way the words spill out automatically now. The lies. But I need them. I know all too well what happens when people like Mrs, Applegarth help. I don't need that kind of help. Not now. I'll be eighteen in less than eleven months. I just have to keep everything together until then.

The bell rings behind me. Has it been fifty minutes already? I have to move. If Sage sees me here…

"I really have to go," I say. "You're a great teacher, Mrs. A. I really enjoyed your class."

"So keep taking it," she urges. "Whatever's going on, you shouldn't quit school. Don't jeopardize your future. It's hard enough to get a good job with a degree, let alone without a diploma."

"See you around, Mrs. A." I turn away, but I know she's right. "Hope whatever's going on with you gets better."

And I bolt.

When I get to the bus stop, I look back and find her in the same position on the grass, head bowed, hair falling around her face like a curtain. It looks like she hasn't even brushed it.

And as the bus pulls in and I deposit myself on one of its hard, cracked, vinyl benches, I swear I see her shoulders shaking.

My last glimpse of the high school is of the sun glinting off the windows and the tear-streaked face of my teacher. I look away, not wanting to stare at her misery. I face forward, looking directly into my future, no matter how bleak and uncertain it looks right now.

Chapter Two

The bus wheezes to a stop a block away from the warehouse. I make the familiar walk slowly, enjoying the fact I'm not running to punch my timecard like I usually am. The streets feel different at this time of day and I look around, trying to figure out why.

There are people around, but they're different people than the ones I usually catch glimpses of while dashing past the small stores lining the street. A pair of elderly ladies pause in front of a delicatessen, studying the goods in the window. I step around a young mother pushing a toddler in a stroller. On the park bench at the corner, an old man sits smoking, his face upturned to the sun.

I see a little kid with dark hair and freckles, a wide grin on his face as he speeds toward me on a scooter, his mother half a block behind, running as fast as she can with a baby in a sling across her front.

"Whoa, kiddo." I grab the scooter before he bowls into me, lifting both him and the vehicle off the ground for a second to slow him.

"Thank you." The mother smiles at me as she drags her kid away with her down the street.

I watch them go, feeling a pang of sadness. Wiley should have someone like that taking care of him. A mother who would run after him if he sped too fast away from her. He should have a shiny new scooter with wheels that light up as they spin. He deserves that much, at least. Instead, he has me and Sage and a bike both of us rode before him. And a mother whose love hurts more than love is ever meant to.

"Blue?"

I'm at the warehouse and reaching for my punch card out of habit.

Jeremiah stands in front of me, a puzzled look on his face. "Don't you usually do the late shift?"

"Yeah." I nod. "I need to see Mr. Carter. Is he in?"

Jeremiah shrugs, still looking at me as if I'm confusing him by being here outside my usual hours. "In the office. And check out the new girl he has workin' for him. She's somethin' else."

"Right. I bet she is." I grin at Jeremiah. I've seen some of the magazines he reads in the break room.

I wave and head toward the back of the building and Mr. Carter's office. I'm sort of curious about the girl now, but when I reach the fake foyer area which acts as reception, no one is behind the desk.

"Hello?" I call, peering around.

Nobody answers. There's no sign of anyone. Mr. Carter is in his office though. For a moment, I hesitate. The receptionist is supposed to announce anyone coming to see the boss. But it's not my fault there isn't a receptionist, is it? I slide around the abandoned receptionist's desk and tap on the window of Mr. Carter's office.

He looks up from his computer screen and peers at me with a confused expression.

I catch him glancing at the clock as he beckons me in.

"You're early," he says, standing and gesturing at the empty chair on the opposite side of the desk. "Please don't tell me you're quitting."

"Uh, no sir." I try hiding the smile threatening to spring to my lips. If he's worried about people quitting, he must have work available. And I need work. "The opposite, actually. I wanted to ask if you might have more hours."

Mr. Carter leans back in his seat. "More hours? I got hours, but they're not gonna work with your availability, son."

For the first time since I left the principal's office, the piece of paper in my backpack feels valuable.

"Availability isn't an issue, sir. I can work whatever hours you have."

"What about school?"

"Not a problem anymore."

"You dropped out?" Mr. Carter's posture changes as he leans forward, elbows on the table.

"I did."

"Why would you do a fool thing like that?"

"I had to," I say simply. It's the truth. Months and months of sleepless nights have led me to this truth. I've tried every other option out in my mind, and at the end of it all, quitting school and getting a full-time job is the only one that makes sense. It's the only way I can keep my brothers safe.

My expression must have tightened or changed in some way because Mr. Carter doesn't ask me anything else. He pulls out his schedule and starts making marks on it with a pencil he pulls from behind his ear.

Fifteen minutes later, I walk out of his office with a new roster. The hours aren't perfect; I've kept two late shifts, but instead of starting at four and working until nine, I now start at one. The other three days are more regular hours, eight to five. It means Sage will have to look after Wiley every day after school, but we can manage. We'll have to.

"I didn't see you come in." A girl's voice startles me so much I jump.

I swing around, confused about who is talking to me. "Huh?"

A girl sits behind the reception desk now. She has

the stool wound up as high as it will go and spins it side to side as she watches me with green eyes ringed with a lot of black makeup.

"You must be the new girl," I say, wishing I'd thought to ask Mr. Carter her name. "I'm supposed to show you around."

"I'm Megan," she says, sliding off the stool and landing on the concrete floor with a clatter of high heels.

Doesn't she know this is a warehouse? Mrs. Wheeler, who has been Mr. Carter's receptionist longer than any of the current employees can remember, never wore anything but sneakers. White sneakers. God only knows what she'd say about this interloper.

"Blue," I say, sticking out my hand.

She cocks her head and raises a single eyebrow. "That your name or your emotional state?"

My face heats up. I hate telling people my name the first time. Why couldn't Mom have been normal and called me Andrew or Steve or Jacob? "It's my name."

I think she's about to say something more, maybe make a comment about hippie parents or something, but she doesn't.

"It's cool," she says. "It suits you."

I never know what to say when people compliment me. Especially girls. And this girl, well, Jeremiah wasn't kidding. She's hot. And it's about ten degrees in the warehouse right now, so that's saying something.

"Aren't you cold?" I blurt out, my eyes fixed on the creamy slice of exposed skin peeking between the hem of her super-short skirt and the tops of her over-the-knee socks.

She shrugs and tugs her cardigan tighter around herself. "Yeah. Kind of. It's like a refrigerator in here. Isn't there any heat?"

"That door stays open all day," I point at the heavy roller-door at the entrance. "So the trucks can back in. If we had heat, it'd all sail out the door. So we dress warm and keep moving."

I shove my hands into the pockets of my coat. I'm wearing jeans, a sweater, boots, and a coat, and I'm still cold. I'm not used to being here and not moving around. I wish I'd thought to wear a hat. Gloves mightn't have been a bad idea either.

"So, what do you do here?" Megan hops back up onto her stool, treating me to a bigger flash of thigh before she smooths her skirt out.

"I'm a picker."

"Sounds sexy." She raises her eyebrows.

I thought she was my age, but when she does that, I realize she has to be at least a few years older. Girls my age don't have that kind of confidence. At least, none of the girls I know. "Sexy?"

"Sure." She smiles.

I shrug. I don't consider anything we do here sexy, but what do I know? "C'mon," I say. "Let me show you around."

"Sure," she says again, jumping back off the stool.

She shivers as we walk into the main warehouse.

I don't want to take my coat off, but I'm not an asshole. "Here." I slide off my coat and wrap it around her shoulders.

"A true gentleman," she says with a laugh in her voice, her eyes twinkling like Christmas lights. "Who knew there were any left?"

"This way," I say gruffly, regretting the gesture already as the cold wind blasts through my sweater and bites into my skin.

As we wander through the maze of shelves, I point out where things are. Cartons of copy paper stacked here, printer toner there, pens, pencils, and notebooks down another narrow row. There's no pattern to what is stored where, but after working here six months, I know where everything is, have figured out the quickest and most efficient ways around the building.

"It's pretty simple," I tell her. "When orders come in, they get put here." I show her the plastic tray full of flimsy paper slips.

"Who puts them there?" she asks.

"You, I guess. If you're on reception." I have no idea if she's a temp, looking after the desk for a few days while Mrs. Wheeler is off, or if she's here permanently. "Anyway, we pick one up, grab a cart, and go pick all the things on the order off the shelves. Once we have everything, we take it down there to the packing area, box it up, and label it. Three times a day a truck comes and picks up the boxes for delivery."

Explaining it makes the job sound even dumber than it really is. And I'm under no illusions about how dumb it is. It's manual labor. About the only skill required is that you can read and write. The rest is grunt work. I don't even get to do something cool like drive a forklift. I'm too young for that. About the most exciting thing I'm allowed to do is use the scissor-lift to reach things on the top shelves. And I only need to do that if whatever I need from up there is heavy. Being 6'5 has its advantages in this job.

"Don't you get bored?" Megan fingers the pile of dockets in the tray. It's thicker than it usually is by the time I get in at four. Guess that's why the day shift has five people, while there are only two of us doing lates.

I run my fingers through my hair. "Bored? Yeah, sometimes. I try not to think about it too much." I try not to think at all. It's hard though, especially when the work is so repetitive. I focus on each individual order and try not to let the rest of the world creep into my head. Packing paper and pencils and manila folders into boxes is way easier than trying to untangle the mess my life is in.

KATE LARKINDALE

Chapter Three

The sun is dropping behind the trees outside the roller-door as I tape up the last box in my final order of the day. I dig through a pile of address labels, searching for the one with the number six in the corner for this, the sixth box.

"You done?"

Megan's perky voice startles me so much I drop the handful of labels I'm holding. They catch in the wind and scatter across the slippery cement floor.

"Aw, fuck," I mumble under my breath as I drop to my hands and knees to chase the still-skittering sheets of paper.

"Oh, god! I'm so sorry," Megan cries. She crouches too, gathering up as many labels as she can without having to crawl. I don't blame her. The floor isn't exactly clean. Grit clings to my palms when she hands me the crumpled labels.

"I'll grab them," I tell her, stuffing the ones in my hands back into their tray. "No point both of us getting dirty."

"Thanks." She straightens and I feel her eyes follow me as I crawl through the dust. It's worse when I have to lie flat to tease one out from under a shelf.

When they're finally back where they should be, I head toward the back of the warehouse and the bathrooms, desperate to wash my hands. As I do, I stare at myself in the mirror. It's the end of my first day as a high-school dropout. I should look different, right? Like a man? I have a full-time job. I'll have money soon. Enough that I can save up for an apartment. Dishes. Cutlery. Towels. The day I turn eighteen, I'm out of

Mom's apartment, and Sage and Wiley are coming with me.

I don't look different though. Tired and dirty, maybe, but no different.

I sigh and splash cold water over my face and drag myself into the office to punch out. Every part of me aches.

"Hey," Megan calls when I step through the door. "I made it through my first day."

"Are you coming back tomorrow?"

Her lips are painted a glossy scarlet, and she's taken her hair out of the ponytail it has been in all day. The thick, dark mane hangs over her shoulders and pours over her breasts. I want to move across to the rack where the timecards are stored, but I can't rip my eyes away. I stumble into a chair and my face burns. Stupid, clumsy oaf.

"So." She darts out and punches my card for me before I can even remember what it's for. "Where are you taking me for a drink?"

"A drink?" I stare at her, feeling awkward and stupid, too large for the small space. I'm not cold anymore. In fact, I'm sweating under my sweater.

"Yeah. Don't you think we deserve a drink? Celebrate getting through the day?"

"Uh … sure." Something about this girl makes my IQ drop about a hundred points. I don't want to go out for a drink—I *can't* go out for a drink; I have to get home. I can't put off talking to Sage forever. Not to mention I *don't* drink. But somehow none of those things mean anything right now.

"Where's your car?" Megan follows me down the short, wide loading dock to the street.

My face blazes again. "I take the bus."

"Better for the environment, right?" Her purple

scarf flutters in the wind, the long fringes tangling in her hair.

"Right," I say with a wry twist to my lips. Good for the environment? Whatever.

"We can take mine." She leads me across the near-empty parking lot to a dusty green VW. "Is Vinnie's okay? I hate how crowded most of the bars get. You can't talk to anyone."

I shrug. "Anywhere's fine." Yeah, as long as they don't check IDs. I'll have to deal with that one when and if it happens. I slide into the seat next to her. It's a compact car, and I'm not a compact person; even with the seat rolled back as far as I can get it, my knees jut toward my chest.

"Sorry." She smiles while I struggle to fasten my seatbelt. "It's not really designed for people over about 5'7" or so... How tall are you, Blue?"

I shrug again. "Around 6'5". I haven't measured myself in a while."

"Wow." She giggles and starts the engine, headlights dazzling me when they flick on and reflect off the snow piled up around the parking lot. "You're a whole foot taller than me."

"You're only 5'5"?" I study her profile. I guess she is only that tall. She seems bigger. Maybe it's her personality.

"Yeah. Don't know why. My parents are both tall. Guess I'm some kind of throwback or something."

"5'5" isn't short," I say. "It's average, right?"

"But who wants to be average?" She grins across at me, and my heart thumps double-time in my chest.

Vinnie's turns out to be a low building, set back from the street with a single string of Christmas lights blinking over its wide front door. I pass it almost every day, but I've never noticed it before.

I follow Megan across the parking lot to the door. With every step I open my mouth to tell her I have to go home, I can't stay for a drink, yet with every step, I get closer to the bar.

She shoves open the door and a cloud of smoky warmth pulses into the cold night air.

A bouncer on a stool gives me a bored look, before turning his gaze to Megan. "ID?" he drawls.

"Sure." Megan rummages through her tiny purse and drags out her wallet. She opens it and hands it to the bouncer.

I shuffle my feet, a hundred lame excuses passing through my skull for why I don't have my ID, none of which will convince this guy. My palms grow damp and I wipe them on my jeans.

"Cool, you can go." The bouncer gestures for us to go through into the dimly lit interior.

Relief cascades over me, and my legs are rubbery as I follow Megan to a booth at the back of the room.

"You must have a good fake ID," I say, watching her slide her wallet back into her purse and pull her phone out.

Her brow furrows and she looks up from the phone screen. "Fake ID?" She studies me carefully, then her face relaxes into a smile. "How old do you think I am?"

I shrug, cramming myself into the seat across from her. "I don't know. Nineteen? Twenty?"

"I'm twenty-three." Her smile drops away and she cocks her head to look at me. "How old are you?"

For a moment, I consider lying, saying I'm twenty-one or twenty-two, but I decide against it. I hate lying and I do enough of it as it is. "I'm seventeen."

"Seventeen!" She stares at me. "But you'll be eighteen soon, right?"

"Is October soon?" I duck my head and stare at the tabletop, which is coated with sticky rings. I trace my finger around one, grimacing at the tackiness trying to glue me to the surface. I've been seventeen less than a month. So no. I'm not going to be eighteen soon.

"You don't look seventeen," Megan says after the silence drags on too long to be comfortable. "How come you're not still in school?"

I pull my finger free of the ooze. "I dropped out." It still sounds wrong. A dropout isn't someone like me. Dropouts are dumb thugs, kids who can't pass their courses and are destined for a lifetime of menial labor or dealing drugs on street corners. That's not me. Maybe I am packing boxes in a warehouse now, but I won't do it forever.

"You did? How come?" Megan waves at a waitress who pointedly ignores her.

I shrug. "I had to. Now, we came for a drink. Let's get a drink. What do you want?"

She gives me a curious glance, but drops the conversation. "I guess I'll take a beer."

I wave the waitress over. She comes, snapping her gum so fiercely I can hear it even over the pulse of music.

"What'll it be?" She pulls a pen from behind her ear.

"A beer for me," Megan says. "Draft."

"Coke," I add when the waitress turns and fixes her eyes on me.

"JD & Coke?"

"No, just Coke." I feel my face redden again. I swear I've blushed more today than I ever have in my life. Must be the shame. Even though I'm proud I've finally done something to change our situation, I don't feel good about quitting school. Every time I remember it my stomach clenches. Or maybe it's from thinking about what Sage is going to say when I tell him. At least this way, Wiley will probably be asleep when I get home so I won't have to deal with the disappointment in his eyes too. But I did want to tell them both together…

"Designated driver, huh?" The waitress jams the pen back where it came from and stomps off.

Megan giggles. "Service with a smile, huh? She looks like she'd taken a bite out of a lemon."

"Guess people leave better tips when they're drunk."

Or not. I can't imagine Mom tipping anyone. Then again, she doesn't usually drink in bars. Doesn't want to be seen. Even now, she clings to her fame, pretending people might still know who she is, and that if they do, they care.

I shouldn't be here. I should be home. I steal a peek at my watch and discover it's after six. Sage isn't expecting me until around ten, but since I finished work early, I should go. I could help put Wiley to bed for once. I could…

"Cheers!" Megan's voice startles me out of my thoughts, and I discover there's a glass in front of me. Megan is already holding hers, a wide grin on her face as she leans in to clink her glass to mine.

"Cheers," I reply without nearly as much enthusiasm in my voice. But I clink and force myself to smile as I take a sip of the watery, over-sweet soda. A small sip. This is my one and only drink for the night. My budget won't stretch to a second, even if I wanted it.

Megan doesn't appear to have any of the same concerns. She downs half her beer in a single swallow. "God, that's good. I needed that."

I force a smile. How many times have I heard that before?

Chapter Four

An hour later, Megan is on her third beer and I'm still nursing my Coke. The ice has melted and it's watery, the fizz mostly gone so it's like sipping on sugar-water. I should go home. I've been telling myself that every five minutes since we got here, but for some reason I haven't left.

"So," Megan says, standing up briefly to tug down her skirt before dropping back to the bench next to me. "My mom's coming to visit this weekend, and I'm kind of freaking out because my mom is like, a total neat freak. You should see my apartment. It's a disaster zone and I'm working every day, so I have no clue when I'm going to get it cleaned up. And my roommate is even worse. Luckily, she got a boyfriend recently, so she's not home a lot, but she never does the dishes."

I let her ramble on. It's actually kind of nice to listen to someone else's problems for a change. Especially when her problems seem so insignificant.

"You could go right home after work tomorrow and clean up," I say absently.

"It's Friday tomorrow," she replies, like it's an answer to what I said. "I'm not going home to clean on a Friday night. Are you kidding me?"

I force a laugh, like I am kidding. I've spent every Friday night for the last six months packing boxes at the warehouse. I usually wind up following that with cleaning at home too. And I bet the cleaning I have to do is way grosser than anything she deals with at her dirty apartment. Not that I'd wish that on anyone.

The lights dim and colored spots swirl across a low stage I hadn't noticed in the corner.

"Karaoke!" Megan squeals. "I forgot it was Thursday."

What have I got myself into? I slurp more Coke, crunching a sliver of ice between my teeth as a pair of overweight guys shamble to the stage.

"Seriously?" Megan groans when they attempt to do an Eminem song, missing most of the lyrics and swinging their hips so out of time with the beat it's comical.

Next up are a pair of girls who giggle their way through a Taylor Swift song. A table of young guys toward the front whoop and holler so loudly I can barely hear their singing. Which is probably a blessing.

"Wanna do a duet?" Megan dumps a heavy book onto the table with a thud and starts poring over it. I look down and realize it's the list of songs to pick from.

"I don't sing," I tell her. "But go ahead if you want to."

She narrows her eyes. "I bet you can sing."

I laugh. "You'd lose that bet."

She shrugs and scribbles a couple of numbers on a slip of paper, handing it to a slim man in a cowboy hat as he passes by.

"What did you choose?" I ask, curious what she might know or like to sing.

"Wait and see." She winks and picks up her phone again, scrolling through it quickly before setting it back down.

"You any good?"

"Better than him." She jerks a thumb at the guy howling into the mic on stage now. I can't figure out what he's singing, even though there's a screen above his head with the lyrics bouncing across the bottom.

A smattering of applause and jeers follows the guy off the stage, and a moment later, Megan is up there.

Her dark hair gleams red, blue, and yellow under the lights. She grabs the microphone with confidence, sashaying around the stage as the intro music plays. She turns and winks at me before lifting the mic and starting to sing.

After the other performers being so terrible, it's a shock when she starts singing, belting out a Sidewalk Regrets song in a voice that's both strong and pure.

A voice eerily like Mom's was before... Well, before.

The room has quietened. No one hoots, jeers, or shouts. Conversations stop and everyone turns toward the stage where Megan struts and swivels and works the crowd as she sings.

When the song ends, she gives a funny little bow before jumping from the low stage.

The bar erupts with applause and whistles.

"Fuck, that was fun!" Megan hurls herself into the booth and downs her beer in a single swig. Another appears in front of her as if by magic.

"From the guy over there," the waitress says, inclining her head toward a table near the door where an older man sits alone.

"Eww," Megan says out of the side of her mouth, even as she lifts the glass and raises it to her benefactor.

"You're good," I say.

"You think so?" She sets the beer down and wipes foam away from her top lip. "I love singing. I'm just not sure I'm good enough."

"Good enough for what?"

She looks down at the table. "To make a career out of it. It's kind of my dream, you know? To sing with a band. Make records. Tour."

My stomach turns to ice. "I gotta go."

"Blue?"

I ignore her as I push through the crowd to the door. I don't look back. I don't even glance through the window to see if she's following me as I run down the empty street toward the nearest bus stop.

The bus is old and creaky, the seats cracked and sticky. I pick one that looks almost clean and lean my head against the freezing glass. I can't get her face out of my head. The joy in her eyes as she sang. The way the crowd hung on every note falling from those perfect, soft lips.

Mom used to look like that. When I was a kid, I loved watching her sing. It was a special treat to sit at the side of the stage. She'd turn occasionally, makeup turning her familiar brown eyes strange and exotic. But her smile was always her own. She'd sing to me, joy and wonder spilling from her as she sang, blowing me a secret kiss before turning back to the audience in front of her.

I try to keep the image in my head, try to cling to the feelings those special nights left me with. But instead, my head fills with other performances, the later ones when she'd cling to the mic stand not out of passion for what she was singing, but because the bottle by her feet was nearly empty.

And then the venues were too. Even the small, shabby clubs that became the only places she could book gigs. Filthy places where Sage and I would curl up in empty booths night after night because she couldn't afford a babysitter.

Until it was over.

I can't think about Megan's dream without visualizing its dark side. And I can't watch while she chases the nightmare.

The wind whips hair around my face as I trudge toward home. I duck my head deeper into my collar in an attempt to keep my ears from freezing solid. Our building is only three blocks from the bus stop. Three long blocks.

When I reach the building, the lights are out in the foyer again. I sigh as I feel my way through the darkness to the stairwell. Those students in 4C must have blown a bulb again.

Wearily, I climb the five flights to our apartment. A single fluorescent on each landing casts shadowy blue light across the steps. But I don't need light to find my way home. I know every crack and creak and broken tile on this staircase.

Outside the door, I pause. Sage will be in there, waiting for me no doubt. And I will have to tell him what I've done. Somehow, I allowed Megan to sweep me up in her tornado-like wake and forgot everything else. Now, it floods back, the guilt and shame, but also the determination and certainty I've done the right thing. I cling to the thought as I insert my key in the lock and let myself into the apartment.

"Blue? Is that you?" Sage's voice is there as soon as I step into the tiny hallway.

"Yeah, it's me." I slide off my coat and hang it on one of the hooks by the door. I step out of my boots and line them up under the coat before padding into the kitchen in my socks.

"You're early." Sage sits at the table, books and papers spread out in front of him. A well gnawed pencil lies across it all.

"Yeah. I changed my hours." I pull out the chair across from him and sit down. "Wiley asleep?"

Sage nods, but he's distracted. "You changed your hours? How come?"

I glance at the stove and find a covered pot sitting there. "That for me?" I ask, getting up and lifting the lid on what appears to be chili.

"Oh, yeah. You hungry?" Sage leaps up and starts

pulling things from cabinets.

I take the bowl he pulled out and wave him back toward the table. "I can get it."

"So tell me about the hours." Sage sits back down and picks up the pencil, toying with it as he watches me spoon chili into the bowl. "You're not going to heat it up?"

I set the bowl on the table and grab a fork from a drawer. "Nah. Too hungry."

And it's true. I'm starving all of a sudden. The smell of meat and spices drifting from the chili makes my stomach growl like a feral dog. I sit down and start shoveling food in practically before my butt hits the wood.

"No lunch?" Sage watches me eat.

I shake my head, realizing he's right. I never had lunch. No wonder I'm ravenous now.

"I was looking for you at lunch. Where were you?" Sage threads the pencil through his fingers.

"You were looking for me? How come?"

He shakes his head. "Nothing important. I needed bus fare for a field trip we're taking next week, but we have until Monday to pay. Where were you, anyway?"

I sigh and set down my fork. "I quit school today."

"What?" Sage stares at me. The pencil drops from his fingers and rolls across the floor.

"I quit school."

"Why, Blue?" Sage's eyes are huge. He looks like a Manga character or something, his blond hair sticking up at the front where he's been tugging at it as he struggles through his homework. He must have been doing math. I can always tell by how mussed up that tuft of hair is.

"Why do you think?"

Sage looks at me, such sadness in his eyes I can barely stand to look at him.

I turn back to my plate instead, but I'm not hungry anymore.

"I had to, Sage. We can't keep going like this." I jam a forkful of meat and beans into my mouth and concentrate on chewing, counting every movement of my jaw so I don't have to focus on Sage and his quiet accusation.

"But you're so close to being done."

"Not close enough." I shake my head. "We have to get out of here. We need money to do that."

"Where will we go?"

I shrug. Does it matter? Anywhere has to be better than this hellhole. "We'll get our own apartment or something. I'll figure it out."

I hope I sound more confident than I feel. I have no idea if I can rent an apartment or not. Even if I have enough for rent, and a deposit, and everything. Do landlords rent to seventeen-year-old kids with two little brothers in tow? Even to eighteen-year-olds?

I have to keep my fingers crossed that money talks.

Sage bends and picks up the pencil from where it's landed near my foot. He says something as he does, but his voice is too low for me to catch the words.

"What?"

He straightens but doesn't look at me. "In three years, you'll hate us," he says, his voice low and strained. "And I won't blame you."

I reach over and clasp his shoulder, forcing him to look at me. "I could never hate you," I say. "This is my decision, okay? I wouldn't do it if it wasn't the right thing for us."

Sage nods, but it's reluctant, like he's forcing

himself to make the movement. "Is it the right thing for you, though?"

Chapter Five

"Where'd you run off to last night?" Megan asks as soon as I walk through the door the next day. "I thought we were having fun."

I punch my timecard without looking at her. "Yeah ... we were."

"So? What happened?"

I take a deep breath before I turn and look at her. She's wearing more sensible clothes today—jeans and boots—but the jeans are so tight they leave nothing to the imagination. Except how the hell she managed to get into them.

"You don't think maybe you're too old for me?" I ask. "I mean... You're twenty-three. I'm seventeen."

She shrugs. "You don't act seventeen. Besides, you're cute."

I raise my eyebrows. Nobody has called me cute since I was about seven. "Cute?"

She nods. Her hair is loose, only a few sections at the front clipped back, and it spills over her shoulders in a shiny cascade. "Yeah. Cute. Don't fight it."

I'm not fighting it. That's the problem. I came in this morning determined to stop this flirtation. To keep things professional between us. Yet already I'm feeling breathless and hot around the collar. What is it about this woman?

"I gotta get to work," I say finally. "Later."

She grins and spins her chair from side to side. "I'll hold you to that."

I bet she will.

Jeremiah grabs me as I leave the office and head onto the floor. "What did I tell you? Hot potato, am I right?"

"Not my type," I lie. "Did those printer cartridges I ordered on Wednesday come in?"

I manage to avoid Megan for the rest of the day. I feel bad about it, but I can't get involved. She *is* too old for me. I wasn't lying about that. Yet in many ways she seems younger. Her worries and concerns are so much smaller than mine have ever been. She doesn't have people relying on her. I won't lie about it; her freedom appeals to me. I wish I could focus on myself like she does. I wish I dared to have dreams and ambitions, but I'm realistic. I've had to be.

The day drags even though the day shift is a lot busier than my afternoon and evening shifts have ever been. The incoming order tray seems to be fuller every time I pass it. I pocket a wad of order forms, wondering about the businesses that order all this stuff. What do the thirty toner cartridges on this order form actually print? Why does this other company require 22 clear files, four boxes of staples, two calculators, and three cartons of recycled copy paper?

By afternoon, I've stopped thinking about the businesses and just pull items from the shelves without considering their use. Instead, I think about my future. Is this what I'll be stuck doing for the rest of my life? This, or something else equally mindless.

Probably.

I bite my lip to keep bitter laughter from spewing from me. I wanted to be an architect. Or a doctor. When I started working after school it wasn't to support my family, it was to save for college. Even back when I was twelve, I knew Mom wasn't ever going to be able to afford to send me to school. If I wanted higher education, it was up to me to earn it. But little by little, the money eked away. Groceries one week, an overdue electric bill the next. Doctor's appointments, school field trips, clothes, and shoes.

I knew college was out of reach before I hit fifteen, yet it didn't keep me from trying. Even if it meant skipping lunch every day for a week, I made sure part of every paycheck was kept for me. Even if it was only a handful of change.

"You know it's after five, right?" Megan leans against the packing table, standing so close I can't finish wrapping the package without elbowing her in the face.

"It is?" I glance at the clock over the office and am surprised to discover it's close to five-fifteen. "I have to go."

And I do. I promised Sage I'd get home early enough for him to make it to his team's hockey game at seven. I'll have to bust my ass now to make sure he has time to get to the flooded tennis court in the park where they play.

Hastily, I finish wrapping the package, using far more tape than is strictly necessary. "Raj," I call to the high-school kid who is my usual shift-mate. "Can you finish up this order for Comsmart? I have to go."

I don't wait for his answer, just shove the order form into his hand and run toward the office.

Megan follows me outside. "Want a ride?"

"Where are you headed?" A ride would be good. Even with the rush-hour traffic, she can save me time.

"Where do you live?"

"It's far," I say quietly. "I don't want you to go out of your way."

"It's all good," she says, not answering my question. "Hop in."

I do. Reluctantly. I don't want to be trapped with her in the small space, yet at the same time, I don't want Sage to miss his game. God knows the poor kid has missed enough of them. It's a miracle the coach even lets him stay on the team after all the practices and games he's had to miss. It's lucky he's good or he would have been cut months ago.

"Big plans for the weekend?" Megan asks once we're inside the vehicle.

"Nothing much," I reply. "You have your mom visiting, right?"

"Don't remind me," she groans. "She's going to be on me all weekend about how I'm wasting my life."

She's wasting her life? She isn't a seventeen-year-old high-school dropout with only a future in stationary delivery to look forward to.

"Turn left here," I say twenty minutes later, as we pass the deli on the corner of Linden and Main.

"You live here?" Megan wrinkles her nose as she stares at the dirty brick facade of our building.

I nod. Unfortunately, I do.

"I couldn't interest you in dinner, could I?" Megan looks away from the building and back at me.

Even with the milky white glow of the streetlight above us leaching her skin of color, Megan looks beautiful. In another lifetime, maybe I could go to dinner with her.

"I'd love to," I tell her. "But I really can't tonight. Raincheck?"

She smiles. "I'll hold you to that."

"I bet you will." I smile back, realizing it's the second time she's said this to me today.

She leans over and drops a quick peck on my cheek. "Have a good weekend."

My face blazes with heat, the spot her lips touched my cheek burning hotter than any other part. I don't want to get out of the car. When I do, the spell will be broken. I'll go back to being plain old Blue Lannigan again, not a guy who could be attractive to this beautiful, vivacious, carefree older woman.

"Thanks," I say a little breathlessly, then, before I can chicken out, I lean over and kiss her cheek. It's cool from the chill in the air, her skin impossibly soft against my lips. She smells faintly of vanilla and apples.

"See you Monday," I say as I slide out of the car. "Have fun with your mom."

She rolls her eyes. "You have obviously never met my mom."

I pretend I didn't hear and hurry up the path to the front door. I can't find my key, so I buzz our apartment, surprised when Sage doesn't open the door for me right away. He has to be waiting for me.

A car horn honks and I glance back at the street. Megan is still there, the car idling at the curb. She raises her eyebrow in a questioning gesture. Where are my keys? I rummage through the pockets of my jacket and jeans before I remember tossing the keys into the front pocket of my backpack when I locked up this morning. I wave to Megan as I dig them out and let myself in. As I do, the car peels away with a squeal of rubber on road.

The lights are still out in the foyer. I can't be the only one who ever shows up after dark. Not at this time of year. Has no one complained to the building manager yet? Or is he not listening? I make a mental note to visit him tomorrow and demand he fixes the lights. I don't like the idea of Wiley coming into this darkness if he's been outside playing with his friends. Anything could be waiting for him in there. Anyone.

"Hello?" I take the stairs two at a time and I'm breathless as I enter the apartment. "Sage? Wiley?"

Nothing.

I frown and peer at my watch. It's only a little after six. Plenty of time for Sage to make it to his game.

"Sage?" I call. "Wiley?" And, when neither of them answer, I call out, "Mom?"

I bite down on my lip as I enter the living room. A bottle sits on the coffee table, an inch or so of amber liquid in the bottom. My stomach curdles at the stench of bourbon clinging to the air. Bourbon and smoke.

"That you, baby boy?" The slurred voice comes from near the door to the hallway. With a drunken giggle, she asks, "Little Boy Blue? Is that you?"

I close my eyes for a second and take a deep breath. It's never good when she starts using those childish endearments. "Yeah, it's me Mom. Are you okay?"

"Fine and dandy, like cotton candy." She giggles again.

I reach over and flick on a lamp. It's then I see her properly, sprawled in the doorway, eyes glazed and face slack. It's a look that's all too familiar. A look that tells me she's had more than the bourbon tonight.

I step over her and into the darkened hallway. A sliver of light spills from under our bedroom door. I installed locks on the inside. I hope Wiley and Sage had the foresight to use them. And they're in there together.

"Where you goin', Blue-baby?" Mom croons. "You're not leaving me here alone, are you?"

I hesitate, my eyes flicking between the slender crack of light and her. She's pulling herself up now, leaning heavily on the wall as she drags herself to her feet. It's awkward and difficult to watch, especially since all she's wearing is a slip. No underwear beneath it. I look away as her knees weaken and she slips down, legs splaying outward.

Why doesn't she have panties on? No guy should be forced to look at his mother's snatch.

"Pull yourself together," I say finally. I hate

seeing her like this.

"I am together."

I could argue with her all night. But I'm not going to. I push past her and head down the hall.

I rap on our bedroom door. "Wiley? Sage? You in there?"

There's no answer, but I hear the snick of a lock turning. The door opens a crack and Wiley peeks out.

"You okay?" I ask as I slide into the room, closing the door behind me. I turn and snap the lock shut too. We don't need her busting in here. When she's like this, it's a toss-up between hysterical tears or fury. Neither is pretty.

I turn away from the door. A single lamp near the door is shining, but the rest of the room is in shadows.

"Sage?" I ask. "Are you here?"

"Yeah." His voice comes from somewhere near the windows.

I snap on the overhead light, bathing the room in brightness. I blink, dazzled for a second. When my eyes have adjusted, I find Wiley perched quietly on the end of my bed. He's pale and far too still, but my all-too-trained eyes don't find any sign of injury as I scan him.

"Okay?" I rest a hand on his head for a second.

He nods and my hand slides off his fine, shiny hair.

"Sage?" I glance around, looking for him.

"Here." The voice comes from behind me.

I turn and find Sage crumpled in the corner behind the bed he and Wiley share, his head resting on the corner of the windowsill. Blood trails down his chin from a split in his lip.

"Shit," I say without really meaning to. "Are you okay?"

The shrug Sage gives sends a stab of terror through me. He's fourteen. No fourteen-year-old should be able to look so resigned. No one his age should have experienced enough to be resigned to anything.

I round the end of the bed and crouch next to him. It's a tight squeeze, but I don't care if I'm uncomfortable, that I feel like a contortionist trying to fit my body into a tiny cube or something. My discomfort doesn't matter right now, not when Sage is bleeding.

Chapter Six

"I'm okay," Sage says as I lift his chin in my hand and study his face. He's going to have a black eye by morning. But the split lip isn't so bad he'll need stitches. This time.

"She hit you anywhere else?" I ask, sitting back on my heels.

"No," he says, but he winces when he moves, his hand reaching over to clutch at his ribs.

"Right," I say dryly. I tug his shirt up gently and run my fingers along his bony ribcage. He cries out and tries to pull away, but I hold him firm. "What did she hit you with this time?" Mom isn't strong enough to do this much damage with her bare hands.

He won't meet my eyes. "Broom."

My fists clench where they're still holding the fabric of his shirt. I force them to relax and let the shirt drop back down over the red and purple marks.

But my fists don't want to relax. No part of me does. Anger burns through me, making my blood feel hot as it surges through my veins.

"What happened?" I ask finally, more to give my brain something else to focus on than anything else.

Sage shrugs again, his eyes bleak. "What do you think?"

"She was trashed when you got home?"

Sage nods. "Completely wasted. It's my fault. I thought she was passed out."

"It's not your fault." I get up, no longer able to stay there, squeezed in against the bed. I need to move. "It's never your fault. I don't want you saying that."

It's my fault. I lingered in the car with Megan,

enjoying the teasing and flirtation. And while I sat there, Mom was beating Sage. And Wiley got to watch. No wonder the poor kid always looks frightened.

Sage just looks at me. He has huge eyes. Dark brown, the same as Wiley's. The same as mine. Mom's eyes. They were her trademark back when she was famous and every newspaper story or magazine article mentioned them, using words like mesmerizing, stunning, or striking to describe them. I feel like she branded us with them, so everyone would know we're her property.

"Stay here," I say after I've paced the tiny square of empty floor between the bed and the door more times than I can count. If I keep going, I'll wear a groove into the hardwood.

"Where are you going?" Wiley leaps up, fear painted across his delicate features.

I glance over at Sage who hasn't moved from his spot under the window. "I'll be back soon."

Sage gives a tiny, almost imperceptible nod.

Wiley's eyes follow me as I cross to the door and unlock it.

Music drifts toward us when I open it a crack. I recognize it and wince. "Lock the door," I tell my brothers.

"Blue," Wiley calls as I'm leaving. "Blue, don't…"

"I'll be fine." I throw him a smile I hope is reassuring. "I'm going to get her to bed. I'll be back real soon."

He doesn't say anything more, but I feel his fear trailing after me as I close the door behind me. Anger surges again. He shouldn't be afraid in his own home. He shouldn't have to lock himself into his room to stay safe. None of us should. When did things get so bad? I listen for the click of the lock before I move out of the hallway.

Mom's dancing when I get back to the living room. She clutches the bottle of bourbon in one fist as she sways to the music. When the verse begins, she raises the bottle to her mouth like a microphone and starts singing into it.

I stand in the doorway for a second, watching.

From the speakers, my mother's voice blazes out, the strong pure alto I remember from sitting proudly at the side of stage after stage. The voice that won her awards and accolades, got her offers of movie roles and sold-out stadiums.

What comes from my mother's mouth now is ragged and raw. She can still hit the notes, but there's no purity now. Her voice is a hoarse, ruined parody of what's playing through the speakers. Like the way she still dresses the same way she did; dresses which flowed around her narrow frame now cling snugly to her drink-bloated stomach, strain across her hips.

She spins around and takes a swig from her "microphone", staggering backward as she does. Her heel catches the edge of the rug and she falls, crashing onto the coffee table on her ass. It cracks under her and dumps her to the ground amid a cascade of old magazines.

I wince.

"Ooopsy daisy!" Mom catches sight of me in the doorway and drags herself up, leaning heavily on the ruined furniture. "Mommy's clumsy today."

"Mommy's drunk," I say. "As usual."

"I'm not drunk, baby boy." Mom sways on her feet and looks blearily around for her bottle. She finds it under the magazines, empty now, the remaining bourbon soaking into the filthy carpet.

"No?" I watch her shaking the bottle over her mouth, trying to get any last liquor out. "Looks that way to me."

"You worry too much. I'm fine, Bluebell. I'm celebratin'"

Celebrating? What the hell does she have to celebrate? Kicking the shit out of Sage? Terrifying Wiley so much he barely speaks? "Don't call me Bluebell."

"Oh, I forgot. My baby boy is too big for pet names."

I roll my eyes but ignore it. There are more important things to deal with. "It's bedtime," I say, tugging the bottle away from her and setting it on the broken table. "You've had enough."

"Darlin'," she snarls, leaping away from me. "I haven't even started yet."

She reaches into the stereo cabinet and pulls out another bottle, this one smaller and slimmer. She unscrews the cap and takes a healthy belt. "Damn. That's the stuff. Here." She holds the bottle out to me. "Have a drink, baby. You know I don't like to drink alone."

I take the bottle, but don't take a sip. For someone who doesn't like drinking by herself, she spends a lot of time doing it. Like, every day. All day. Since giving up singing, drinking has been her career.

Who am I kidding? She never gave up singing. People just didn't want to listen to her anymore.

I dump the booze I'm holding into the pot holding a dying plant.

"What are you doing?" Mom shrieks. She lunges across the room, arm outstretched, palm ready. She swipes at me, but is so unsteady she misses and hits the plant instead. It tumbles off the table and lands on the floor with a thud. Bourbon-scented dirt streaks across the floor.

"You little…" Mom's fury overwhelms her and she lashes out, slapping, scratching, and punching at me.

I take it, letting her wear herself out. She only

lands about one in four hits, and they don't hurt much. When her efforts don't move me, she claws at my face.

"Ow!" I grab her hand and hold it away from me. My cheek stings and when I reach up to touch it, my fingers come away scarlet. "Okay. That's it."

Keeping her hands trapped in one of mine, I push her out of the living room and down the hallway to her bedroom.

"Let me go," she hollers. "If you know what's good for you, Blue…"

"I do," I say, through gritted teeth.

It takes some time for me to manhandle her to her room, but we make it. She fights me every step of the way, but I'm bigger than she is and much stronger. When we reach her bedroom, I scoop her up and carry her the rest of the way to the bed. She's exhausted now, still struggling, but ineffectually now, her arms and hands weak and floppy as noodles.

"You're mean," she murmurs as I drop her onto her unmade bed. "I only wanted to party."

"Party's over." I tug the covers up over her. "Go to sleep, okay? You'll feel better in the morning."

I'm lying. She's going to have the hangover from hell in the morning, but that's normal.

"Oh, baby!" She sits up and cups my face in her hand. "You're bleeding. Did I do that?"

"I'm fine." I push her hand away. "Just go to sleep."

Tears fill her eyes. "But you're bleeding. I hurt you. I'm such a bad mother sometimes. I'm sorry, baby. I don't mean to be bad. I…"

She breaks off, tears choking her voice. I hate this part almost more than I hate the hitting.

"It's okay, Mom. I forgive you."

"I'm sorry. I'm so sorry. It's hard, you know?

One day you're at the top and everyone loves you. Everyone threw money at me. And other stuff. Men wanted me. And then … nothing. No man. Three kids and a job in a goddamn supermarket. I need a little help sometimes. A little taste of the old days, y' know?"

I push her gently back onto the bed. "Yeah, I know. But you had too much of a taste tonight. Get some sleep and feel better tomorrow."

She's crying for real now, big ugly, drunken sobs. If I hadn't seen it a thousand times before, I might feel sorry for her. But it's not real. By tomorrow she will have forgotten all of this, and it'll start all over again. And maybe next time it'll be Wiley she slaps around instead of me. She's not that strong, but if she can give Sage a black eye and cracked ribs, she could kill Wiley without any thought. She'd be sorry after, of course…

It feels like only a few minutes later that Mom's sobs have turned into snores and I breathe a sigh of relief. She's out. And she'll stay out until morning. I get up and leave the room, turning the light off as I close the door behind me.

"She's out," I call through our bedroom door as I pass. "You can come in here."

I head to the living room and switch off the stereo. I'll never be able to listen to those old records without anger twisting my insides. Anger and sadness. She had so much talent. So much potential. Yet she pissed it away. And when she drinks, she likes to blame her downfall on us, not the drugs she took or the booze she swilled day after day. The cigarettes. The men who rode the coattails of her fame then left her when things got serious. She blames everyone except the person who actually orchestrated every failure—herself.

Sage and Wiley join me. Without a word, Wiley scoops up the magazines and books scattered across the floor around the broken coffee table.

"You're bleeding," he says when he looks at me.

I rub at my cheek, feeling the rough edges of the scratches she's left there. "It's nothing," I say. "Her nails caught me."

Sage drops onto the couch, curling up around his bruised ribs. "I hate her," he whispers. "I used to feel sorry for her, but I hate her now. I wish she'd just die or something."

I stare at him, unable to believe Sage said this. Sage, who is the kindest, most generous person I know.

"No," I say helplessly. "Don't wish that."

And then I know what I have to do.

KATE LARKINDALE

Chapter Seven

I finish straightening up the living room, my mind racing at about seven-hundred miles an hour. I've left it too late. We can't afford to wait until I have enough money saved for an apartment. We can't wait until I'm eighteen. Mom's killing us. The injuries aren't serious, at least not this time, but if Sage is talking like this... I shudder. She's poison, pure and simple. And I won't let her poison spread any further. I won't let Sage and Wiley be ruined by her.

No. We have to leave. We have to leave now.

I close the stereo cabinet and look around the room. There's nothing here I'll miss. There's nothing here I value at all. Except my brothers. I look at them, my throat suddenly thick with emotion. Wiley sits on the floor, his back against the couch where Sage remains curled. He reminds me of a guard dog, the way he sits there, all frightened eyes and too-long dark hair.

I turn my attention to Sage. He's blond, like his father, but his coloring is all he got from him. I was only five or six when he left Mom, but I remember him as an overbearing bully. Nothing like Sage whose gentleness is as much a part of him as his hands or lungs.

I head out of the room.

"Where are you going?" Wiley sits bolt upright, hands white-knuckled around his knees.

"I'll be right back," I promise.

In the kitchen, I dampen a dishtowel in the sink and rummage through the junk drawer until I find some aspirin. There are no clean glasses in the cabinet, so I rinse one of the dirty ones, sniffing them until I find one which may not have been used for booze recently.

Back in the living room, I perch myself on the arm of the sofa next to Sage. "Can you sit up?"

He winces and groans but manages to pull himself upright.

I tilt his face toward me and dab at the blood on his chin with the towel.

"Ow!" He flinches away from me when I touch his cut lip.

"Sorry." I hate that I'm hurting him. "Take these. It might help."

Sage stares at the pills I hold out to him, and I think he might not take them. But he sighs and snatches them out of my palm, gulping them down with the water like they're poison.

"Are you okay to walk a bit?" I ask after a minute.

"Now?" Sage stares up at me. "Why?"

I shift down so I'm sitting next to him and beckon Wiley to join us on the couch. He does, sliding in beside me and so close I can feel his ribcage move with every breath.

"We gotta get out of here," I start. "I thought we could hold out a little longer and wait until I'd saved some money, but I was wrong. We have to leave."

"Now?" Sage repeats. "Tonight?"

I nod. I'm angry now. I'm ready to do it. If we wait until tomorrow, things might feel different, safer, and it will be too easy to put it off again. I've already put off doing something for too long. The next time I come home, someone could be dead, not just bruised or bleeding. And it won't be Mom.

I've been selfish. It's been bad here for years, yet I've kept making excuses for her behavior. Not because I wanted to protect her, but because I wanted to get through school. I left quitting until too late. If I'd dropped out as soon as I recognized how impossible our situation was becoming, I would have some savings now. Instead, I have half of my last paycheck sitting in my bank account and a couple of hundred emergency cash hidden in our room. About enough to feed us for a week. Ten days if we ration carefully.

"Where are we going?" Wiley asks.

I bite my lip. That's the big question. Where *are* we going to go? It's not like we can pitch a tent and camp out in the woods for a while. We'll freeze to death. Where can we go? Think, Blue. Think.

"The lake." The words pop out of my mouth and as soon as I hear them, I know I'm right. The summer houses up there will be empty now. No one much goes there in the winter. It's too bleak. We'll pick the most remote, isolated property and hide out there until I can figure out something more permanent.

Sage opens his mouth as if he's about to protest, but he doesn't. He nods instead. "Sounds like a plan."

And just like that, it is.

" It'll be cold," I say, already making lists in my head of what we need. "So make sure you pack your warmest clothes. Nothing else. We can't afford to be too weighed down with stuff. Only the essentials."

"Can I take Honey?" Wiley asks.

"Of course," I say. I may be practical, but I'm not heartless. Besides, the stuffed dog won't take up much space.

"Thank you, Blue." He gives me a brief hug as he slides off the couch and heads toward our room to pack.

I watch him go, grateful for some time to speak to Sage alone. Wiley won't question me. He's always looked up to me. In his eyes, I can do nothing wrong.

"I'll help you pack," I say as I help Sage to his feet. "And I'll carry your stuff."

"I'll be okay," he says, but I recognize the careful

way he's walking, his posture very erect as he attempts to keep pressure off his bruised ribs.

In the hallway closet, I find an old hiking pack I think belonged to Wiley's father. It's dusty and smells of mildew, but it's big enough to fit most of what we need.

"It's freezing out there," I tell Sage as I toss underwear, socks, and jeans into the pack. "You should probably put on a few layers."

Sage doesn't move. "So we're going to go up there and break into someone's house?"

I nod as I lever up the floorboard at the back of the wardrobe and pull some cash out of the hollow underneath. "It won't be for long. Only until I can figure something else out."

Sage nods, but I don't think he's heard me. I lift my mattress and pull out more cash. I learned a long time ago not to keep all my money stashed together. When Mom needs something—booze, drugs or whatever—she'll toss the house looking for cash. So I keep a little bit in an obvious hiding place, like under the mattress, so she'll take that, leaving the bulk of it safely hidden elsewhere.

"D'you think she'll come after us?" Sage looks thoughtful as he struggles to pull a pair of sweatpants on over his jeans. "Will she even care we're gone?"

I stop what I'm doing and stare at him. "Do you care?"

"She is our mom."

I spit a bitter laugh through my teeth. Didn't he just say he hated her? "Yeah, she really acts like it. Sage, she hit you tonight. And I bet you didn't do anything to deserve it."

He shrugs, but doesn't say anything. If I know Sage, he jumped in to keep Wiley from taking the brunt of her anger. Not that Wiley would have done anything to deserve getting hit either.

"I bet she won't do shit," I say finally. "She'll be glad we're gone. You've heard her talk about how we've done nothing but hold her back for years."

Now it's Sage's turn to laugh. It comes out more like a snort though. "Yeah. Once we're gone, she can make that comeback she's always telling us about."

"She'll be back at number one in six months." The idea is so far-fetched, so ridiculous. A hysterical bray of laughter escapes my lips.

Once I start, I can't stop. I drop the backpack and collapse onto my bed, doubling over with the force of my guffaws. It's not good laughter though. It doesn't make me feel lighter or better about anything that's going on. No, this laughter hurts. It rips through my belly like a knife. Tears roll down my cheeks, and I discover I'm not laughing, I'm crying. Crying. Me. I haven't cried in years. I can't even remember the last time I did. And now that I am, I can't figure out how to stop.

"Hey." Sage sits next to me and rests a hand on my back. "Blue, it's okay."

"It's n ... n ... not," I manage to choke out. I hate this. I'm always in control of myself. I have to be. I have to stay strong for my brothers. They need me to do that, to be the dependable one. God knows everyone else has failed them in that respect. So why am I falling apart now? When they need me the most?

I sit up and wipe savagely at my tears. "I'm sorry," I say.

"Don't be," he says, still keeping his hand on my back where he's tracing circles between my shoulder blades. "You don't have to be tough for me. You're allowed to be scared. I'm scared too. But we'll be okay as long as we stick together."

I hope he's right. We don't have anything else, so

he has to be right.

I swallow hard, struggling to get myself back under control. "Why don't you go see how Wiley's getting on?"

Sage nods, but he glances back at me a couple of times as he crosses the room and crouches next to Wiley who, oblivious to us, is sorting through his small box of toys.

I get up and finish stuffing clothes into our bag. That will have to do. I glance around the room, searching for anything else we might want to take with us. Surely there's some personal memento or childhood treasure worth holding on to.

There are a couple of photographs pinned to the wall over Sage's bed. I pull them down and glance at them. One is an old publicity photo of Mom. She's very young, her dark hair in long braids hanging almost to her waist. She's wearing a red dress and black boots, smiling at the camera in a way I haven't seen for years. A cigarette burns between her fingers, but instead of looking like a lifeline, it looks like a prop, something she's holding because it makes her look more mature or something, not because she wants to put it between her lips.

The second picture is a wedding photo. Mom is in a white dress, her hair shorter. I expect the man standing at her side to be blond—Sage's dad—but instead I find myself looking at my own father. He left Mom a couple of years after I was born, not willing to keep following her around the country while she performed. Not prepared to spend his nights stuck in a hotel room with me while she flirted with other guys and drank into the wee hours. He died in a car wreck when I was about six, so I barely remember him. Only that he was big and spoke in a voice which boomed through whatever room he was in. His laugh boomed too, and he laughed a lot. I remember falling asleep to the sound of his laughter.

"I think I have everything." Wiley drags a garbage bag stuffed full of clothes and dumps it at my feet, his stuffed dog tucked neatly under one arm.

"Even your toothbrush?" I stuff the pictures into the backpack I'm still holding and look down at it so Wiley won't see the evidence of my tears. "Can you grab mine and Sage's too?"

He drops the bag and runs off, taking the dog with him. At eight, he's probably too old to still be sleeping with that thing, but I'm not going to take it away from him. Everyone needs something to make them feel secure, even if it is a ratty old plush toy.

I slip the backpack onto my back, adjusting the straps so it will fit me. Picking up Wiley's bag, I'm surprised at how light it is. His whole life shouldn't be so insubstantial. All our lives.

I sigh and switch off the light as I leave the room.

I won't miss it. I may have called this place home, but it's never really been one.

KATE LARKINDALE

Chapter Eight

I feel nothing as we leave the building. Nothing except the bitter wind biting through my clothes. We could have chosen a better time of year to run away from home. Summer maybe. Then shelter wouldn't be such a big concern. For a moment, I doubt myself. Maybe this is a stupid thing to do. Maybe we just need to be more careful... But, no. This is why we've stayed as long as we have. Because I've been too scared to make this move. And that's why Sage is limping next to me, his eye rapidly swelling shut.

"C'mon," I say and lead the way up the street, shouldering Wiley's garbage bag.

"How are we going to get to the lake," Sage asks quietly.

"Hitch?" I don't mean it to be a question, but that's how it comes out. And I wish it didn't. I've made this decision for all of us. I need to be confident about it. My brothers are trusting me to do the right thing, so I need to be confident about the decision. Even when I'm not.

"Is that a good idea?" Sage's face wrinkles as he considers it. "I mean, people will remember a bunch of kids hitching, right? Especially with all this stuff."

He's right. We need to fly under the radar here. Standing on the side of the road with all our possessions is going to draw attention.

I sigh. "I guess we're walking ... at least part of the way."

There's a bus that goes as far as Warrington, but it's still at least another three or four miles to the lake from there. I didn't think this through. It's almost eight and Wiley should be in bed. Sage should be at his hockey game. We could have left in the morning instead of now. Mom's passed out and is likely to stay that way until morning. I'm such a goddamn hothead sometimes. I need to learn to think before I act. It's too late now though. No way am I telling my brothers we have to go back. We've made a break for it. We have to push forward from here.

"Let's head down to Mornington Road. We can check the bus schedule," I say. "Warrington isn't too far from the lake."

Sage raises his eyebrows but says nothing as he takes Wiley's hand and starts down the street.

It's brighter once we hit the main road. People mill about under the orange glare of the streetlights and walk through the brighter puddles of light cast by store windows. Cars crawl the street, adding to the glare with their headlights. I've never noticed the contrast between our shitty, dark street and the main drag before. At least, not this acutely.

It's not far to the bus stop, but weighed down under our accumulated belongings, it feels like a long way. Sage doesn't move with his usual speed or grace either, favoring the side where he took the bulk of Mom's beating. Wiley stumbles along in his wake, never letting go of Sage's hand.

People stare at us as we move along the crowded sidewalks. Whether it's because I look kitted out for a camping vacation or because there aren't any other kids as young as Wiley walking the streets at this time of night, I have no idea. I stare down a couple in their forties who look like they're about to approach us.

Don't come up to us, I urge in my head. *Don't ask me what we're doing.*

My thoughts must show in my face because they drop their gazes to the pavement and hurry away, not even glancing back once they're past us. I watch them go. I don't need any fucking do-gooders butting in. I've been there. *We've* been there. Back in middle school, I made the mistake of answering truthfully when someone questioned me about my bruises. That night a social worker showed up at the apartment and took the three of us away from Mom.

There are worse things than living with an alcoholic mother given to occasional violent rages.

"There's a bus to Warrington in twelve minutes," Sage says, peering at the timetable.

I shrug the backpack off and set down the garbage bag, keeping everything tucked tightly between my feet. This area isn't as shitty as the one we've been living in, but at this time of night, I'm not taking any chances. Even if our stuff is worthless, it's still all we have.

Sage and Wiley drop down on the bench. They both look exhausted, and I'm suddenly overcome with guilt. What was I thinking? Who am I to drag these children away from the most permanent home they've ever known? Especially when we have no place to go, no money, and no hope of earning any. There's no way I'll make it to work if we're at the lake. Not without a car. And a car wouldn't do me any good anyway. I've never learned to drive. There wasn't any point in forking out for driving lessons when I was sixteen because I knew I'd never have access to a vehicle to practice in.

I shuffle over to the bench, dragging all our stuff with me as I do. "Look, maybe I made a mistake," I begin. "Maybe we should go back."

Sage sits up straight, untangling himself from Wiley, who has sagged against him. "I'm not going back. You can, if you want. But I'm not going back there."

I take a step backward, surprised at the venom in his voice. Sage doesn't talk like this. He's the gentle one, the peacemaker. If anyone can talk Mom down when she's in one of her rages, it's Sage.

"Me neither," Wiley pipes up, the same determination in his voice I recognized in Sage's.

"I don't want to fuck up your lives," I plead. "And I don't know what I'm doing right now. I had a plan for us. One that would have worked. At least in theory. But that went out the window when we walked out tonight. We're in unchartered territory here. It's not going to be easy."

"Being at home isn't easy," Sage says quietly. "You're not going to fuck up our lives, Blue. Not any worse than they already are. How could you? You actually care about us."

He looks down, like he's embarrassed to have brought something so personal up. But he's right. I do care about them. I care about them more than anything else in the world. And it's because I care about them that I'm so determined not to let them be hurt again. Not by Mom or one of her so-called boyfriends. Not by bullies in some residential 'care 'facility. Not by anyone.

"It's not going to be easy," I say finally. "I hope you're prepared for that."

Sage shrugs, a crooked grin twisting his mouth. "When has anything ever been easy for us?"

His eyes meet mine and in them I find more trust and love than I deserve. More pain and sadness than he deserves. I have to look away. If I don't I'll cry again, and if I start crying, I'll probably never stop.

"I'm going with you," Wiley says, his jaw jutting skyward. "I don't care where. I want to go where you are."

Sage wraps an arm around Wiley and draws him close. "That's right, Wiley. Because home isn't a place."

I bite my lip. Hard. How can these two trust me

with their lives? It's not like I've done such a great job protecting them up to now. I've tried. God knows I've tried. How many afternoons have I dragged them to the park or the public library to keep them away from Mom until we could be sure she'd drunk enough to pass out? How many times have Sage and I stepped in and taken beatings Wiley would have otherwise endured?

"Are you guys sure?" I have to ask again. I won't force them to come with me. I don't want to go back, but for them I will.

Sage gets up and walks toward me. I'm struck by how small he still is. At fourteen, I was close to six foot; Sage is nowhere near that. He's closer to Wiley's eight-year-old height than mine.

"I'm sure," he says. "Wiley's sure. We're coming with you."

I want to question him further, dig deeper into his reasons for following me on this potentially foolhardy journey. It's great they trust me, but I'm still only seventeen, still a child in the eyes of the law. If we get caught at any point...

The bus rumbles up the street and I scramble to gather our stuff while Wiley and Sage wave it down.

"Warrington," I mutter as I drop money into the tray beside the driver.

Sage and Wiley have gone ahead and found seats toward the back of the bus. I stuff all our baggage onto an empty seat across from them and squeeze myself in next to it.

"Too late to change your minds now," I say as lightly as I can.

"Why would we?" Sage asks and leans his head against the window.

I can think of about a million reasons why. But I don't articulate any of them. Instead, I settle my weight against our luggage and try to relax as the bus takes us farther and farther away from our lives.

I can't though. Every mile the bus takes us, my anxiety deepens. We're breaking the law. We're runaways. I guess technically we're thieves too, for taking things from Mom's house, even if they are things we've considered our own. We're planning to break into one of the summer houses at the lake—another crime.

How did it come to this? I'm not a criminal. I've never wanted to be one, anyway. I've seen what a life of crime can do. Sage's dad was a criminal. That's why he's not around anymore. Mom's manager was too, although in not such an obvious way. In a way hers was the worse crime. The way she siphoned money away, little by little, cheating Mom, and us, out of the future we should have had available to us. Sage's father was just a stupid, violent thug who didn't know any better.

I glance over at my brothers, wondering how such sweet, smart kids could have come from such assholes. I was so young when my own father died, I barely remember him. But from what Mom's said, he was a good guy. At least until he left her. If he really was, he's probably the only good guy she's ever hooked up with. The ones I remember since haven't been worth much.

Sage's father, Errol, was a drug dealer. He traveled alongside Mom's band, showing up backstage whenever she or any of the band or hangers-on needed a fix. It didn't take long for him to wrangle himself onto the band's payroll, or into Mom's bed.

Wiley's dad wasn't a drug dealer; what he shilled was worse than cocaine or smack. He was a promoter and promised Mom the world. In reality, he booked shitty shows in ever shittier venues and took a cut of whatever she got paid. He disappeared from the scene not long after Mom's pregnancy started showing, not even bothering to stick around long enough to meet his son.

In between these two charmers, and after them, were a string of losers who liked to drink Mom's booze, take her drugs, and bask in the tattered remnants of her fame. I hated them, not only because they didn't hesitate to slap us around if they felt we got in their way, but because they'd do the same to Mom. I never understood how on one hand they could brag to their buddies about getting to be with the great Tabby Lannigan, then turn around and knock her into a wall the very next day.

Is that love?

KATE LARKINDALE

Chapter Nine

"Blue. Hey, Blue... Wake up." Sage shakes me and I blink, unable to figure out where the hell I am.

"Huh?" I sit up and rub at my eyes. They're gritty with sleep and so exhausted the lids feel too heavy to hold up.

"We're here. In Warrington." Sage reaches across me and drags a heavy, black garbage bag over my knees.

Warrington? I struggle to make sense of what's going on while my eyes adjust to the flickering light of a failing fluorescent overhead.

"Oh!" It floods back to me and I'm suddenly wide awake. "Wiley?"

"I'm here." Wiley stands behind Sage, his face, always narrow and angular, looking even more drawn than usual.

"Let's go," I say, dragging myself and the backpack off the seat and heading down the too narrow aisle toward the doors at the front of the bus.

Sage struggles along behind me, dragging the garbage bag until I reach over and take it from him.

"Thanks," he mutters as we clamber down to the street. The bus pulls away almost as soon as our feet hit the ground, leaving a cloud of foul exhaust trailing in its wake. It accelerates up the street, taillights flashing briefly as it turns a corner and disappears into the night. My stomach contracts and for a second, I want to drop everything and run as fast as I can after that bus. It's my last link to the city and my life.

I turn my back on it. "C'mon," I say. "We should keep moving or we'll freeze to death."

I'm not kidding. The air up here feels several

degrees colder than it did in the city. I guess maybe the buildings and pollution back there keep the heat hanging around longer. Out here, where there's a great expanse of clear, starry sky above us, and the tallest building in view is maybe four stories, there's space for the wind to whip around us, its chill slicing through our clothes to settle into our bones.

"Which way?" Sage jams his hands into his pockets and looks both ways along the deserted street.

I frown. I have no idea. I've never been here before. The two times I've been to the lake with friends, we've shot straight past Warrington on the highway, the signs indicating its presence little more than a reminder the town is the butt end of one of the city bus routes.

"Let's try this way," I say, pointing back the way the bus went. I was asleep when we came up, but it would make sense the bus route would follow the highway. Once we get back there, finding the road to the lake won't be hard. I settle the pack on my back and try to find an easier way to carry Wiley's garbage bag. The plastic's so shiny and slippery, it keeps wanting to slide right out of my hand, and I have to adjust my grip on it every few seconds.

We walk in silence down the street, not seeing a single person or vehicle. The quiet is so unlike the city it's unnerving.

"I'm scared," Wiley says after a few minutes. "Is everyone dead?"

I force a laugh. His idea seems all too plausible right now. "Of course not. This is a small place. Everyone's probably at home in bed."

Which is where I wish I was. It's cold out here, and I'm so sleepy I can't keep myself from yawning every few minutes. The bags over my shoulders feel heavier with every step I take. Whose stupid idea was this anyway?

"Is that a cow?"

Sage's voice breaks through my half-asleep brain and I stumble to a stop, almost tripping over him.

"Over there." He points to something on the other side of the fence we're walking alongside. Something large.

"A real cow?" Wiley sounds awed and I realize the poor kid has probably never seen a cow or a horse or a sheep up close. Sage and I spent so much time on the road with Mom as little kids, we've probably seen half the livestock grazing between the coasts. But touring stopped after Wiley was born, so he never got to experience life on the road.

Whatever is behind the fence snorts softly and Wiley shrinks into my legs.

"It can't hurt you," I say, pulling him close and moving forward with my hand on his shoulder. "Look."

We peer through the fence at the black and white beast standing there. In the dark, it's hard to see much more than a hulking shape in the field. The moon is still too low in the sky to cast much light, and even when it does rise, it's not full.

"Hey," Wiley says softly, peeling himself away from me as he steps toward the fence. "Hi, there."

The cow snorts again and thuds its feet against the ground.

Wiley looks back at me, a look of absolute delight and wonder on his face.

"Uh…" Sage glances over at me. "Maybe we should get out of here. I think that cow might be a bull."

I look back through the fence Wiley has started climbing. His feet rest on a slat of wood about a foot off the ground and his upper body hangs over the top of the fence.

"Wiley…" I begin, but it's too late. The bull charges at him before I've managed to get the word off my tongue.

"*No!*"

It's Sage's voice, but I barely hear it. I drop the bag I'm carrying over my shoulder and tear Wiley from the fence in a single movement. My heart thuds heavily in my ears, its pulse far quicker than it was seconds ago.

"Run!" I scream at Sage.

But Sage can't run. At least not well. Or fast. Even though he was ahead of me, and I have Wiley slung over my shoulder like a sack of potatoes, plus the backpack, I pass him in seconds. I look back over my shoulder and find him struggling, hands clutched to his bruised ribs, just as the bull crashes headfirst into the fence with a cacophony of splintering wood and tortured wire.

Then there's silence. My heavy breathing and too-quick pulse is all I can hear. There's another thud, this time followed by a loud snort. I hear the sickening creak of boards splintering.

"Sage!" I shriek as the beast attacks the fence again, its hooves thudding against the ground as it scrambles free of it.

I don't know what to do. I can run fast, but won't that tease the bull into chasing me? And Sage is right behind me, directly in the huge beast's path. I stop running. I am not letting this animal bully my brothers. I'll stand up to it the way I never had the guts to stand up to Mom.

Sage staggers past me and as he does, I swing Wiley from my shoulder and push him to go with Sage. Away from me.

"Blue," Wiley say.

"Go," I say. "I'll be fine."

But I don't feel fine. My stomach is cold and writhing with snakes. Under my clothes my skin prickles with gooseflesh. I have to stand my ground. If I'm still enough, it may not see me. I wish I had one of those red flags bullfighters use. I'd distract it with that. Then Sage and Wiley would have plenty of time to get away.

But I don't have a flag. I don't even have the stupid garbage bag to flash around anymore. It's sitting in a lump just outside the fence.

The fence.

I rub at my eyes for a second.

Didn't I hear the fence crack and splinter? Didn't I hear the bull coming right for us?

A laugh explodes out of me when I recognize my overwrought mind must have been playing tricks on me. The bull—if it even is a bull—stands by the fence, pawing pathetically at the ground. Air puffs in and out of its nostrils in small clouds which drift quickly away into the night air.

I walk slowly and carefully back to where Wiley's garbage bag lies, spilling its contents across the ground. I scoop everything back in and sling it over my shoulder again.

"Thanks for the scare, dude," I say to the bull. "I needed an adrenaline kick."

I'm not sleepy now. Not even close to it. I'm super-awake, everything I look at extra sharp and clear in the brightening moonlight.

I find Sage and Wiley hiding in some bushes lining the road. "False alarm," I say sheepishly as I help them out of the broken branches and falling leaves. "I swear I heard the fence break."

"Anyone ever tell you you're paranoid?" Sage says with a grin.

I lean over and pull some leaves out of his hair.

"Yeah. You."

Sage slaps my hands away. "I'm glad you are though."

I brush Wiley down, considering what Sage said. I don't believe I'm paranoid. Concerned, maybe. Worried a lot of the time. I don't go looking for disaster around every corner. I'm just unsurprised when I find it. That's what seventeen years on this planet has taught me. I hate that I think that way, but unfortunately, I've had to.

"Come on," I say once everyone is largely tree-free. "It's getting late and we still have a way to go."

"I'm tired," Wiley says. He's not whining, or complaining, only stating a fact.

"I know," I say. "Me too. But once we get there, we can sleep for as long as we like."

Sage is the first to start moving again. "I could sleep until next month."

Again, it isn't a complaint, just a statement. And one I believe. In the cool, pale light the moon casts over the street, Sage looks exhausted. No, he looks old. It's like a worn fifty-year-old man has taken up residence in my fourteen-year-old brother's skin.

We walk in silence for a long time. And it is silence. There is no traffic on the road we're following, no people, no voices. The only sound is the faint scuff of our shoes on the tarmac. I find myself counting the rhythm of our steps, mine sure, heavy, and even, Wiley's so light I have to strain to hear them, and Sage's unsteady, one shoe dragging across the ground every few steps. It's an odd symphony, but it's all I have to hold onto, so I do.

"Anyone need a rest?" I have no idea how far we've come, but my shoulders ache from the weight of the bags. We've come over a small rise and I scan the dark landscape, searching for any kind of landmark. But there's nothing but a couple of pinpoints of light, both so far off I can't be sure what they might indicate.

Sage and Wiley both collapse where they're standing, dropping to the ground with matching grateful sighs. I kick myself as I shrug out of the backpack and join them. I should have stopped sooner to let them rest.

"Water?" I pull a plastic bottle from the backpack and pass it to Wiley. He unscrews the cap and takes several long gulps before handing it on to Sage. When it gets back to me, it's close to empty so I tip the rest of it into my mouth.

I should probably have thought to bring more water. My stomach growls. I never ate dinner and I'm hungry. Yet I have no food packed. We should have stopped somewhere and bought food before we headed out to the middle of nowhere. I was so focused on getting away, and where we might go, practicalities like food and water never even crossed my mind.

Sage scrambles to his feet, dragging Wiley up with him. "Car," he says as the headlights spill over the crest of the hill.

KATE LARKINDALE

Chapter Ten

The car is driving too fast for the narrow, badly-sealed road. We're already on the very edge of the asphalt, but I grab Wiley and pull him farther off the road with me, hoping Sage has the sense to do the same. It roars past. Loud music pulsing through the windows competes to be heard over the noise of a shot muffler.

I'm prepared to watch the taillights blink away into the darkness, but seconds after it passes us, the brake lights come on. The car reverses, too fast again, and pulls up across from us.

"Are you guys lost or something?" It's a man and his voice is preceded and followed by a cloud of pungent smoke that bolts out of the window as soon as he opens it.

"Something like that," I say cautiously.

"You're going to Bradshaw's party, right?" The guy's wearing a baseball cap backwards and he reeks of pot. But he has a car and could give us a ride to somewhere a little closer to the lake than we are now.

"Of course," I say, chuckling as if to say, why else would we be heading out to a summer resort if not to party with someone called Bradshaw? At the same time, I try to shuffle Wiley behind me. If the guy doesn't look too closely, Sage might pass as being old enough to hang out with this guy and Bradshaw, whoever he is.

"Well, hop in. Can't let you walk the rest of the way. Party'll be over before you even get there."

I grin. "Thanks, man. I appreciate it. I have a couple of things here. You got room in your trunk?"

As if in answer, the guy pops the trunk. I grab the bags, which feel like they've grown heavier in the few minutes we've rested at the side of the road. I slam the trunk closed over them, ridiculously glad I'm not going to have to carry them too much farther.

"We're going with him?" Sage whispers as I open the door to the backseat.

I nod. "Better than walking, right?"

Sage frowns but follows me to the vehicle. I jump into the empty passenger seat and make a big show of shaking hands with the driver while Sage and Wiley climb into the back. I gesture for Wiley to duck down behind the driver's seat. If we're lucky, this guy will never know there was a little kid in his backseat.

"Really appreciate your picking us up," I say, keeping one eye on the rearview mirror. "Was starting to feel like a long walk."

"No problem," the guy says. "Plenty of room, as you can see. My buddies bailed on me tonight. I was going to skip the whole shebang too, but my girlfriend's already out here. And she'll have my balls if I don't show. I'm Rick, by the way."

"Nice to meet you, Rick." I do some fast thinking, trying to decide how to introduce myself and Sage. Our names are so distinctive, people either remember them instantly, or only remember they were something weird. And I don't want this guy remembering us as anything other than a couple of guys going to a party. "I'm Dave, and back there is Steve."

In the rearview, I catch Sage cringe when I call him Steve. That was Wiley's dad's name. Maybe that's why it came to me right away.

Rick reaches down and turns the volume up on the music again. "Tell me if it's too loud," he yells.

I nod. The bass thrums through the car, making the seats vibrate. But I don't care. The less I have to talk the better.

About ten minutes later, Rick turns the music back down a fraction and turns off the road.

"Is this it?" I ask as we bump our way along a dark, tree-lined alley.

"I think so," Rick says. "I only came here once before, but I'm pretty sure this is it."

We drive a little farther before the trees end and we pull up in front of a huge house with lights blazing in every window.

"I guess we found it," Rick says with a grin.

"Looks like it." Sage climbs out of the backseat. "This place is huge."

"It isn't even the biggest one on this side of the lake either." Rick flips off his cap and runs his fingers through the thick dark hair beneath. "There are some fucking palaces down that way." He gestures vaguely to the right. "Seems stupid to have something so big when you're only going to use it a few weeks in the summer. I'll never understand rich people."

"No, me neither." I pop the trunk and pull our bags out, racking my brains for something else to talk to Rick about while Sage sneaks Wiley out of the car. "How do you know Bradshaw?"

"I don't really." Rick looks a little sheepish. "But Nina's been friends with him since they were both in diapers. Nina's my girlfriend. How about you?"

"Me? Oh, we go way back." I can't come up with any kind of association I might have had with this guy, any way I might know him so I'm stalling while my brain tries out different stories and rejects them. "We were lab partners in chemistry."

Rick looks suddenly impressed. "Oh. You're that Dave? You're a fucking legend, man. A real honor to meet you."

Fuck. Why did I say my name was Dave? Oh,

right … because it's a normal, innocuous name that wouldn't draw too much attention. How was I to know this Bradshaw character had a legendary lab partner called Dave? This is why telling the truth is way easier than lying. Way simpler too.

"Thanks?" I say. "Look, we should go see if we can find the Brad man. Enjoy the party, okay?"

Rick nods. "You too, man. And if you need a ride back into the city tomorrow, look for me. I have work at three, so I'll be heading out around eleven or twelve."

"We're good for a ride back. But thanks. And thanks so much for the ride up here." I want him to go inside. Or around the back of the house. Anywhere other than here. I don't want to have to go inside and try to figure out who this Bradshaw is and how to bullshit my way through a potentially awkward situation. It's late and all I really want is to get out of here and find a safe place for my brothers and I to sleep tonight. A safe place as far away from this party as we can get.

"All good, man." Rick clicks a button on his keyring to lock the car. I hope Wiley's out by now. I can't see him or Sage, so I have to imagine they're together somewhere.

I reach out and shake Rick's hand. "See you around."

"Yeah. Will do." He slaps my palm as he withdraws from the shake, then he walks off.

I wait until he's disappeared into the house before moving around the car. "Sage? Wiley?"

"Here." Sage's voice drifts toward me, but I still can't find him.

"Where?"

"Here. Behind the hedge."

I look around. Light shines from the house's windows so it's plenty bright out here. Yet I can't find my brothers. Behind the hedge? I can see the hedge, a huge, impenetrable mass of evergreen which grows in both directions as far as the light spreads. How the hell can they be behind it? How would they have got through?

I push against a section of hedge, wondering if it might not be as impenetrable as it looks. Branches groan under my weight, but don't give. No way did my brothers push their way through this. Not without making a sound.

"Sage?" I call again.

"Follow the hedge," he says and it sounds like he's trying to hold back laughter. Glad he's finding this so funny. Now is not the time for hide and seek.

"Which way?"

"Toward the house." Sage's voice has shifted a little, so I pick up our things and start moving in the same direction.

The music and voices grow louder as I get closer to the house. I do my best to ignore them as I follow the hedge. Broad pools of golden light flood the hedge and the narrow, bricked path which runs alongside it. I pause before I walk into the first one. If anyone looks out the window as I walk by, I'll have to figure out some way to explain why I'm lurking behind the house with a backpack and an overstuffed garbage bag. Now I think about it, I'm surprised Rick didn't say anything. I mean, who brings this much stuff to a party? Even if the plan is to stay overnight? Guess we're lucky he was so stoned.

I make it through the first pool of light without any problem. When I reach the second, I move closer to the house, pressing myself against the wooden boards so if anyone does glance out, they won't catch me. I'm halfway across when I see what Sage was talking about—a narrow doorway cut into the hedge.

"Great," I mutter to myself. Now I'm going to have to risk being seen. I take a deep breath and dive for the cutting, running across the soft grass, the brick path, and more soft grass until I'm on the other side.

"So you finally found us." Sage's voice startles me when it comes from right beside me.

"Don't want to do that again in a hurry," I say, gulping air and trying to slow my racing heartbeat. I must have been more tensed up than I thought.

"You were funny when you couldn't find us," Wiley says, his elfin face lit up with a grin.

"Well, you hid pretty well," I tell him. "Now, let's get out of here."

I look around, trying to get my bearings. The lake is right in front of us, the lights from the upstairs rooms of the house reflecting off its gently rippling surface. The cold night air smells fresher or something, damp and clean and somehow green. I don't know how to describe it, but I guess it's what the lake smells like.

"Look." Sage has moved to the waterline and is cracking the thin film of ice growing along the edge with his foot.

I frown. "We need to find somewhere to stay." It's only November, yet already the lake is starting to freeze. It's only going to get colder from here.

I focus on that, trying to figure out which way we should go. Rick pointed right when he was talking about bigger houses. Bigger houses are likely to be owned by rich people and will no doubt have better security. We're better off finding something less fancy and more likely not to get us caught by security guards or the police.

"Let's go that way," I say finally, pointing to the left and picking up Wiley's damn garbage bag again.

There's a rough path worn into the grass, and we follow it along the lake's shoreline. The hedge continues for a long time, shielding the houses behind it from view. I understand wanting privacy, but if you're buying lakeside property, wouldn't you at least want a view of the lake?

The hedge finishes and we find ourselves walking right into someone's backyard. Outdoor furniture is stacked up against the weather and there are no lights on inside. An abandoned swing set sits lopsidedly on one side of the frozen lawn. The swing drifts backward and forward with the wind. A shiver rolls up my spine. It's creepy in the moonlight, like someone has jumped from it and may be lurking somewhere in the yard.

I tell myself not to be stupid, not to let my imagination run wild. I've just managed to convince myself there's nothing to be afraid of, when the night's silence is torn apart by a loud, ragged bark.

KATE LARKINDALE

Chapter Eleven

I freeze. My heart stops beating for a second. Out of the corner of my eye, I see something coming toward us. Fast.

My head whips around as the small white dog gets pulled up by the chain attached to its collar. It whines once, then resumes barking.

My feet unfreeze from the ground. "Just a dog," I say quietly. "And it's chained up."

"That scared the crap out of me," Sage says with a slightly hysterical laugh.

"Me too," Wiley adds. He's very pale and his eyes are wild. I think the dog scared him more than the rest of us.

"Let's get out of here," I say. "That dog's barking loud enough to wake the dead."

Yet strangely, no lights go on in the house beyond the yard and the chained-up dog. Nor do they go on in any other houses.

"Weird," I mumble as we continue along the rudimentary path.

"What's weird?" Wiley is walking right beside me now, almost running so his shorter legs can keep pace with mine. I force myself to slow down, although every instinct tells me to get away from that house and the dog as quickly as I can.

"What?" I look down at Wiley and find him looking expectantly at me.

"What's weird?" he repeats.

"Oh…" I shake my head. "The dog. It's weird no one came to check what it was barking at. Most of these houses are probably empty at this time of year, but there must be someone in that one. You don't leave your dog chained up and head home."

As soon as I say the words, I wish I could take them back. Some people do. They think a puppy is a nice idea, but once it's grown up and not so cute anymore, the novelty wears off and the dog gets neglected or abandoned.

It happens with kids too. I should know.

I make a mental note to sneak back in daylight to check the poor mutt isn't starving or injured or something.

"Maybe the owner sleeps real hard. Like Mom does sometimes," Wiley says. "That's why they didn't wake up."

"Maybe," I agree, rubbing at Wiley's hair with the hand which isn't tangled in his garbage bag. "Hey, if you see a house you like the look of, tell me." We're far enough away from both the dog house and the party now. And the houses whose yards we're crossing now are modest. Short jetties jut out into the water from some.

"Shouldn't we find somewhere to go soon?" Sage asks from behind me. "It's freezing out here."

I look back over my shoulder and see the way he has his arms wrapped around himself. I'm not cold, probably because of all the extra weight I'm carrying, but my breath puffs into the night air in visible clouds.

"Yeah. You're right. Which one looks good?" I stop and look around at the houses nearby. They all look much the same in the darkness. Small, wooden cottages with a long strip of lawn leading from the back door to the lake. No fences mark the boundary between properties, so it's like the entire lakeside is one gigantic backyard.

"That one?" Sage points at one with a wooden picnic table sitting in the center of the lawn. I study it for a second.

"Why not?" I say. They're all pretty much alike. Probably painted different colors, but I can't tell in the moonlight. Everything looks cool and milky.

We walk cautiously up to the back door. I'm sure it will be locked, but I try the door handle anyway. Unsurprisingly, it doesn't turn. On either side of the steps leading to the door are flowerbeds, slightly raised and lined with bricks. I step down and try lifting the nearest brick. It doesn't budge. Nor do the next three I try.

Sage and Wiley must catch on to what I'm doing because they take the other side of the steps, trying each brick in turn.

"Found it," Sage says a second later, holding up the brick he's managed to slide out of place. Under it, in a small hollow in the mortar, a house key gleams in the moonlight. "People are so obvious."

I nod. They are, but I'm grateful for it. I scoop up the key and try it in the lock. It doesn't even stick, just turns like the lock was oiled yesterday. Is it even breaking in if you have a key? Semantics, I know, but somehow it feels better this way.

We walk inside, taking care to close the door behind us. Sage fumbles along the doorframe for a light switch, but I pull his hand away before he can find it.

"We don't want to advertise we're here," I say in a low voice. "So no lights until we're sure there's no one around."

"How are we going to find out if we have no lights?"

"Candles?" I say, looking around the small kitchen we're standing in until my eyes have adjusted to the dimness enough I can recognize cabinets and drawers. I pull open the first drawer I come to and find cutlery. In the next one down are bigger kitchen tools—spatulas, whisks, and tongs. I find what I'm looking for in the third drawer down—a box of ten single white candles like the ones they stick in wine bottles at Italian restaurants. Jammed in beside them are several books of matches.

I light a couple of candles. The first I hand to Sage. The second I hold for a second, letting wax melt and pool along the base of the wick. Once a generous amount has collected there, I pour it onto the edge of a countertop and settle the candle in before the wax hardens. There. Now we have a candle and a candle holder.

"That looks cool," Wiley says, staring at the candle's flame as it bobs and weaves with the air currents moving through the room. Shadows stretch and grow against the walls. It's a little unsettling. I understand how ghost stories came about. Candlelight is spooky as hell.

I find saucers in one of the cabinets and use wax to fix Sage's candle to it. Then I light another and do the same for myself.

"Let's explore," I say, picking up the candle and walking to the wide arched doorway on the far side of the kitchen. I feel like I've stepped back in time or something. My shadow on the wall does nothing to change this impression. With the candle in my hand, I look like an illustration I vaguely remember from an old children's book.

I shake off the thought. Thinking about books like that only reminds me of the times Mom used to read them to me. To us, once Sage was born. I wonder if he remembers it at all. I don't recall exactly when she stopped the bedtime story routine, but he can't have been much more than three or four. I tried to keep it up for a while, reading to Sage in the back of vans, in motel rooms, and in filthy backstage areas at bars, but it didn't last long.

We move out of the kitchen into a large open-plan space set up to be both dining room and living room. There's a heavy wooden table at one end, and a pair of long couches set into an L-shape separating the living area from the eating one. Colorful beanbags litter the floor in front of the couches and bookshelves line the walls.

"Nice," Sage says, looking around. His candle's flame reflects off the glass in the floor-to-ceiling windows looking out over the backyard and the lake.

"Yeah," I agree. In summer, this place must be amazing. Now though, it's cold. Warmer than outdoors of course, but still cold.

Another broad, arched doorway leads out of this room and I marshal my brothers through it. We find ourselves in a small hallway, a staircase leading to the upper level, and a couple of closed doors. I cross to the first one and find myself in a tiny bathroom, just a toilet and a sink. The next one over is a closet, and when I open the door, a tennis racket and a hiking boot tumble from an upper shelf and almost catch my head. I put them carefully back, taking care not to let my candle's flame get too close to the nylon rain jackets hanging there.

The last door is the entry to the house.

Sage slides the bolt open and pokes his head out the door.

"See anything?" I ask as I step behind him to peer over his shoulder.

"Nope. Doesn't seem to be anyone around."

He's right. The street beyond the small front yard is empty. The other houses are dark and sit there, as silent as tombs. I wish I could be certain there's no one in them, but it's late at night. Even if people are living in them, chances are at this time of night they're asleep.

"Keep it closed," I say, pushing the door shut.

"We'll stick to the back of the house." Although I'm not sure it's much safer, given the wall of glass looking out over the lake.

"Come on!" Wiley has already scampered halfway up the stairs and is waiting for us to join him.

"Yeah, yeah…" I pretend to be irritated, but I'm not. We've only been away from Mom a few hours, and already Wiley is starting to act more like the eight-year-old kid he is. For the first time, I start feeling like I've done the right thing.

A small landing like the hallway below sits at the top of the stairs, several doors branching from it. Wiley opens one at random and finds a small bedroom, the two single beds made up with colorful quilts. A few worn stuffed animals are collapsed against the pillows on one. A tin robot and a toy dump-truck missing one of its front wheels sit on the dresser. Wiley's eyes widen, but he doesn't touch anything, just closes the door behind him.

The next door reveals a bigger bedroom, this one with a large double bed scattered with cushions. A large bay window looks out over the lake, a window-seat with more cushions sits in the alcove.

On the opposite side of the hallway, we find the bathroom and a linen closet filled with sheets, blankets, and towels. I run my hand across one of the towels, wondering at the soft thickness of it. My fingers almost get lost in it.

At the far end of the hall is another bedroom, but it looks like whoever owns the place uses it as an office or study. A desk is pushed against the wall under the window and the bed is kind of squished in amongst more overflowing bookshelves. I feel a sudden surge of pride in myself. If nothing else, we won't get bored here. There's plenty to read.

"Can I have this room?" Wiley asks, sitting down

on the narrow bed and bouncing once or twice.

I wish I could say yes, but something about the idea of us being separated makes me uneasy. Wiley deserves his own room. We all do. But I'm not sure about taking over this space. Breaking into someone's house is one thing, sleeping in their beds is another. It feels like too much of a violation.

"Let's go back downstairs," I say. We have shelter and that's the main thing. We can work out details later. Now we need to see if we can find the other things we need: food and heat.

KATE LARKINDALE

Chapter Twelve

Downstairs again, I walk back through the living room and draw the heavy curtains across the huge windows, shutting out the night sky, stars, and rippling lake. I move back toward the doorway and search for a light switch. With the curtains drawn, I doubt anyone will see the light.

Blinking in the sudden brightness, I blow out my candle and gesture for Sage to do the same. I'm actually a little surprised the power is still on. Relieved, but still surprised. I would have thought shutting off the electricity was part of closing up a summer house for winter. But I've never had a summer house, so what do I know?

"Look, there's a fireplace over here." Sage pulls something back and reveals a wide stone hearth behind it.

"Weird," I say. "I thought that thing was a TV cabinet or something."

A fireplace solves our heating problem. Well, it will if we can find some wood.

"Wiley." I turn to find him digging through boxes stacked in one of the shelves. They rattle as he files through them. "What did you find?"

"Games," he says. "And puzzles."

"Anything good?"

Wiley shrugs. "I don't know what most of them are."

" Can you go outside and see if you can find any wood? There's probably some stacked up somewhere around here."

"On my own?" He looks up at me and his eyes glitter with excitement.

"You think you can?" I walk back through the archway into the kitchen and to the drawer I found the candles in. Rummaging around, my fingers find a cylindrical object. "Ah ha!"

I set the unlit candle down on the counter and thumb the button on the flashlight, hoping the batteries are fresh. I'm rewarded with a beam of bright white light.

"Here," I say, handing the flashlight to Wiley. "Safer than candles."

"Brighter too." He flicks the thing on and off, clearly delighted by the responsibility I've handed him.

"Probably not such a great idea to do that, buddy," I say, reaching out and stopping him from flicking it again. "Might draw attention to us. And be careful with it while you're outside. Don't flash it around too much. Just at the ground and whatever you're looking at."

Wiley gives a solemn nod and heads for the back door, the flashlight trained directly at his feet.

I leave the door open, despite the chill coming in from outside. I want to be able to hear if anything happens to Wiley.

There are no curtains in the kitchen, so I re-light the candle before heading to the cabinets. I'm not hopeful there will be food there, but there's no harm in looking. We might have lucked out and picked a house belonging to one of those survivalist types who have enough food and water stashed away to last the apocalypse. On second thought, I didn't find any guns while we explored the house, but that doesn't mean they're not here. Or these survivalists are the pacifist type. I must be tired. My thoughts aren't making any sense.

"Found anything good?" Sage opens a door and peers at what's inside.

"Haven't started looking, really," I say, throwing

open the nearest cabinet. "Anything in that one?"

Sage pulls a couple of things off a shelf and peers at them in the wavering light. "Couple of cans. They look pretty old though."

I go over to him and check out the labels. They do look old, the paper faded and peeling away from the can underneath. "In a pinch, maybe?"

Sage sets them back on the shelf and continues rummaging. I move back to my own cabinet. Cereal. That's good. Even if it's stale. A couple of packages of crackers. Not much to live on, but enough to get us through until I can get back to Warrington to get supplies. Or find out if there's somewhere closer I can go.

"I found it!" Wiley races back inside, the flashlight's beam bouncing off the walls and ceiling in exactly the way I didn't want it to.

"What?" Sage looks confused.

"Wood. Lots of it." Wiley grabs my hand and drags me outside, leading me around the house to a small shed. A tarp flaps idly in the wind, and under it are neat stacks of logs.

"Good work!" I pile as many logs into my arms as I can carry and gesture for my brothers to do the same. Wiley manages four. Sage picks up one, grimacing as he reaches for a second.

"Don't," I say quietly. "I'll come back."

"Sorry." Sage drops the one log he had back.

"Don't be," I say, more savagely than I mean to. "It's not your fault. I shouldn't even have asked you."

Inside, I busy myself building a fire. I've never done it before, but I keep that fact to myself. It can't be that hard, can it? I've seen people do it on those stupid reality TV shows, not to mention, even the cavemen managed, and they were outdoors and didn't have matches.

Yet even with matches, it isn't easy. I keep getting the paper I'm using as tinder to light, but can't get any of the wood to catch before the paper turns to ash.

"Goddamn it!" I shout when the tiny flame I've conjured up goes out for the fifth time. "What the hell am I doing wrong?" I've blown gently on my flames, blown harder, blown them out, yet nothing seems to work. The log doesn't look or feel wet, but I'm starting to believe maybe it is.

Sage and Wiley are curled on the couch, not asleep, but getting close to it. A clock on the wall says it's almost three in the morning so no wonder they're tired. Maybe I should go and get some of those blankets from upstairs and leave fire-making until tomorrow.

But I don't give up. I keep trying, this time peeling some bark off one of the other logs and tossing it on once I get the first tongue of flame licking up the paper. The bark catches quickly, but doesn't burn up at the same speed the paper does. And this time the log catches. It's slow, but little by little the log starts burning.

"Yes!" I give myself a fist pump.

"Good work," Sage says sleepily.

"I know you guys are tired," I say. "I am too. But if you go upstairs and get some blankets and stuff, I'll make us some beds down here. Probably better to stay together. And where it's warm."

Where I hope it will be warm. So far, my fire isn't emitting much heat. I throw another log on, watching to see if it will catch, then add another once it looks like it's burning well.

"C'mon, Wiley." Sage hauls himself off the sofa and heads for the stairs.

Wiley yawns but follows.

Once they're gone, I muscle the couches around so they're still in the L-shape, but facing in the opposite direction. I pull the cushions off one and lay them end to end. Probably about long enough for Sage; plenty long enough for Wiley. I flop down on the remaining couch, testing its length. If I rest my head on the arm and curl up a little, I'll fit. Just.

Sage and Wiley come back with some pillows and a couple of blankets. Not enough for all of us. I get up and head back upstairs, grabbing the quilt from one of the beds and dragging down duvets and blankets from the linen closet. I take one of those super soft towels too. Simply because I like how it feels against my skin.

In less than fifteen minutes we have cozy beds made up. Sage is in the kitchen mixing up some hot chocolate powder he's found in one of the cabinets.

"Stove works," he says approvingly as he sets a pot on it.

"Good." I yawn. The fire has taken the chill off the air a little and casts a warm glow across the room. I throw another log on before heading to my place on the couch.

"Look," Sage says as he comes in with three mugs of hot chocolate in his hands. "It's snowing."

I go to the kitchen window and look. He's right. Outside, snowflakes drift past the window. They're not sticking to the ground though. Not yet.

"Made it just in time," I say with a smile.

"You're not kidding." Sage glances back at the window. "Wouldn't want to be out in this."

"Is there anything to eat?" Wiley asks hopefully.

I grab one of the boxes of cereal I found earlier. There's no milk of course, but I prefer dry cereal anyway. It's a little soft, but not as stale as it could be. We sit there, huddled in our blankets around the fire, sipping watery hot chocolate and eating handfuls of dry cereal. It's not luxurious. It's not even good. But to me, it's the best meal I've ever tasted. It tastes of freedom.

Wiley falls asleep before he finishes his hot chocolate. I take the dangerously tilting mug out of his hand and set it on the coffee table before lying him down on his mattress and tucking blankets around him.

"Thank you," Sage says once I've settled myself back onto the couch.

I give him a funny look. It's not like I haven't tucked Wiley into bed before. I mean, sure, Sage does it most of the time, but it's not unheard of.

"No, seriously," Sage says. "Thank you for getting us out. I was scared."

My heart seizes in my chest. "You never said anything.",

Sage gives a funny little shrug. I hate that he's been scared. Not surprised, of course. I've been scared too. For years, I've been scared. But I never told them. How could I when I asked them to be brave every single day?

"You don't have to be scared anymore," I tell him. It's a lie of course. There are actually more things to be scared of now. At home there was only Mom and we knew what to expect from her. Mostly. She sometimes threw us a curveball.

Now, I have so many things to be scared of I don't think I've even thought of them all yet. Money, food, shelter, being caught, where we go next, jobs… But I'm not going to share that with Sage now. I will of course; I don't keep secrets from Sage, but he deserves at least one night where he can sleep without being afraid.

"Let's go to sleep," I suggest. I'm too tired to consider any of this right now. I'm warm and sleepy, and for the first time in years I actually feel safe.

I hold on to the feeling as I curl up under my blankets and let my eyes drop closed.

Chapter Thirteen

I wake up cold. I open my eyes and blink around, unsure for a moment where I am. It's not until I catch sight of my brothers, sprawled out on the floor in a tangle of blankets, that I remember.

My stomach turns to ice. I tighten the blankets around me, trying to keep from trembling with terror as I try to forget what I set in motion.

It's no good though. I'm not getting back to sleep. So I get up and pull the curtains open a crack. Just enough for me to see outside. When I do, I'm practically blinded by the sudden brilliance. The sky is blue and the sun shines on the lake in a way that sears my eyes. The snow hasn't come to anything, hasn't stuck, and for that, I'm grateful. I wish I'd thought to bring sunglasses. I make a mental note to look around for some later. Sunglasses are exactly the kind of thing people would leave at a summer house.

The fire appears to have burned out and it's frigid in the house, despite the sunlight. I get up and poke at the ashes with the heavy poker hanging from a hook beside the fireplace. Nothing even glows. The remains of the logs sitting in the grate crumble into dust at my touch.

I sigh and try to build a new fire as quietly as I can, not wanting to wake the others. This time I manage to get it lit on my first attempt. That bark makes all the difference. I make another mental note, this time to find some small twigs to use as kindling.

I sit back on the couch and cover myself again, waiting for the fire to warm the air a little before I get up and do anything.

I'm too antsy to stay still, so I get up, wrapping a

blanket around my shoulders as I do. It'll be easier to assess what we have and what we need in the daylight.

In the kitchen, I throw open all the cabinets. Cereal in this one, as I discovered last night. Only two boxes now, both already opened, plus a plastic bag of oats. Crackers. An airtight container that, when opened, reveals a half-empty bag of shredded coconut. The pantry has a whole collection of spices in a Tupperware container. The ancient cans Sage showed me. Jars of dried beans and lentils—those will be useful. A couple of boxes of macaroni. A package of instant soup sachets.

The refrigerator is, surprisingly, switched on, but there's nothing in there except four bottles of beer and a box of baking soda.

Okay. So I need to get to a store. We can probably live off what's here for about two days, and we'll be hungry most of the time. Leaving without food was stupid, especially when I knew we were coming somewhere so remote. I'll probably have to walk back to Warrington, and that could take several hours. Maybe it's worth heading back to the party house. I could try to catch the guy who drove us up here and hitch another ride.

I open the back door, squinting against the brightness of the sun. It's cold even though the sun is high in the sky. High enough I suspect I've slept through most of the morning and it's now early afternoon. Probably too late to catch anyone leaving the party. The lake sparkles invitingly at the end of the yard, but I'm only wearing socks. I head back to the couch for my boots.

My brothers are still asleep, but they've moved since I left. Sage has turned onto his back and in the harsh daylight, his face looks horrible. One cheek is purple and his eye is grotesquely swollen. If he can see out of that thing today, I'll be surprised.

I slip on my boots at the door and step outside. In the shadow of the house the dry grass is crisp and frozen. My feet leave marks in the frost. As I move into the sunlight, the ground grows softer, the grass damp enough to leave wet streaks across my boots.

Closer to the lake, the grass stops, replaced by pebbles and slick mud. I wander toward the water's edge, looking out at the clear, still expanse of blue. The ice Sage commented on last night is gone here, in the sun, but I'm sure some lingers in the darker places where trees or reeds filter away the light and warmth. I've never been up here in the winter so have no idea if the lake freezes over during the coldest months.

I walk a short way in one direction, eyeing the houses for signs of life. There's no one around. The only sounds are the cries of birds in the trees and the constant lapping of the lake against the shore. As I head back, I notice clouds building on the horizon, looking like puffs of cotton sitting on the surface of the lake. I cross the lawn toward the back door and a cold breeze fingers the back of my neck. I shiver and open the door to the kitchen.

Sage is in there and as I suspected, his eye is black and swollen almost closed.

"Ouch," I say as I close the door behind me. "Does it hurt?"

Sage reaches up and probes the area around his eye gingerly with his fingertips. "That bad, huh?"

I can't do anything other than nod. He's been here before, so he knows what it looks like. There's no point lying to him about it.

"What are you making?" I nod to the water on the stovetop.

"Oatmeal. It's cold!"

"I know. I was out there checking if anyone else is around. I need to go get supplies. There's only enough here for a day or so."

"Think you'll make it into town?" Sage looks concerned. I recognize it even through the bruises.

I shrug. "I'll give it a go."

Sage goes to the door and peers out. "Looks like this weather isn't going to last."

I glance over his shoulder and see he's right. The lake that was glassy smooth only a few minutes ago is now rippling as wind blows across it. The clouds that looked so pretty are piling up now and darkening to gray. Yet over the house, the sun still shines brightly.

Wiley wakes up just as Sage finishes the oatmeal. There's no sugar or syrup or anything to put on top, and no milk, so we scatter coconut over it and get out the box of spices to experiment with.

"Do you think cardamon will taste good on oatmeal?" I ask, sniffing one of the boxes with suspicion.

Sage shrugs. "Only one way to find out."

I pinch a small amount of the powder out of the box and sprinkle it over a corner of my oatmeal. "Not so good," I say after a mouthful. "Maybe I'll try cloves instead."

"Cinnamon's good," Wiley says with his mouth full.

I try some, but I'm pretty sure I still prefer my oatmeal with bananas and brown sugar. But I'm not in a position to complain. Having something in my belly is better than nothing.

After breakfast, Wiley drags one of the puzzles from the shelf and dumps the pieces out on the dining table. He's deeply involved in it within a few minutes, and doesn't even seem to notice when Sage and I leave the room to go and explore the upstairs again in daylight.

This time we open all the closets and drawers. Most are empty although we find several old bathing suits—both men's and women's—and the sunglasses I wanted.

"Do I look cool?" I ask Sage, sliding them on.

"Like one of the Men in Black," Sage replies. "There's nothing very useful up here."

I shrug. It's a summer house. It has summer stuff in it.

We're about to raid the bathroom cabinet when I hear something that sounds like the crunch of gravel under a car's tires.

"What's that?" I ask.

Sage looks stricken. "It sounds like…"

"I know!" I go to the bathroom window, but it's frosted and I can't see out. I open it a crack. "Oh, shit."

"What?" Sage pushes me aside and peeks out. "What do we do?"

I stare at him, my mind whirling at about seven million miles an hour. It comes up blank.

"Wiley!"

"Oh, shit," I repeat.

We run for the stairs, but before we reach the top, the distinctive sound of a key turning in the lock stops us in our tracks.

"Back," I hiss and drag Sage away from the stairs and toward the small study at the end of the hall. I pray Wiley heard the same thing we did and has the sense to hide. It's not going to keep us from getting discovered, but I'd rather whoever this is meets me first.

We huddle by the desk under the window. I try to keep still, but my blood and every nerve in me quivers under my skin. After a second, I raise my head and take a peek out the window. A dark blue car is parked at the side of the house, right under the window I'm looking out of. The trunk is open and I catch sight of brown grocery bags lined up in there. A lot of brown grocery bags. Whoever this is, they're expecting to stay a while. Or they're having a party. Maybe both.

"What do we do?" Sage whispers, his voice squeaky with panic. "Wiley…"

"Shh. I know." I snap and I don't mean to. It's not Sage I'm mad at. It's myself. "I'm thinking."

"Well, think fast!"

I glare at him. What does he think I'm doing over here? Maybe he could come up with something instead of leaving it all to me.

I crawl back toward the doorway and listen hard.

Nothing.

I'm not sure if it's a good thing or a bad thing. On the plus side, Wiley isn't screaming in fear or pain. On the downside, I have no idea where he is or what he's doing.

I have no idea what the owner of the car is doing either. They can't have come inside yet. The bedding on the living room floor and Wiley's puzzle on the table would have been obvious as soon as anyone stepped into the room. Not to mention the dishes in the kitchen and my wet, muddy boots left inside the back door.

These thoughts dart through my head at lightning speed. They're not giving me any solutions. I have no idea what to do here. We're going to get caught. Maybe shot even. Definitely arrested.

Think, Blue. Think.

And then I hear it. The sound of a door handle turning. The creak of the door being pushed open.

My heart hammers in my chest. I can't breathe. My chest aches with the air trapped within it. I fight to swallow, to loosen the lump of breath sitting somewhere between my lungs and my throat.

"Blue…" Sage's unswollen eye is huge and terrified in his pale face. "Blue, what…"

He doesn't finish.

There's a scream from below and I bolt to my feet, running toward the staircase before I even realize it's not Wiley's scream.

Before I can think anything further, before I can analyze the timbre and pitch of the voice, there's another sound, a dull metallic clang. This is followed by a strangled choke and a heavy thud.

It's quiet. Too quiet. My pulse thumps in my ears and I can almost hear the swish of blood racing through my veins, the tuneless twang of my overstretched nerves.

I glance at Sage, unsure if I should go down there, unsure what I'll find when I do.

Then, Wiley shrieks.

KATE LARKINDALE

Chapter Fourteen

I've never heard Wiley make a sound like that before. I've never heard any human being make a sound like that before. It's a ragged, tortured howl. It's the kind of sound a trapped animal might make. A trapped animal in terrible pain.

I fly down the stairs. I'm not even sure my feet touch any of the steps, but one moment I'm at the top, the next I'm at the bottom. I skid to a stop in the hallway when I find the crumpled figure sprawled face down on the floor. Two bags of groceries lie on either side, their contents scattered across the rug. A single orange rolls to a stop against the side of my foot.

Wiley stands in the center of the room, his shadow falling across the prone figure, the fireplace poker still in his upraised hand.

"What did you do?" I ask, not believing the scene before my eyes. "Oh, Wiley... What did you do?"

Sage must have followed me down the stairs because suddenly he's there too, pulling the poker out of Wiley's unresisting hand.

"I... I... I..." Wiley chokes. He glances down at the unmoving figure on the floor and bursts into tears.

I let Sage take over with him. I can't deal with him right now. There's a dead body in the hallway. I gulp. Maybe not dead. Hopefully not dead. Wiley's only eight. Surely, he's not strong enough to kill someone.

I drop to my knees next to the figure. It's a woman, I think. Long dark hair hangs down, obscuring her face. She's wearing jeans and boots with one of those colorful puffer jackets over them.

I brush aside some of the hair, searching for her

neck and the pulse I hope to find beating steadily there.

"Is she dead?" Sage whispers from where he's crouched with Wiley sobbing against his chest.

"Not sure yet," I mutter.

Wiley howls again and Sage tightens his arms around him.

"Get him out of here," I say. "Take care of him." I can't do this with him in here. Every sob tears another piece of my sanity away. How scared must Wiley have been to have done this? I've never heard him talk back to anyone, let alone lash out.

"C'mon," Sage murmurs, gathering Wiley into his arms. "It's okay, Wiley. She's okay."

And they're gone, into the other room. Wiley's wails are still audible, but they're quieter now, less piercing. Sage will look after him. He's good at it.

I turn back to the woman on the floor. The way she's fallen, I can't reach the pulse points on her neck without turning her over. And I hesitate to do that. When someone's hurt, aren't you supposed to leave them where they are in case you do more damage moving them?

I debate myself for about thirty seconds before deciding I need to turn her over. Her face is mashed into the carpet, and I'm afraid she'll choke or suffocate if she isn't already dead.

If… Why am I thinking if? She can't be dead. Wiley couldn't kill anyone.

She's not a large woman, but unconscious, she's heavy. I'm suddenly grateful for all the lifting I do at the warehouse. It's given me the strength to do this. Who needs a gym?

I groan as I roll her onto her back. Her hair flops forward with the momentum, keeping her face concealed. Unfortunately, it isn't enough to conceal the bloody wound above her temple. I feel for her pulse first, breathing a sigh of relief when I feel a heartbeat. It's slow, but there.

She's not dead.

"Thank god!" I say out loud.

"What?" Sage calls from the other room. "Blue? Did you say something?"

"She's not dead," I call back. "Wiley? It's okay, kiddo. She's not dead. You just knocked her out."

I have no idea if Wiley can hear me, but I need to say it aloud. My relief is so great, my entire body goes limp with it. I have to sit back on my heels for a moment, balancing my weight on my hands to keep from falling flat on my face.

Once I've regained my equilibrium, I lean back over the woman. She seems to be breathing normally too. I push her hair away from the wound on her head. The blood has run down over her cheek and into her ear, but it's already slowing. It's not deep. Scalp wounds bleed a lot. I know from experience.

I brush away more hair, revealing her face for the first time.

"Fuck!" I jump to my feet, my hand clawing through my own hair as I look down at the figure on the floor. "No fucking way!"

"What?" Sage is suddenly there, inside the archway, still holding Wiley against him. "What is it, Blue?"

I stare down at her, unable to tear my eyes away. "I know her. That's Mrs. Applegarth. She's my English teacher."

"What?" Sage repeats himself. "Are you serious?"

I nod, my tongue suddenly too thick and heavy to form words. Of all the houses up here, of all the places to choose from, I had to go and choose hers.

Sage crosses the room and stands by my side,

Wiley crying quietly into his shirtfront. "Mrs. Applegarth? Does that mean there's a Mr. Applegarth about to show up?"

"Maybe?" I've always liked Mrs. Applegarth. We got along. But we talked about Dickens, Shakespeare, and poetry, never anything personal. I'm not sure if there even is a Mr. Applegarth.

"Help me get her onto the couch," I say finally. "We can't leave her here." The hallway is cold and drafty, the front door still open. Whatever heat my fire managed to generate has drifted into the great outdoors by now.

I kick the door closed as I round Mrs. Applegarth to grab her shoulders.

"Wiley?" I say quietly. "Can you do me a favor?"

Wiley manages to dig his face out of Sage's front long enough to nod.

"Can you go upstairs and find a washcloth?"

I get another nod.

Sage squeezes him tightly for a second and drops a kiss on his head before releasing him.

Wiley walks off, not running this time. His footsteps are heavy as he climbs the stairs, his shoulders hunched as if he's carrying a heavy burden.

"I hope he'll be okay," I say quietly.

"Yeah." Sage wipes at his eyes hurriedly. "Me too."

It takes the two of us several minutes to maneuver Mrs. Applegarth to the couch. I try to take the bulk of her weight, but even lifting her feet makes Sage wince and gasp with pain.

"I'm so sorry," I say as we lie her on the cushions. "I know you're hurt. I shouldn't keep asking you to do all these things."

Sage shakes his head, his teeth gritted. "I'm fine."

I glare at him. "No, you're not. You're in pain. There's gotta be some aspirin or something around here. Go find it. She's going to need some when she wakes up too. She's going to have one hell of a headache."

"I don't need any," Sage says. "I'm okay."

I take one look at his pale face, at the beads of sweat on his brow. He's hurting. I bet Mom cracked a rib or two last night. It wouldn't be the first time. When she gets really riled up, she sometimes throws furniture. Or us at it.

Wiley slips back into the room and presses a washcloth into my hand.

"Thank you," I say, trying to smile. I don't feel much like smiling though. We're in my English teacher's house. Wiley knocked her out cold. Her husband could be here any minute. When she wakes up, she's going to be scared. And mad. She'll call the cops on us for sure. Wiley and Sage probably won't go to jail, but I will. And I can't take care of them from jail. They'll either get taken back to Mom or put in some boys' home. I couldn't tell you which is worse.

"Sage?" I look around for him and find him in the kitchen. Despite saying he wouldn't take them, he's swallowing aspirin with a glass of water. Good.

He sets the glass down as I walk into the room. "Yes?"

"Can you and Wiley pack up our stuff? We have to get out of here." I want to make sure Mrs. A is okay, but once I'm sure of that, we need to get gone. And fast. I only wish I could figure out somewhere to go. Another lake house maybe? That's not going to work. As soon as Mrs. A wakes up, she'll call the police, and they'll likely search every one of the houses for the thugs who broke in and assaulted her. So we have to go somewhere else. Anywhere else. Well, anywhere except back to Mom. I'd rather go to jail than take my brothers back there.

I dampen the washcloth under the tap, wringing it out well.

"I don't think we're going anywhere," Sage says quietly from where he's standing by the kitchen windows.

"Huh?" I drop the washcloth in the sink and join him by the windows. The blue sky has disappeared, replaced by a thick blanket of steel-colored clouds. Below them the lake shifts and tosses. Small white-capped waves tumble across it. All around the house trees shake and rattle their bare branches, and I realize the roaring sound I thought was coming from my own head is, in fact, wind.

"Fuck," I say, as the first drops of rain splatter the glass.

"What are we going to do?" Sage asks, his eyes wide with panic again. "Blue?"

Running my hand through my hair, I look around.

Wiley is standing by the sink, seemingly oblivious to our conversation. He's stopped crying, but his face is still puffy and streaked with tears. He sniffs and wipes at his nose with the back of his hand.

I glance out into the living room. Mrs. Applegarth hasn't stirred, but that doesn't mean she won't. And when she does...

"Can you go look in the shed around the side? See if there's some rope or something?"

" Rope? You're not going to..." Sage looks horrified.

"I don't think we have much choice."

"Jesus, Blue." Sage shakes his head. "Really?"

I bite hard on my lip. "Really. Do you want to go back to Mom? Or to Dunstan again?"

Sage cringes at both suggestions, his hand

unconsciously drifting toward the bump at the bridge of his nose. "Okay. I get your point."

"Good," I say grimly. Sage always sees the best in people. I wish I still had that ability. I wish I could still look at the world the way Sage does. I don't even believe Wiley has his innocence and at eight, he should.

Sage disappears out the back door, letting it slam behind him. I wince at the noise.

"Are you going to tie that lady up?" Wiley asks.

The kid doesn't miss a trick, does he?

I nod. "Yeah. Only for a while. She's going to be mad when she wakes up. And probably kind of scared. I don't want her to do anything to hurt us."

Wiley nods. He understands anger, fear, and getting hurt.

After pulling the damp washcloth from the sink, I head back into the living room to wipe the blood away from Mrs. Applegarth's face. It has stopped flowing already, and when I examine it, the gash isn't too bad. Wiley must have been lucky with the angle he caught her at. It doesn't look like he's done a lot of damage.

Of course, internal brain damage might not show. But let's not think about that right now. I don't want Wiley to have to live with knowing he's done someone permanent injury.

"Is she going to be okay?" Wiley asks, when I return to the kitchen to rinse blood from the cloth.

"Yeah," I tell him. Until we know differently, why scare the kid? He looks terrified enough as it is with his bloodshot eyes and tearstained cheeks. I rest my hand on the top of his head for a second. "She'll be fine."

I hope I'm right about that.

KATE LARKINDALE

Chapter Fifteen

I've just tied the last knot securing Mrs. Applegarth's legs when she begins to stir. Her eyelids flicker a couple of times, then she tries to raise her hand to her head. She can't though, because I've tied both of them together. So she ends up raising both hands and almost punching herself in the face.

That wakes her up.

Her eyes pop open and stare around, a panicked look in them. I'm standing behind the couch so she doesn't see me right away. She takes in the room. Her face registers her recognition of the space and the tension in her jaw relaxes a little. She looks down and catches sight of her bound hands and the tension is back, exaggerated now. It's not only her jaw that's tight now, it's her entire body. She looks like a coiled spring, ready to be let loose.

She shifts around, wincing with the movement of her head. Headache. Like I predicted. She sees me and she freezes. The look of utter confusion on her face is almost comical. It's not just confusion, it's disorientation and disbelief. It's like she's seeing two disparate images and is trying to justify their juxtaposition. Or something like that. If we were in class right now, she'd be trying to explain how when an artist or a writer place two entirely different ideas or images next to one another, it can create a meaning that isn't implied by either individual idea or image.

Except in this case, the familiar place and the familiar face don't create any coherent meaning. The two worlds colliding here should never have met.

"Blue?" Her voice is horse and scratchy, and my

name is said in a kind of unbelieving whisper, like maybe she thinks she's hallucinating.

"Hi, Mrs. Applegarth," I manage. My mouth is suddenly so dry I can barely form the words. It's like I've swallowed a mouthful of sand or flour or talcum powder. My tongue sticks to the roof of my mouth, and the words I want to say are trapped there.

"It *is* you," she says in the same, raspy voice. "How…"

I shift from foot to foot, uncomfortable. There's no easy way to explain how this came about. Choosing her house was a coincidence. An accident. An unfortunate one. And we're only still here because of the storm brewing outside. If I had any other choice, she'd be waking up here alone.

"Look…" I step around the couch so she doesn't have to crane her neck at such an awkward angle to see me. "I'm sorry. We… I … didn't know this was your place." There's no point letting her know there's more than one of us here. If I handle this right, I can keep Sage and Wiley hidden until the storm breaks, and we can get the hell out of here. She doesn't ever need to know I wasn't here alone.

"Did I leave it unlocked?" She shifts uncomfortably on the couch, her eyes not leaving my face. She looks frightened, but somehow not as frightened as she should look given she's tied up on a couch, bleeding from a head wound with one of her former students standing over her. A large, male, former student.

"Uh… No." I jam my hands into my pockets so neither she nor my brothers who are lurking inside the kitchen door will see how much they're shaking. "But you probably shouldn't hide your spare key in such an obvious spot."

She gives a humorless laugh which sounds almost like a cough. "Jeremy!"

"Jeremy?" It's my turn to be confused.

"My husband." It's like a tsunami of emotion floods over her. Her body goes limp and tears well in her eyes. She still looks scared, but that expression is almost overwhelmed by the other emotions which flit across her face—sadness, anger, resignation, and something I can only describe as loss.

"Mrs. Applegarth?" I lunge forward, but stop short of touching her. She's my teacher. I can't forget that. Or, she used to be my teacher. I guess I still haven't quite managed to get it through my thick skull that I'm a dropout. "Are you in pain?"

For a long moment, she says nothing. She does nothing. I feel big and clumsy, and helpless standing there. "No," Mrs. Applegarth says finally. "At least, not the way you're probably thinking. My head hurts a little. But I can bear that. The rest of it..." She trails off. I'm missing something here. Maybe because it's suddenly so dark in here I can't easily read her expression anymore.

"Uh ... yeah." I ignore the conclusion to what she said and focus on the part about her head. I have aspirin which can help with that. "I'm sorry about that. Do you want some aspirin?"

She rolls over onto her side. It's not an easy move with her hands and legs bound, but she manages. I should probably have roped her to the couch. It didn't seem necessary when she was unconscious. Now it feels like an oversight on my part.

" I don't believe aspirin will do the trick," she says. "Maybe morphine."

"I'm pretty sure I didn't find any in your medicine cabinet."

"No," she says. "I don't doubt that."

The room falls silent. I have no idea what to do. I have no idea what to say. Should I grab Sage and Wiley and leave? No. She's seen me. She knows me. If we leave now, she'll no doubt figure out a way to get free of the ropes, and the cops will be looking for us in hours. Even if we leave the lake area, they'll be on our tail.

Not that we can leave the lake area. One look out those floor-to-ceiling windows tells me that. It's not raining anymore but snowing again. And this time it's not only a few flakes drifting past the window and melting into the ground. The wind howls, sending great flurries of snowflakes whirling past the glass and flinging handfuls against it. The sky is as dark as iron, the clouds heavy and low in the sky. It looks like they're pressing down on the landscape outside, shrinking what seemed expansive to something flat, gray, and lifeless.

I reach over and turn on a lamp, flooding the room with intense golden light. It's not much, but lifts the sense of claustrophobia the relentless, heavy gray gave me.

"Is everything okay, Mrs. Applegarth?" I ask finally. She doesn't seem like the strong, sassy, confident woman who managed to stand in front of my class day after day, spouting Shakespeare like it was everyday slang. She seems sadder, older, and more broken than that woman.

I guess she has a right to though. She's tied up. She has no idea what my plans are. She has reasons to look broken. Yet, I remember the way she looked the day I left school, the way she appeared to be crying as the bus carried me away. This broken expression isn't all about me.

I back carefully away from the couch, keeping a close eye on her. If she tries to move, I'll stop her. I doubt she can do much except roll—Sage and I tied her hands together in front of her, and her legs are bound at the ankles and knees—but it could be enough for her to get to a phone and call the police. If there is a phone here. I haven't seen one. Maybe they rely on cells up here. If cell service reaches this far.

I go into the kitchen, grab the package of aspirin, and fill a glass with water.

The routine motions calm me. I'm still uncertain what to do with her, with us, but I feel more in control.

"Stay out of sight," I whisper to Sage and Wiley as I move through the kitchen.

Obediently, they move away from the doorway and huddle together under the windows. It's so dark now they are little more than shadows against the wall. The wind makes an eerie whistling sound as it fights to make its way through the cracks around the door and windows.

"I want to go home," Wiley says, his voice trembling a little. "I'm scared."

"Don't be. There's nothing to be scared of." To chase away the shadows I turn on the overhead light. "It's just a storm."

When I get back to the couch, Mrs. Applegarth hasn't moved. I show her the small white pills. "Want some?"

She doesn't say anything. She doesn't even nod. She opens her mouth and lets me drop the pills in. Then she lets me put the glass to her lips and sucks back enough to swallow the pills.

"So," she looks around at herself, catching sight of the knotted ropes around her ankles and wrists. "Are you going to untie me?"

"I don't think I can," I say and I hate that I sound apologetic. "I'd be gone, but it's storming out there."

"I know," she says. "The news said they're expecting at least six inches of snow. It's going to last until Monday."

"The storm?"

She nods and winces again. Guess the aspirin isn't doing its work yet. "Early in the year for a blizzard, isn't it?"

"Yeah." What am I doing here, talking to my teacher about the weather? We're trapped here, at least until Monday, possibly longer if the storm is worse than predicted. And I never got any supplies.

Supplies! I remember the groceries Mrs. A dropped in the hallway. Maybe we aren't quite as bad off as I thought.

Chapter Sixteen

The hallway is dark and I kick one of the fallen grocery bags as I search for the light switch. I find it and turn it on. At least with Mrs. A's car parked out front no one is going to find it weird the house is lit up like a Christmas tree. I scoop the spilled groceries back into the bags and carry them into the kitchen.

"I think there are more in the car," Sage whispers when he sees what I've brought in. "There were more than two sacks."

"I'll get them," I say, stepping into the boots I left by the back door earlier. "Can you guys check what's here? Just be quiet, okay?"

Wiley's eyes widen as he watches Sage pull stuff from the sacks. Boxes of crackers, packages of spaghetti and rice, cans. Sage opens some crackers and drops a handful into Wiley's palm. I grab a couple myself and nibble on them as I pull the door closed behind me and head back into the living room.

The fire has almost burned out, so I throw a couple of fresh logs on. I'll need to go out and get more before too long.

"Thank you," Mrs. A says. "It's chilly in here."

I nod and blow on the fire until I'm sure the wood has caught enough to keep burning. I'm going to need to figure out some way of moving her out of here. This is the only room with a source of heat, so this is the room my brothers need to be in. But first, I need to get the rest of the groceries in from the car.

The wind is strong enough to fight me as I pull open the front door. A small pile of snow that has drifted against it collapses onto the carpet at my feet and more tries to follow, circling and spinning on the bitter wind. I close the door behind me to keep both the snow and wind out and make my way to the car. It's freezing and I wish I'd thought to put on my coat. The snow is wet, slushy, and slippery underfoot. It's not the time to discover a hole in the sole of my left boot, but there must be one because it takes only a few seconds for my sock to grow damp and my foot ache with cold.

"Great," I say aloud, watching my breath appear in a cloud in front of me. "Just what I need."

I forget my discomfort when I open the trunk and find it filled with bags of groceries. I take as many as I can carry and dump them in the hallway before going back for the rest. Mrs. A's purse sits on the front passenger seat and I take that too, and the thick woolen blanket I find draped across the back seat. The car keys are in the ignition, and I use the button on the key to lock the car as I head back inside.

"We have plenty of food," I say as I ferry the bags of groceries to Sage in the kitchen. "And Mrs. A says the storm is supposed to die out by Monday."

"We're going to keep her tied up until then?" Sage stacks cans in the pantry, neatly, labels facing out. The sight of all this food seems to have calmed him a little.

I scratch my head, finding my hair damp with melting snowflakes. "If we have to, I guess."

"I'll make us something to eat," Sage says, checking packages of meat for expiry dates and filing them in the fridge or freezer. "Wiley can help."

Wiley looks up from where he's crouched on the floor with the crackers. "We'll be quiet."

"I know you will." I smile at him and bend down to take the cracker box away before he eats them all.

I take Mrs. A's purse out into the living room

when I go back in there. She hasn't moved, which surprises me.

I sit down in the armchair next to the couch, right in her line of sight, and rifle through the purse. As I suspected, there's a phone in there along with a charger for it.

"Hope you don't mind if I take this," I say, showing her the phone and pocketing it.

She closes her eyes for a second, shrugs. "It's not like I can stop you. I'm the one who's tied up here."

"That's right," I say in a way I hope is at least a little threatening. I have to remember I'm the one in charge here. Or I'm supposed to be.

"There's no other phone here?" I ask. I haven't seen one, but there could be one hidden somewhere, or disguised as something else. "And don't lie to me."

"I don't lie."

That makes one of us. "That's not an answer."

She sighs. "There's no other phone here. Jeremy never wanted one up here. It's supposed to be a place for getting away from everything. If he could have, he'd have left the cells at home too. Will you untie me now?"

I waver for a moment. I have her phone and her car keys. There's a blizzard outside. Even if she tried to make a run for it, she wouldn't get far.

But I decide against it. I'm sure I'm stronger than her and could overpower her if she tried attacking me, but Sage and Wiley probably aren't. She's not a big woman, but Sage is hurt and Wiley's only eight. And she doesn't know about them. If she is taken by surprise the way Wiley was, she may react the same way and lash out at him. I know who'd come off second best in that fight. Better to keep her tied up for now.

"You're going to have to untie me," Mrs. Applegarth says, her cheeks reddening. "I really need to use the bathroom."

"Oh…" I wasn't expecting that, but of course. "Okay."

I untie her feet first, taking care to stay well clear of kicking range, but she doesn't even try. I help her up. "You're not dizzy?" I ask when she's on her feet. I have one hand at her back in case she falls backward.

Her face screws up a little, the way Wiley's does when he's thinking hard about something—a math problem or reading a word he doesn't recognize. "No. Not really. Kind of light-headed."

"Sorry," I say gruffly. "I didn't want to hurt you."

I walk with her to the tiny bathroom in the entry foyer. I'm hesitant to untie her hands, but there isn't much choice. There's no room for a second person in the room. Not that I really want to go in there to help my English teacher pull her pants down anyway. Maybe some guys would get off on that, but the thought makes me feel skeevy.

So I untie her hands too. This time I do stay close, using my body as a barrier in case she decides to bolt for it and head for the door, blizzard be damned. But she doesn't. She rubs at her wrists and shakes her hands a couple of times to get the blood flowing again. She walks into the bathroom and closes the door behind her. I don't even hear her lock it. I guess she knows not to. Not that there's any way out from in there. There's no window in the bathroom. Only a narrow vent, high up near the ceiling. Not even the slimmest super-model would have a hope.

I stand there, leaning against the wall, waiting for her to finish. The smell of something delicious cooking drifts from the kitchen. My stomach growls. I could use a meal. A big one. The oatmeal I ate earlier only took the edge off my hunger for an hour or so. I sniff at the fragrant air, trying to figure out what they might be making. I can't tell really. The scent of cooking meat mingles with spices, onions, and garlic. It doesn't matter really. Sage is a good cook. I'm not sure where he learned that. It's certainly not a skill Mom could have taught him. Mom's idea of cooking is throwing a frozen burrito into the microwave.

I snap out of my daydream and realize Mrs. Applegarth has been in there a long time.

"Mrs. A?" I rap on the door gently with my knuckles. "Are you okay in there?"

When there's no answer right away, fear starts nibbling at my gut. She could have passed out in there. She could be lying there, sprawled beside the toilet, choking on her own tongue.

"Mrs. A?" I rap harder, with more urgency. "Mrs. A, are you okay?"

I press my ear to the door and hear a small snuffling sound.

"Out in a second," Mrs. Applegarth says, her voice thick and choked with tears. A loud sob issues from behind the door, followed by some softer sniffing. Another sob follows.

"I'm coming in," I say, wrapping my fingers around the doorknob.

The only answer is another of those deep, gut-wrenching sobs, so I pull open the door.

Mrs. Applegarth is sitting on the closed lid of the toilet. Her head is down, her face buried in her hands. Her shoulders shake with the force of her tears.

Touching her feels wrong, not just because she's my teacher, but because we tied her up, made her a prisoner in her own house.

Yet she's crying in a way I can only describe as heartbroken. These tears are nothing like Mom's drunken ones. She controls those like a faucet, turning them on when she thinks it might help her get her own way. I guess it works on some people, or she wouldn't keep doing it. It only pisses me off more because when I see them, I know she's trying to manipulate me.

Mrs. A's tears are nothing like that. These are coming from deep inside her and look almost painful in the way they wrench her body on the way to escaping.

"I'm sorry," I say finally, unable to find anything better to do or say. "You have no idea how sorry."

She looks up, forcing a ghastly smile through her tears. She grabs a handful of toilet paper and blows her nose, loudly and messily. "It's not you, Blue."

Chapter Seventeen

I help Mrs. Applegarth out of the bathroom and back to the living room. She makes no move to escape or to rush for the door, so I feel comfortable enough to leave her alone for the time it takes to grab a box of Kleenex from the small table by the front door.

She hasn't moved when I get back. I guess she isn't as scared of me as we are of her. Which is good, I guess.

"Wanna talk about it?" I ask, handing over the tissues.

She takes a handful and looks up at me, an almost grateful look on her face. "It's a hard day for me," she says, wiping at her red, swollen eyes. "I lost my family six months ago today."

Crap. That's what it was. I remember now. She wasn't in school the first week or so we were back after summer vacation. *That's* the tragedy that wound its way along the school grapevine as quickly as any lurid story does.

"Oh," I manage. "I'm really sorry. I didn't know."

But I did. At least a little. It was a car wreck, I think. A drunk driver. She wasn't in the car, but her husband and kids were.

She doesn't seem to hear me. "They loved this place. All three of them. They'd come up without me if I was busy. Even when it was really too cold for fishing or any of the other things you do at the lake. That's why we put in the fireplace when we renovated."

I glance toward the fireplace and find the fire is almost out again. I move around the couch and throw the last two logs on, waiting until the first licks of flame curl around them before looking back at the figure on the couch. She looks so small huddled there. So broken.

I do my best to shake off the pity I'm feeling. She's a threat. I have to remember that. She may look pathetic, but my life and the lives of my brothers are in her hands right now. Hands I haven't tied back up since returning from the bathroom.

Reluctantly, I reach for the ropes again. Tying her up again feels unnecessary, but I'm too frightened of what might happen if she gets out of here to leave her unbound.

"I'm sorry," I tell her as I wind the cord around her wrists. "I wish I didn't have to do this."

She nods, not struggling or fighting me. I move cautiously to her legs and bind those too, certain she's going to kick me in the teeth at any moment. But she doesn't. She lies there, limp and unresponsive, her face stony beneath the streaks her tears have cut through her makeup.

"Do you need anything?" I ask once, she's secured again. "Hungry? Cold?"

She shakes her head and lets her eyelids drop down over those red, swollen eyes.

I move toward the door to the kitchen, then stop, taking a step back toward her on the couch. I'm not sure I should leave her, even if she doesn't look like she's going to try and escape. She could be fooling me though, lulling me into believing she's helpless so I'll drop my guard. It's the kind of thing Mom does all the time, saying one thing to get her way, then doing exactly what she wants almost as soon as the words have left her mouth.

The logs in the fireplace shift as they crumble into ash. I whirl around at the sound, remembering once again I need to get some more wood. A glance out the window tells me the wind has strengthened. It's hurling great handfuls of snow at the glass. So much I can barely glimpse the lake through the spiraling flakes. The light is dim and flat, partly because of the thick, heavy clouds blanketing the sky, but also because it's getting dark. I pull the phone I took from Mrs. A out of my pocket and glance at the time. Incredibly, it's almost five. I should go and collect that wood before it gets completely dark.

I stuff the phone away and look back at the woman on the couch. Her eyes aren't closed anymore. She's watching me. But when she clocks me noticing, she lets them close again.

"Don't move," I growl as I move toward the kitchen door and the good smells drifting from behind it.

"Not much chance of that," she says, her voice low. And as if to prove it, she lifts her bound legs and lets them fall back on the sofa with an audible thud.

The kitchen is warm and steamy, the windows fogged with condensation.

"What are you making?" I ask, pulling the door closed behind me.

"Spaghetti," Wiley says, for once managing to get the word out without mangling it beyond recognition. "And salad and garlic bread."

My mouth waters at the thought of real food. Substantial food. The few crackers I nibbled earlier have done nothing to curb my hunger.

"How long until it's ready?" I ask, looking to Sage, who stands by the stove, stirring something in a big pot.

He dips his spoon in and regards the contents thoughtfully. "Maybe another twenty minutes?"

"Perfect." I reach for my coat which I left hanging by the door this morning.

"Where are you going?" Sage glances at the closed kitchen door before looking back at me.

"To get more wood. I used the last of it. Doesn't look like the storm's letting up anytime soon."

Sage nods. "Need help?"

"I'll be fine." I throw him a fond grin. "No point two of us getting cold." Not to mention he can barely carry himself around with those bruises, let alone an armful of logs.

The wind tries to tear the back door from my hands when I push it open. It takes some effort to get it closed again, but I wrestle with it until it remains shut. The cold is enough to take my breath away. I duck my head into the collar of my coat and move down the stairs. My eyes water from the combination of cold and wind. I'm grateful we decided to stay put in Mrs. A's house. There's no way we could have survived long in this.

Wind howls along the side of the house where the shed sits. Snow lies in uneven piles against the walls, but the path between the structures is largely clear. And icy, I discover when I step off the grass and onto the paving stones leading to the woodpile at the rear of the shed. It's more sheltered by the woodpile, and I'm grateful for a moment's respite from the savage wind tearing at my hair and clothes. I brush snow from my coat with fingers which have already stiffened from the cold. Gloves would have been a good idea. I flex my hands a few times and jam them into my coat pockets to warm them up a little before reaching for a log.

I stack as many as I can into my arms, cursing myself for not looking for a box or basket. I'm going to have to take a second trip just to stock enough for tonight. Gritting my teeth against the freezing wind, I round the shed and make my way carefully back toward the house. Not wanting to let any more cold air in than necessary, I dump my load by the steps and head back toward the shed. My coat isn't doing a lot to keep the cold out. Icy fingers of wind grab at the back of my neck, dipping under my collar to trickle down my spine. I shiver and shrug my shoulders up toward my ears. A scarf would have been a good idea too. Not to mention a hat.

I ignore the pain in my frozen fingers this time and pile as many logs as I can into my arms. They sit precariously on top of one another in an uneven stack high enough it's difficult to see around. I hesitate a second, wondering if I should leave a couple behind. They're heavy and my arms ache beneath the load. But I don't have to take them far. I stagger into the wind, eyes burning with tears and cold. The logs at the top of the stack totter before settling again. My boots crunch across frozen grass as I keep my eyes on the brightly lit windows.

My foot comes down on something hard. Icy. My worn boots have no traction on this surface. I try moving back onto the grass, but my other foot finds the stone path too and slides out from under me. I scrabble for purchase on the ice, my ankle turning as I skid off the edge, back onto the grass. The armful of wood tumbles around me when I fall.

Suddenly, I'm on the ground. Half on the path and half on the grass, my left leg folded under me.

"Fuck!" The wood is all around me and I have the vague thought that I'm lucky none of it hit me in the head. My ass is freezing and snow has already started seeping through my jeans. I notice those things first. It's only when I move to lift myself from the ground that the pain hits me. It bolts up my leg, a glassy agony that forces me to give up any attempt at moving and drop back onto the frozen ground.

I open my mouth to cry out, but the wind tears my breath away and all I manage is a gasp. Now that it's registered, the pain is all I can think about. A deep-rooted, dull throbbing centered somewhere near my left ankle. The left ankle that's still twisted under me.

Using my hands, I lift my weight off that leg, forcing myself to straighten it in front of me. The movement sends another monumental wave of pain toward my hip. I groan as I fall back onto my ass. My cold, wet ass. I shiver again. I can't stay out here much longer. Busted ankle or no busted ankle, I have to get back to the house.

I take a deep breath and prepare myself for the pain as I try to pull myself up onto my uninjured foot. I manage to get about halfway before my boot slips on the icy surface and sends me crashing back to the ground. I scream when my injured foot slams into the edge of the stone path.

And then I keep screaming, hoping Sage or Wiley might hear me. But even to me my screams sound pathetic, the sound disappearing into the howling wind almost before it leaves my trembling, frozen lips. The house is so near. I'm only a few feet from the bright patch of snow beneath the kitchen window. In daylight, my brothers could glance out and see me. But it's dark now and the kitchen windows are clouded with condensation.

"Sage!" I call, my throat aching from my screams and the icy air. "Wiley! Help!"

There's movement behind the glass, but nobody appears. How long have I been out here? Long enough for Sage to start wondering where I am? I'm not sure if I can wait that long. My entire body aches, is jerking uncontrollably in the cold. Each shiver sends another intense wave of pain through my leg and foot.

I look around for something else I could use to get my brothers 'attention since my voice doesn't seem to be doing the trick. My fingers feel brittle enough to break off as I scrabble through the snow in search of a pebble or something. They come up empty, too stiff and sore to dig into the frozen ground beneath the snow. I catch sight of one of the logs I was carrying and I reach for it. I have no idea if I'm strong enough, but it's all I can think of.

Biting my lip, I raise the log above my head and heave it toward the house.

It falls short, but not by too much.

I reach for another log, this one a little smaller than the first. My arms are trembling so much I'm not sure if I can even lift them above my head, but I force them to move. I fix my eyes on the spot below the kitchen window I want to hit and hurl it with all my strength.

There's a satisfying thud as the log makes contact with the windowsill.

KATE LARKINDALE

Chapter Eighteen

The back door flies open and Sage shoots out, leaping off the back steps into the snow, head swiveling this way and that.

"Sage!" I call. "Over here!"

He turns at the sound of my voice and freezes.

"Blue?" He blows on his hands as he skids toward me. "What happened?"

"I slipped," I say, but I'm shivering so much the words rock and roll all over the place.

"Are you hurt?" He studies me in a way that's too knowing. He shouldn't recognize so well how I wear pain.

I nod. "My ankle."

He glances at my feet, which are stretched out in front of me. "Broken?"

I shrug. "Maybe?" From what I can see, my ankle doesn't look any different; it's not sitting at a weird angle or anything. My boot feels tight around it though, so I know it's swelling.

Sage hugs himself, already shivering in the freezing wind.

"Go get your coat," I tell him. "You'll freeze to death."

He shakes his head. "I'm not leaving you here like this."

"You're not leaving me. You're going to get your coat and you're coming back." I'm trying to sound authoritative, but my teeth are chattering so hard it's difficult to get the words out. "Now hurry. I'm freezing my ass off."

He hesitates, but goes, running across the snow-covered lawn and back up the steps. I wish I'd asked to him to check on Mrs. Applegarth too. I've probably been gone long enough for her to figure out how to free herself. She could be in there now, the poker in her own hand this time, waiting to clock the next person to enter the room.

Before I can think much more along those lines, Sage is back. Wiley trails him down the steps, zipping up his jacket as he comes. His eyes are wide and frightened.

"Go back inside, Wiley," I say before he gets close enough to get a proper look at me. "It's too cold out here."

"But…"

"Now!" I shout the word, louder than I meant to.

Wiley's face crumples, but he climbs back up the steps and disappears back through the door.

"Shit," I mutter. "I didn't mean to yell like that."

Sage shakes his head. "He'll be okay. Let's get you inside."

He crouches next to me and settles his arm around my waist. I manage to sling one of my own arms around his shoulders and use the other to lever myself off the ground and onto my uninjured foot. At the same time, he tries to rise to his feet, lifting me with him.

I hear him gasp and try to bite it back. Under my arm, his shoulders tremble. I'm hurting him, but I try not to dwell on it. Once I'm up, it'll be easier. I won't need to lean on him so much. I hope.

"Sorry," I say through gritted teeth.

That makes him tighten his arm around me.

Once again, I get about halfway up before my foot skids on the icy surface. I grab at Sage, hoping he'll be able to keep me upright. He tries, and, for a brief second, I believe we're going to make it. But he cries out. His arm disappears from around my waist and I crash back to the ground. At least this time my injured foot just slides across the grass. It still hurts, but not as bad as it did when it came in contact with the stone path.

"I'm sorry!" Sage cries, crouching back down in front of me. "Are you okay? Did I hurt you? I was slipping. I couldn't keep hold of you."

"And I was hurting you," I add.

His face is white and despite the freezing wind, sweat stands out on his forehead. "Let's try again," he says, wiping the sweat away with the sleeve of his coat. His eyes are bigger than Wiley's and dull with pain.

But what choice do I have? The cold has penetrated my clothes, dug through my skin, and is probing my bones in a way that's almost as painful as my injured foot. My fingers don't ache anymore. They're numb and unfeeling. I shake my hands a couple of times, hoping to get some blood flowing back to them, but they hang there, limp, almost like they're not mine.

"Okay." I settle my arm more firmly across his shoulders this time, forcing my unfeeling fingers to close around the far one. He shifts closer to me and slides his arm around me again. He's scared. I can smell it on him. A scent like burning rubber drifts from him each time he moves.

I bend my knee and press my good foot into the ground. It's as numb as my hands, but I sense the ground, firm beneath me.

"One, two, three..." I push upward, trying not to put too much of my weight on Sage as he strains to lift me.

And then we're both on the ground.

I cry out when my hurt ankle wrenches.

"I can't do it," Sage cries. He gasps for breath, frustration etched into his features alongside the pain. "I'm sorry, Blue."

It takes a moment before I can speak without screaming. I'm shivering harder than ever, despite the exertion. "It's okay," I say, wanting to calm Sage. "I don't want to hurt you."

But it's not okay. It's not even close to okay.

"I'm going to get that lady," Sage says finally. "She'll be able to help."

I want to protest, but I'm too cold, too wet, too sore.

So I nod and watch as Sage limps his way back to the house.

He's back more quickly than I thought possible, tugging Mrs. Applegarth along behind him.

"Good lord!" She cries, letting go of his hand and dropping to her knees beside me. "How long have you been out here?"

I shrug. Too long.

"And he says you're hurt?" She glances at Sage, who hovers over me like protective hawk.

I nod. "My ankle," I say, through chattering teeth. "I think."

She frowns. "Well, let's get you inside."

She crouches next to me the same way Sage did, but on the opposite side. He does the same and this time I sling arms across both their shoulders. As I grab at Mrs. Applegarth's shoulder, I wonder what Sage said to get her out here. I don't imagine helping me was one of her top priorities. My freezing to death could not have been a bad thing in her books. But, when the blizzard clears, she'd have a lot of explaining to do.

"Focus," she says, slapping my cheeks, first one and then the next. "C'mon, Blue. Stay with us."

I shake my head. Was I drifting off? Maybe. I'm not cold anymore. Just sleepy. I could use a nap. Maybe after that I'll have the energy to get myself up.

"C'mon, Blue!" Sage begs. "You gotta help us."

I bite the inside of my cheek. Hard. The pain clears my head a little, and I tighten my hands on each of their shoulders.

"Now," Mrs. Applegarth says in a voice I wouldn't argue with.

And then I'm up., swaying a little and leaning heavily on both of them.

Sage trembles under my arm and I try to shift my weight away from him and onto Mrs. A.

"Good boy," Mrs. Applegarth says. "Now let's get you inside."

I try putting my injured foot down, but even the slightest pressure sends stabbing pain through it.

"Hop," Sage says. "And lean on me."

I shake my head. He's shaking almost as hard as I am. I won't hurt him any more than he's already hurt.

Somehow, we make it to the steps, slipping and sliding in the thickening snow. Every movement makes the pain in my ankle worse, but I bite back the screams collecting in my throat. I grab hold of the railing and let Sage duck out from under me. He runs ahead and wrestles the door open while Mrs. A stays where she is, supporting me as I use the wooden rail to drag myself up the steps.

KATE LARKINDALE

Chapter Nineteen

The steamy heat in the kitchen sears my freezing skin.

"Blue?" Wiley runs up to me. "Are you okay, Blue?"

I try to smile at him, but my lips are trembling too much to make the movement. I can't speak.

"Let's get him into the other room," Mrs. A says, motioning Sage to support my other side again. My good leg is shaking so much it's barely holding me up, but somehow they get me into the living room and set me down on the sofa where I'd left Mrs. A tied up.

I sit there shivering, the warmed air like acid against my skin.

"You." Mrs. A points to Sage. "Can you get these wet clothes off him? And you." She turns to Wiley. "Can you go and get some of the firewood I saw by the back door?"

Both my brothers nod. Wiley disappears back into the kitchen. He's still wearing his coat, I'm pleased to see.

Mrs. Applegarth shrugs out of her jacket and tosses it across the second couch, the one we pulled the cushions off to make a bed for Wiley and Sage last night. Was it last night? I feel like days have passed since we left the apartment, but it's been less than twenty-four hours.

"I'll go get some more blankets," Mrs. A says and leaves the room.

Sage tugs the boot off my good foot before turning his attention to the other one. "I think this is gonna hurt," he says.

I nod. It will. But the boot is uncomfortably tight. Even loosening it will be a relief.

Sage unties the laces and works them through the eyelets. The small movements hurt, but not too much. I grip the arm of the couch as much as I can with my stiff, aching fingers and watch as he tries to slide the boot off my foot.

"Okay?" He glances up at me, worry tightening his features.

I nod and dig my fingers deeper into the arm of the couch.

It isn't enough to keep me from crying out when he jerks the boot all the way off. "*Ow!*"

Wiley dashes into the room, dropping an armful of logs in the doorway as he runs toward me.

"I'm okay," I say, holding my hand out so he won't jump on me. "I'm okay, Wiley."

He stands next to Sage and looks at me with those huge, frightened eyes. "True?"

"He's cold," Sage says. "We need to build the fire bigger to warm him up. Can you go get the wood?"

Wiley nods and backs up, not taking his eyes off me as he goes back to the doorway and the three logs he dropped.

"How's the foot?" Sage sits next to me and unzips my coat. I'm still shivering uncontrollably, so he helps me slide it off.

"Hurts," I whisper. "You think it's broken?"

"Can you undo your pants?" He ignores my question and watches me fumble with the buttons on my jeans. My fingers tingle like they've gone to sleep, pins and needles prickling through them. They feel as large and clumsy as sausages, and I can't seem to grab hold of the buttons.

When Mrs. A comes back, Sage has pulled off all

my soaked clothes and wrapped me in the quilts and blankets from the makeshift beds we slept in last night. My injured foot is propped on the arm of the couch, swollen and misshapen, the entire outside of my foot and ankle already darkening with purple bruising.

"Can you make some tea?" Mrs. A says to Sage, draping more blankets over me. "We have to get him warmed up."

She tosses a few more logs onto the fire and shifts them around using the poker.

Wiley, who has parked himself on the floor beneath me, makes a tiny squeak.

I reach down and stroke his hair with fingers that still feel weird, but maybe a little less weird than they did fifteen minutes ago. I'm still shivering though. It feels like I'll never stop shivering. My skin is warm, but underneath it, my bones feel like ice and chills keep running through me.

"Can I look at your foot?" Mrs. Applegarth asks, moving toward it.

"I guess…" My voice is faint and I'm not sure if it's because of the pain or the chills. Or both. How quickly things change. Less than an hour ago, she was the one trapped on this couch, helpless. Now it's me. How's that for irony?

Sage comes in with a tray of mugs. "I made hot chocolate too," he says and sets a mug next to Wiley. "Careful, it's hot."

"It's got marshmallows!" Wiley says, his little face brightening with delight. "Look, Blue."

"Nice," I manage through my still-chattering teeth.

"Try and drink some tea," Mrs. A says, taking one of the mugs and blowing on it before holding it to my lips. "It'll warm you up inside. Afterward, we'll get you into a hot shower. Wish we had a bath up here, but…"

I suck at the rim of the mug, taking a little scalding tea into my mouth and swallowing it. It burns a path down my throat and into my gut, but it feels good. I sit up a little straighter and take the mug into my own hands, folding my fingers painfully around it.

Mrs. A watches, her brow knotted with concern until I take another sip. She turns back to my foot.

"I'll take that," Sage says with a wry grin, tugging the mug from my hand. "For a second."

I'm about to protest, but Mrs. Applegarth touches my ankle and I jump. God, that hurts.

She does it again, holding my foot in both hands and shifting it from side to side.

"Can you stop that?" I gasp.

She drops down on the couch next to me. "I don't think it's broken," she says. "It's sprained. I'll wrap it for you after you shower and it should feel a lot better."

"Are you sure?" Sage hands back my tea and moves to the end of the couch to study my ankle. "It looks broken."

Mrs. A stands and joins him by my foot. "You see how all the swelling and bruising is down this side?" She points to the outside of my ankle and foot. "That's generally a sign of a lateral ankle sprain. If it was broken, it would be swollen all around."

"Huh." Sage looks over at me, clearly impressed with this new knowledge.

I take another sip of tea and almost feel the hot liquid melting the frozen parts inside me. The warmth spreads from my gut, but it only seems to reach my chest. The rest of me—my arms, my legs, my hips, my ass—remain freezing. I'm not shivering as hard as I was before, but I'm still trembling and every once in a while, a larger chill rolls through me like a localized earthquake.

Mrs. A frowns down at me the way she does when she hands back a quiz or paper she's not happy with. "Are you okay to move again? You need to get in a hot shower."

I gulp some more tea, then nod. It's going to hurt, but I can deal with it. It's not like pain is anything new to me. It's finite and I can survive it. My entire life is testament to that.

Sage lets me finish the tea before taking the mug and setting it down on one of the small tables by the couch. I use the arm of the sofa as leverage and pull myself onto my good foot. I'm very conscious I'm not wearing pants, that under the layers of blankets and quilts draped over me, I'm naked. I grab at the blanket around my hips to make sure it's not going to slide off me. I'm embarrassed enough right now, without Mrs. Applegarth getting a peek at my junk.

"Lean on me," she says, moving around to my left side and inserting herself under my shoulder. "Unfortunately, we're going to have to go up the stairs. We've been meaning to put in a downstairs shower, but..." She trails off, and when I look over at her, her eyes have filled with tears again.

Somehow, we make it up the stairs, and somehow the blanket stays secure around my hips.

Mrs. A eases me down on the closed lid of the toilet and bustles around the bathroom, turning on the shower and opening cabinets.

"Here's a towel," she says, setting a large, fluffy one next to the sink. "I'll see if I can find some of Jeremy's sweatpants for you to wear. They'll be a little short, but they'll be warm."

"Thank you," I say, finally. She shouldn't be doing all this for me. I tied her up. I broke into her house. The last thing I deserve is this kindness.

She tosses me a weak smile, turning to Sage who is hovering in the doorway. "Stay in here with him," she says. "Just in case."

I stay in the shower a long time, letting the water's heat work its way to my bones. I lean against the wall and let it pound on my shoulders and back. I focus on the way it feels against my skin, on how my muscles loosen and the shivering ceases.

When I shut off the water, the room seems eerily quiet.

"Sage?" I reach for the steamed-up glass door. "You still here?"

"Yeah," he says. "Want your towel?"

"Please." I push open the door and let him pass the towel into my hand. I run it across my arms and chest, relishing how soft and plush it feels against my skin. When I'm as dry as I'm going to get in this sauna, I wrap the towel around my waist and make my way carefully from the shower. My ankle throbs and when I look down at it, it appears to have swelled even more. The bruising has spread across the top of my foot and darkens my last three toes.

"That looks awful," Sage says.

I shake my head. This is the last thing we need. No way I can run anywhere now.

"Does it hurt?" Wiley asks and I realize he's in here too, tucked in beside Sage who's perched on the closed toilet lid.

I gesture for them both to move so I can sit down. Sage reaches out to help me cross the room, but I shake him off and use the sink for balance until I can lower myself to the closed toilet.

"You didn't happen to take the phone out of my jeans pocket?" I ask Sage.

"Phone?" Sage looks confused. "You don't have a

phone."

"I had *her* phone." I sigh. It's too late to do anything about it now. She's somewhere out there in the house alone and has probably already called the cops on us. It might take them a while to get up here with the storm and all, but that's not going to matter. We can't go anywhere. Even if there wasn't a storm still raging outside.

"I'm hungry," Wiley says, breaking the tense silence seething between Sage and me. "When can we eat?"

Sage's eyes meet mine and he grins. "I did cook," he says. "And I remembered to turn off the stove when I came out to rescue you, so it won't be ruined."

"Even Mrs. Applegarth needs to eat," I say and drag myself up once more. "Wiley, can you find my pants? It's not polite to eat dinner with no pants on."

KATE LARKINDALE

Chapter Twenty

Mrs. Applegarth is waiting in the living room when we get back downstairs. I'm wearing nothing but the sweatpants Wiley brought me—my own, not Mr. Applegarth's—so my chest is bare. My ankle aches and throbs from the journey down the stairs. I leaned on the banister and tried both hopping and putting as little weight as possible on the hurt ankle on the way down, but neither was successful. Hopping jarred it, and even the small amount of pressure from balancing on my toes hurt. I'm still not certain it's not broken. I hope like hell it isn't. I can't afford four to six weeks in a cast.

"Warmed up?" Mrs. A asks as Sage helps me back onto the couch. "How are you feeling?"

"I should be asking you that," I say with a glance at her temple. There's a faint smudge of bruising around the cut, but it doesn't look too bad.

Sage's face looks much worse.

She waves the comment off. "I'm fine. A little bit of a headache, that's all."

A little bit? I wonder if she's lying. I can't tell from looking at her. Either she's telling the truth, or she's way better at hiding her pain than most people are. She just looks sad. No, sad's too small a word for how she looks. Devastated might be better.

"You didn't answer me," she says, opening the large first-aid kit she has on the table next to her. "Do you feel warmer?"

I nod. I am warm. The fire no longer feels like it's gnawing at my skin, and my bones don't ache. I feel like me again. Even my fingers have stopped with their maddening pins and needles sensation. She searches through the first-aid kit, pulling out packages and setting them aside as she delves for what she needs. The phone I had in my pocket sits on the table next to the red plastic box.

So she does have it. I consider leaping up and grabbing it, but my ankle gives a huge throb at that moment and I bite back a gasp, deciding to stay put.

She moves toward me with rolls of bandages in her hands. "You should…" She pauses and blushes, looking away. "Um… Maybe put on a shirt?"

Sage goes to the backpack I left by the windows. Clothes spill out from it across the floor. Wiley must've been in a hurry to find these pants I'm wearing. He tosses me a t-shirt and a faded hoodie before gathering up the rest of the spilled clothing and shoving it back into the pack.

"Better?" I ask once I've pulled the clothes on.

She presses her lips together and doesn't meet my eye. "Much."

Without another word, she crouches down and lifts my injured foot into her lap.

I dig my fingers into the arm of the couch and bite down on my lip to keep from making a sound. The pain must show on my face though, because Sage comes and sits by me.

"Okay?" he asks in a low voice, reaching up to brush the hair away from my eyes.

"Yeah." I wrap my arm around him and pull him in closer to me. When Wiley crawls up onto the couch on my other side, I draw him close too. We sit there in silence, listening to the wind blast its way around and across the house. It whistles in the chimney, an eerie sound like the moan of a ghost. Wiley presses himself more firmly into my side at the sound, but he doesn't say anything.

"There," Mrs. A says, straightening up. "That should feel a lot better."

I look down and find she's strapped my ankle. My toes poke out from the layers of bandages, the last two black with bruising, the others various shades of purple. But she's right. It does feel better. I almost feel like I might be able to walk on it some. Or at least limp. I'm not ready to test the theory yet though.

"Thanks," I say, looking up at her gratefully.

"Keep it elevated," she says, dragging a pile of cushions over and settling my foot on them. "It'll help with the swelling."

"You know a lot about this stuff." Sage looks impressed as he studies the way she's wound the bandages.

She shrugs and sits down in the armchair across from us. "Teachers have to learn first aid. And, unfortunately, we get a lot of opportunities to use it."

I thought it was only the school nurse who knew first aid. And maybe the gym teachers.

"So," she says, looking from me to Wiley and then to Sage. "Are you going to tell me who you are? And what you're doing in my house?"

I figured we'd have to have this conversation sometime. I was hoping it wouldn't be now. I'm exhausted suddenly. It's like everything that's happened in the last twenty-four hours has suddenly caught up with me. I can barely keep my eyes open.

"It's just me and my brothers." I gesture at Sage and Wiley who are still tucked in under my arms. "This is Wiley," I say, with a squeeze to his narrow shoulders. "And this is Sage."

Mrs. Applegarth's eyes dart from face to face, studying us, taking the three of us in.

"You're brothers?" she asks finally.

I nod. "Yes."

People never believe we're related. We look too different to one another. At least, on the surface we do. If you take the time to look more closely, you'll realize despite the differences in coloring, in skin tone, the three of us share the same bone structure, the same almond-shaped eyes, the same single dimple in our left cheeks.

Her eyes shift between us.

"Different fathers," I say to help her out. "Same mother."

"How old are you?" She looks at Wiley.

He glances up at me, silently asking if he should answer. I nod and he turns back to her. "Eight."

"My sons never got to be eight," she says wistfully. She stares toward the fireplace, and for the first time I notice the photographs clustered on the mantelpiece. Photographs of her and a tall, muscular guy with a mustache. Photographs of two little boys, maybe two or three years apart, both dark-haired and unmistakably her sons.

"Caleb was so close," she says finally. "He wanted a skateboard for his birthday. I was supposed to take him to pick one out. He didn't trust me to get the right thing."

She stops and shakes her head, wincing and reaching for the spot Wiley clocked her. I guess it hurts more than she's letting on.

He makes a small sound like a frightened whimper then falls silent, pressing himself more firmly against my side.

She lowers her hand and looks at me in a way that makes me instantly guilty. It's the look she uses on kids who talk or chew gum or play with their phones in class.

I wince.

"I'm sorry," I say finally. It's worthless and

stupid, but there's nothing else to say.

Sage shrugs off the arm I have around him, gets up, and moves away from the couch. "I'll go get dinner," he says. "Wiley, come help me."

The kitchen door swings closed behind them, and I'm alone with Mrs. Applegarth once more.

"So…" I have no idea what to say here. Her misery is palpable. I can feel it against my skin, a dark, heavy pressure which won't let up, even when I shift into a new position on the couch.

"I needed some time out to clear my head," she says, not looking at me. "The house… Our house… It reeks of them. I can't open a cupboard or a door without some reminder slapping me in the face. So I decided to come here."

I look around at the shelves of books, the framed paintings of boats on the walls. The photographs in their dusty frames. "This is better?"

Mrs. Applegarth shakes her head. "Maybe not."

We're silent for a minute, listening to the clatter of pots and dishes coming from the kitchen.

"Your little brother's cute," Mrs. Applegarth says.

"Wiley?" I ask, assuming he's the one she means.

"Is he the littlest one?"

I nod.

"He's adorable." The smallest hint of a smile curves her lips. "And what an unusual name. Is it short for something?"

"My mom's kind of an unusual person." It seems weird to be having this reasonable, ordinary conversation with someone whose house we broke into. Who Wiley assaulted. Not just weird—wrong. "Look, I'm really sorry about all this."

"About what?" Mrs. Applegarth looks startled, her eyes wide.

I make a gesture with my hands, including us, my busted foot, her cut and bruised temple, the house—everything. "All this. It's… It's not me. I'm not some psycho thug who breaks into summer houses and kidnaps people."

But I am. Even if it's not who I want to be, not who I've ever considered myself, here I am, in a virtual stranger's house, uninvited. Worse, I tied her up on her couch. And to add insult to injury, I had to ask her for help.

"No," Mrs. Applegarth says. "I never figured you to be that person. So I'm guessing there has to be a good reason why you're here."

I shake my head, disbelieving. She doesn't sound mad. Or scared. If anything, she sounds concerned.

She gives a small laugh. "Come on, Blue. Don't look so shocked. Now, I'm guessing this has something to do with why you dropped out of school? And maybe something to do with the fact your brother looks like he went three rounds with the heavyweight champion of the world?"

I drop my eyes to the floor. Her gaze has suddenly become too sharp, those clear blue eye drilling right through my skin and piercing my soul. I hate the idea of her seeing the black secrets I hide there, the various poisons I filter from my thoughts on a daily basis.

"Whatever it is," Mrs. Applegarth says in a low voice, "I might be able to help."

That pulls me back into myself and I feel my protective walls rebuilding around me. It must be something about the word help. As soon as anyone offers it, I pull away. Probably because the last time anyone offered any real help, we wound up in that terrible group home which was more like a prison than anything else. And not one of those nice prisons they send white-collar criminals to either.

"Doubt it," I say finally, assuming the tough, hard voice I usually only use around Mom's boyfriends.

Mrs. Applegarth is silent for a moment, shifts again, this time pulling her legs up so she's curled up in the armchair, hugging a cushion. "Try me," she says simply.

KATE LARKINDALE

Chapter Twenty-One

I stare down at my hands. They're large, the fingers long and blunt. My nails are bitten to the quick. I don't even remember doing that. The cuticles are ragged. Dark hair dusts the back of each hand, not thick enough to hide the raised humps of vein crisscrossing the back of each.

"Things..." I start, stopping again almost immediately. I can't talk about this. I've drilled it into Sage and Wiley for years. We don't talk to outsiders. Not about this. It's too risky.

"Blue," Mrs. Applegarth says my name so gently it almost brings tears to my eyes. "You can trust me."

I look back at her. "Can I?"

She nods, but makes no move toward me.

I study her. There's no malice in her face. No fear. Nothing but an open and genuine curiosity. That and the pain clinging to every part of her. This is a nice woman. Smart, classy, and clearly generous. Look at the way she helped me after I tied her up. After Wiley hurt her. She didn't have to. She could have left me out there to freeze to death, but she didn't. That's class.

"We ran away," I say finally. "Things at home... Well, they've been bad for years. I've wanted to get the kids away for a long time, I just didn't have a way to do it. I had a plan. Quitting school was part of it, but I left it too late. And then something happened last night, and I didn't want to wait any longer. So we left. I figured no one would be using the houses up here, so it was a good place to hide out while I figured out where to go next."

"And have you?" The question is asked so

casually it's almost not a question at all.

"No." How could I? We'd barely had time to settle ourselves in here before she showed up, let alone make a longer-term plan.

"So, you'll stay here? Until you come up with something better?" She gets up and moves toward the windows, drawing the curtains against the darkness and the storm.

My face burns. "That was the plan. But we can leave…"

But we can't. The storm still raging outside tells me that. The snow quietly piling up outside the windows. Not to mention the persistent ache in my bandaged ankle.

Mrs. Applegarth shakes her head. "You can stay here. I'm not about to turn a bunch of kids out of my house into the snow. Especially not hurt kids."

"You won't call the cops?" My fingers itch to reach for the phone. It's lying there out in the open. I could reach it in one or two steps. It would hurt, but I can deal with pain. Then I'd have control again.

Wiley comes into the room with a handful of cutlery and starts setting the table. Mrs. A watches him, a wistful expression on her face. Wiley doesn't notice. He's intent on getting the table right, holding the knives up as he reaches each chair to make sure he gets them on the right side of the placemats.

"My boys were younger than your brothers," she says. "Harry was five and Caleb was seven. One day, they were running around the house like a pair of noisy little aliens, the next they were gone. I had to leave. The silence was too much for me."

" What happened to them?" Wiley asks, and I realize he's been paying attention to us after all.

"Car wreck," she says in a low, broken voice. "They'd been up here for the weekend. I didn't come because my mother had just had surgery and needed help around the house. It was late when they headed home. They were always late heading home. Jeremy never wanted to waste a drop of daylight. So it was dark. A woman in an SUV drove right into them. She'd been at her sister's bridal shower, drinking champagne cocktails all afternoon. She broke her leg. Jeremy died instantly, according to the police. Harry and Caleb weren't so lucky."

I wince. I don't want to know anything more. The pain in her voice is so intense I can feel it like a film across my skin. It's like her loss is a black hole in the center of the room, sucking out any joy or happiness that might have once been there.

But she goes on. "Harry died in the ambulance on the way to the hospital. Caleb hung on for three days. I sat beside him in the hospital room the whole time, holding his hand and begging him to stay. The doctors kept telling me the chance of him waking up was minimal, but miracles happen every day, right? I had to believe he'd be a miracle."

Maybe miracles do happen every day. Just not to me. I can't think of a single thing I'd call a miracle in my own life.

Perhaps that's what keeps us all going though, an innate belief a miracle is right around the corner. We keep pushing through each day, holding onto the faint hope tomorrow will be better, will somehow miraculously be different.

"After three days I lost faith," Mrs. Applegarth says. "I kissed him and told him he could go. It's like he was waiting for permission, because he died right after that. And I've been alone ever since."

"You're not alone now," Wiley says. I'd almost forgotten he was there, and it's a surprise to find him by my side, his eyes wide as he looks at her. "We're here now."

Mrs. Applegarth manages a real smile through her tears. "Yes. You are."

"Me and Sage made dinner. Are you hungry?"

"Sage and I," Mrs. Applegarth corrects, wiping away the tears and giving Wiley a shaky smile. Once an English teacher... "You know what? I *am* hungry. What did you make? It smells delicious."

It's like talking to Wiley has brought her back to life. The sadness doesn't disappear exactly, but it recedes so it's not the only thing you can see in her. She looks the way she did in the classroom again, like she did while she was dealing with me and my injured foot. A little worn and tired, but present. If her eyes weren't so bloodshot, she'd look completely normal.

"Spaghetti," Sage says, setting a huge bowl onto the table. "Garlic bread and salad. Come and eat."

I don't need a second invitation. I pull myself onto my good foot and use the couch to lean on as I hobble across to the table. I'm pleased to discover that with the ankle bandaged, I can put a little weight on it, can use my toes for balance. Maybe it isn't broken after all.

Wiley follows and Mrs. Applegarth trips behind him as if Wiley is a magnet dragging her in his wake. As I pass the table where the phone sits, I palm it and slide it into my pocket without anyone seeming to notice. I feel better with its weight tugging at the left side of my pants.

"This looks good," Mrs. Applegarth says when she reaches the table. "Thank you."

Sage gives an embarrassed shrug. "S'okay," he says.

Mrs. Applegarth sits down at one end of the table and reaches for a serving spoon. "Say when," she tells

Wiley as she spoons noodles onto his plate.

She's slipped so automatically into this role. After serving Wiley, she doles out a generous portion for Sage and slides it toward him. "Blue? How much for you?" She dumps a huge pile of spaghetti onto a plate. "Big guy like you must have quite an appetite."

"Yeah. Mostly." I take the plate and add a hunk of garlic bread. I'll have salad after.

We eat in silence for a few minutes. Once my stomach has something in it, it quiets somewhat and I can consider the weirdness of the situation. I'm not sure if we kidnapped Mrs. Applegarth, but she doesn't seem afraid of us. Maybe because she knows we can't go anywhere. Maybe because she knows she could probably get the better of any one of us in a fight right now. But there doesn't seem to be any fight in her. She seems completely at ease, showing Wiley how to spin his spaghetti around his fork.

I look at Sage.

He catches my eye and shrugs, as if to say, he doesn't get it either, but he'll roll with it.

Mrs. Applegarth slides out from the table and my shoulders tense. But she doesn't head for the table where the phone sat or the front door. She goes into the kitchen and opens a cabinet. She pulls out a bottle of wine that she brings back to the table with a wine glass. "I'd offer you some, but you're underage," she says to me.

"I don't drink," I say, watching as she takes a sip, swallowing it with obvious enjoyment.

"I probably shouldn't. Especially after being hit in the head." She shrugs and takes another, bigger swallow.

"I ... I ... I didn't mean to," Wiley says, his face twisting in fear.

Well, now he's done it. Now she knows which one of us clocked her. I'd planned on taking the rap for it, but now it's too late.

Mrs. Applegarth sets the wine glass down and reaches for Wiley.

He cringes, every muscle tensing as he waits for the blow he's certain is coming. When Mrs. Applegarth merely strokes his hair, he relaxes, his face melting into an expression of wonder. He glances my way and my throat tightens at the incredulity painted across his features. Kindness shouldn't be such a surprise. Not to a kid.

"I know you didn't mean to, Wiley," Mrs. Applegarth says, her voice gentle. "I'm not angry at you."

Wiley looks relieved.

"Anyone want dessert?" Sage starts clearing our now-empty plates from the table. I hold mine back, eyeing the last little bit of spaghetti in the bottom of the serving dish.

Sage sighs and lets go of my plate, shoving the serving dish toward me with his other hand. "Blue here, is a human garbage can," he tells Mrs. Applegarth. "He'll eat anything."

"That's not a bad thing," Mrs. Applegarth says. "My Harry was the pickiest eater. The only vegetable he'd eat was broccoli. You have no idea how tired of broccoli I was after a few years."

I grunt as I inhale my second helping of spaghetti. None of us are picky eaters. We can't afford to be. We've always had to eat whatever we were given, whatever we could get our hands on. There hasn't always been a pantry full of food waiting for us. When we were on the road, Mom would sometimes forget she had to feed us and leave us alone in motel rooms for days without anything.

So now I eat anything I'm given. So do Sage and Wiley. Being picky about food isn't something I've ever considered.

"I like broccoli," Wiley says. "And other vegetables."

"What's your favorite?" Mrs. Applegarth asks Wiley.

He screws up his face, thinking about this. I'm not sure he's ever decided on a favorite. When you're grateful for every mouthful, liking one thing more than another isn't really a consideration.

"Maybe … spinach?" Wiley says finally. "The creamy stuff Sage makes."

Mrs. Applegarth looks at Sage. "You're quite the chef, apparently."

Sage ducks his head, his face reddening. "Not really."

"You don't need to be ashamed, Sage. It's a good thing. Too many boys never step into a kitchen because they believe cooking is women's work."

Sage blushes even more deeply. "Someone has to do it."

Mrs. Applegarth looks at all three of us in turn. "Your mother doesn't cook?"

Sage opens his mouth to say something, but I cut him off. "She's not exactly the domestic type."

Mrs. Applegarth glances at Sage for a second, her gaze lingering on his blackened eye. She frowns and looks thoughtful. She takes another sip of wine. I glance at the glass, surprised when I discover it's still more than half full. Mom would have knocked two glasses back by now and be working on a third, maybe even a fourth. And wine isn't even her drink of choice.

"I don't believe I've met your mother," Mrs. Applegarth says slowly. "I don't think she's ever come to any parent-teacher meetings."

"You don't say?" Sage says, sarcasm dripping

from every word. He gets up and starts clearing the table again, rattling the dishes together more noisily than is strictly necessary.

I wait until he's back in the kitchen before I speak again. "Mom… She doesn't do that kind of thing."

"What does she do?" Mrs. Applegarth's mouth is grim now. "If she doesn't cook and she doesn't take an interest in her children's education?"

I bite my lip to keep myself from spitting out the truth. Lying is so ingrained in me now. Protecting her, even when she doesn't deserve my protection.

"She's a singer," I say finally, but it sounds like a lie. Mom's as much of a singer these days as I am. And I couldn't carry a tune if it was strapped to my back. "At least, she used to be."

"And now?"

Now? Good question. What does my mother do now?

Chapter Twenty-Two

An uncomfortable silence settles over the room as Mrs. Applegarth waits for an answer. Wiley looks at me, his eyes even bigger and rounder than they usually are. Sage, who has stepped back into the room, freezes, his gaze flicking toward me. I feel like I'm in a spotlight with all these expectant eyes on me, waiting for me to speak. And I don't know what to say.

The truth?

She drinks. She takes drugs. She cries and listens to her old records on repeat. She screams at us, blames us for her career being over. She hits us. Usually not hard enough to do any real damage. Not really. Bruises heal pretty fast even if they are ugly to look at. Even broken bones heal, and it's not like she's done that more than a handful of times.

She was always sorry afterward. Not sorry enough to quit with the drinking or anything, but sorry all the same. And she never hit one of us when we were already hurt. I guess that's a positive.

Is that what I'm supposed to tell Mrs. Applegarth? Why Wiley and Sage are looking at me like that?

"She's..." I stop.

I'm tired of lying. I've been lying for as long as I can remember. Lying to motel managers about being alone in rooms. Lying to well-meaning bar owners who'd ply Sage and I with sodas when Mom snuck off between the soundcheck and the actual gig to score. Lying to neighbors who enquired about the noises coming from our apartment. Lying to teachers about everything under the sun. I've lied to doctors, to social workers, to my boss, and even to the few people I could call my friends.

And I'm tired of it.

Lying takes so much energy. First you have to dream up a story, then you have to remember the details of the story. All of them. And if it's one of those stories where you've told different things to different people, it's hard to keep track of the lies.

"She drinks," I say finally. "A lot. Like … all the time. If she's not high."

No one says anything. What I've said hangs in the air, the words so heavy I can practically see them dangling there before they fall to crash on the floor.

"And she hits us," I add. Now I've started, I may as well lay the whole lot out there. Mrs. Applegarth can decide how she wants to take it.

I don't want pity. We're not pitiful. We're just a bunch of kids who got a shitty lot in life.

Mrs. Applegarth nods and when she speaks again, it's slow, thoughtful. "I should have known."

"How?" I ask. There's no way she could have known. I kept my hoodie on when it was eighty degrees out so the bruises wouldn't show. If Mom got careless and left a mark on my face, I always had a good excuse—a cupboard door left carelessly open, a trip on the living room rug—anything but the truth. When she broke my wrist, I told everyone I fell down the stairs in our apartment building because the landlord hadn't replaced the busted bulb over them. No one ever questioned me. No one even looked interested once I started telling whatever mundane story I'd made up.

Mrs. Applegarth looks at me, agony in her eyes. "You came to class pretty bashed up a couple of times last year, and you were absent a lot. I should have suspected."

Sage's face flushes, but this time it's not with embarrassment but with rage. His eyes burn with it. "You could have helped us!" he says, his voice low, even in fury. The words hiss between his clenched teeth. "You're a teacher."

It's startling and I'm more than a little shocked to find this level of anger in Sage. I'm the one with the short fuse. Sage is calm and gentle, always. Even when he's upset about something, he never raises his voice.

Mrs. Applegarth lowers her head. "I should have done something."

The room falls silent again, but this time it's even more uncomfortable. The only sound is the wind blasting across the windows. Wiley slides out of his seat and heads for Sage, the person he's always gone to for comfort. But at the last minute, he veers away and comes to me instead, tucking his skinny little body in against mine. I put my arm around him. He's trembling.

Mrs. Applegarth looks up again and her eyes are shiny with tears. Great. Now we've made her cry again. "I'm so sorry," she says. "I guess I was afraid. In case I was wrong about what I thought I was seeing. You can make a real mess of people's lives that way."

"Couldn't be much worse than the mess we're already in," Sage mutters, but he's calmer now, the rage already fading out of him.

"Yes, it could," I break in. "It could be a whole lot worse."

"Yeah?" Sage challenges me. I shake my head, trying to recognize the boy standing before me. This is not Sage. Sage never questions me. I sometimes wish he did because I don't have all the answers. In most cases, I'm going into things as blindly as he is. I hide my fear of the unknown better, I guess.

"We're together," I say. "We're not dead. And we're not in the system."

Sage flops back into his seat. "Yeah... You're

right."

Mrs. Applegarth gets up and starts stacking the remaining dishes. Her hands shake a little. "It's probably not enough to make up for anything, but you can stay here. For as long as you need to. I won't tell anyone."

"You mean it?" I ask. It could be a trick. She could be lulling us into some false sense of security. When we're asleep, she'll make a run for it, or call the cops.

"Yes, Blue. I mean it. It's the least I can do."

Wiley wriggles closer, practically climbing into my lap. "We're not going back to that place are we?"

I shake my head, smoothing the back of his hair. "No, Wiley. Never, I promise."

"Sage?" Mrs. Applegarth stands inside the kitchen door. "Did you say something about dessert?"

"Yeah," he says. "I did." Sage gets up and heads toward the kitchen.

The lights flicker once and I glance up at them. I've almost decided I imagined it when they do it again. Then they flick off and stay that way.

"What happened?" Wiley whispers into the darkness.

"I thought that might happen," Mrs. Applegarth says with a groan. "It's a blackout, Wiley. The storm must've blown down the power lines somewhere."

Now Wiley does climb into my lap. He's a little big for that, but the darkness *is* frightening, so I let him, even though his extra weight makes my ankle throb. It's not dark like it is at home where the streetlights and lights from buildings and signs keep the darkness from being truly dark. Up here, darkness is really blackness. With the curtains drawn against the storm, there's no difference between having my eyes open or closed.

"It's okay," Sage says. "There are candles,

remember?"

"And the fire will keep us warm," adds Mrs. A.

****

An hour later, bellies groaning with spaghetti and the apple cobbler Sage managed to throw together, we're all in the living room. Candles flicker on the small tables, giving just enough light for us to see one another and move about without tripping over something. The fire blazes, throwing intense heat into the room. Wiley is curled up on his makeshift bed next to the fireplace, the covers tucked up under his chin. He's struggling to keep his eyes open, and as I watch he blinks slowly. Once. Twice. Three times. The fourth time, his eyes fall closed and stay that way.

Sage, sitting on the cushions next him, yawns. I know how he feels. My own limbs feel heavy with exhaustion and spent adrenaline. I can't believe it's been only twenty-four hours since we left home. It feels like a lifetime has passed since I left work on Friday night, yet it's only Saturday now.

Work. I'm going to have to decide what to do about that. Call in sick on Monday? I guess I'll have to. Even if I did have a way to get back into the city, I'll be no good with this ankle. I've never missed a shift before. Even when I was so bruised I could barely move, I made it in to work. Even when I've been up all night with one or the other of my brothers, or stopping Mom from giving in to her worst instincts I've made it. I didn't even miss a day with that broken wrist. I kept my sleeve tugged down over the cast and shuffled through the order forms to find the ones that didn't have anything too heavy included.

Yet I don't really care if I lose the job. I chuckle to myself.

"What?" Mrs. Applegarth asks from where she's curled next to me on the couch. She has the stereo on low, some kind of smooth jazz playing through the almost-invisible speakers dotted around the room.

"I was thinking about my job," I say quietly. "And how I really don't care if I lose it."

And I don't. Apart from the money, of course. I'll miss that. And maybe Megan, a little. But nothing else. If I never lift another ream of paper again, it will be too soon.

"What were you doing?" Mrs. Applegarth puts down the magazine she was holding and peers at me over her glasses. A moment later, she pulls them off and sets them on the arm of the couch beside her.

"Picking and packing," I tell her. "In a stationary warehouse."

She grins. "Sounds scintillating."

"It really isn't."

"I was kidding," she says. "But you knew that."

I nod. I did. She has this sly, quiet sense of humor. The kind where you're never quite sure if she's fucking with you or not. I get that kind of humor, but other people don't. There were kids at school who didn't get it and were convinced she was out to get them.

"I'm glad you're out of that house," she says after a long moment. She glances at Wiley's sleeping figure, and at Sage who has settled down next to him, one arm slung carelessly across him.

"Yeah. Me too." I smile down at my brothers. Even if we did everything wrong, we're safe now. Or at least, safer. I don't think Mrs. Applegarth is going to turn us in. "Thank you, Mrs. Applegarth. I don't know how to thank you…"

"Please." She reaches for my hand, trapping it beneath hers. "You can call me Jude. I'm not your teacher anymore."

"Okay … Jude." I try out the name. It feels

unfamiliar to my tongue and to my brain. I've only had her as a teacher the last two years, but for all that time she's been Mrs. Applegarth. It might take a while to adjust.

"What place was Wiley talking about before?" she asks a moment later. "The place you promised he'd never have to go back to."

"Oh..." I forgot she heard that. "A ... a group home. The one and only time I ever talked to someone about what was going on in our house, we got taken away from Mom and sent to this home for unwanted kids. It was... Well, it was bad."

I don't want to talk about it. It was worse than bad. It was hell on earth.

KATE LARKINDALE

Chapter Twenty-Three

I shiver as I remember the way the heavy doors clanked shut behind us, blocking out the daylight and leaving us in a cold florescent glare.

Footsteps echoed through the oversized foyer. The heavy scent of disinfectant hung over everything, layered with the smell of stewing meat and unwashed socks.

"I don't like this place," Wiley whispered, clinging to me. He was four, and not given to clinging, so I paid attention.

"Me neither." Sage's eyes were huge in his pale, pinched face, wild with fear.

"It'll be okay," I told them. "We're together, so it'll be okay."

But it wasn't.

Wiley was taken away to another part of the building, wherever they kept younger kids. He cried when the woman in blue pried him from my arms. His sobs echoed through the hallways even after Sage and I were taken in the opposite direction by another blue-clad woman.

"Will he be okay?" Sage kept glancing over his shoulder at the corridor Wiley had been taken down.

"He'll be taken care of." I hoped I was right. It wasn't as if I'd ever been here before either. "We're gonna be fine, Sage. I promise." I reached down and squeezed his bony shoulder in a way I hoped was reassuring.

The room the lady took us to was huge. Rows of narrow cots lined each wall, no more than a foot or two between them. Kids of different sizes wandered through the room, none of them bothering to look up for more than a second when we passed.

"These will be yours," *the woman said, gesturing to two beds in the middle of the row on the left side. She turned and for the first time I was able to read the name-tag pinned to her faded t-shirt: Jeanette.* "Don't keep anything of value in your lockers. If you have any valuables, hand them in to the matron in the office." *She gestured to an open door at the far end of the room.* "Bathrooms are down the hall. Dinner is at six. Lights out at nine. Any questions?"

"Where did they take my brother?" *I asked.* "Can't he stay here too?"

"This dorm's for kids ten and over. We keep the younger ones separate. It's safer." *Her words sent chills running down my spine. Sage had turned ten about three days earlier and still looked like a child. He could have passed for eight if not for his eyes. A boy slouched past, staring at us. Sage shuffled closer to me, dropping his gaze from the hostile glare the heavy-set kid tossed our way.*

I thought I'd never get to sleep. The thin blanket did little to keep me warm, and the tasteless meatloaf and mashed potatoes we'd been served for dinner sat in a lump in my belly. All around me kids shifted and snorted their sleep. Over the racket, I couldn't hear the familiar sound of Sage's snoring from where he lay on my left. We couldn't stay here. No way. I'd go crazy. I had to figure out a way to get out of here.

I rolled over, pulling the flat pillow in its bleach-smelling pillow case over my head. It helped block out the noise of the ten or twelve kids sleeping around me, but did little to silence the panicked voices in my head. What if I couldn't get us out of here? What if we got split up? Sent to different foster homes? I shivered, pulling the blanket around me more tightly. With the pillow still over my head, I drifted into a restless sleep.

I woke up when someone crawled into bed next to me.

Sage shook, his bony body jerking against mine.

"What's up?" I whispered. "You scared?"

"Yes." Sage's voice sounded thick, choked, as if he'd been crying.

"Well, don't be." I wrapped an arm around him and held him close, wanting to stop the tremors which shook the bed with their intensity. He was so thin I could feel each of his ribs pressing against my forearm.

Something liquid trickled down my chest. "Are you crying?"

"No." Sage pressed closer into me, still shivering a little.

"It's okay, Sage. I'm going to take care of you, okay?" I pulled the pillow off my head and put it back on the bed, making room for Sage on it too. It was not until he lay down on it that I realized what the wetness on my chest really was—not tears, but blood. It stained the white pillowcase in seconds.

"What happened?" I sat bolt upright, pulling Sage with me. The room was not completely dark; nightlights burned in the corners of the room, and moonlight trickled through the narrow windows above us.

"I had to go to the bathroom..." Sage's voice shook as he whispered the words. Blood coursed from his nose.

"I'll go get the..." I said, one foot already on the floor.

"No!" Sage grabbed at me. "I'm okay. I don't want anyone. Just... Can I stay with you?"

"Are you sure?" I peered at him in the dimness, wishing I could turn on a light to see him better.

"I'm sure." He pulled away and lay down, curling up on the very edge of the cot to make room for me. I stayed upright for a long moment, conflicted as I watched the bloodstain spread across the pillow case. Finally, with a sigh, I lay back down, curling myself around him.

I awoke early. Flat early morning light was drifting through the windows. Next to me, Sage slept. He lay on his back, breathing deeply through his mouth. His nose was misshapen and swollen. In the brightening daylight I could see a darkening smudge of bruise across his left cheek. Fury surged into my throat, hot and poisonous on my tongue. I fought it back, not swallowing it, but caging it somewhere deep in my stomach, containing it until I needed it. I knew I would later, although I wasn't sure when or how yet.

All around me the room came alive. People stirred and shifted in their beds, some rose and walked drowsily toward the bathrooms. A loud fart tore through the air, making me jump. I wondered where Wiley was. Whether he was awake. If he was scared. I couldn't help thinking he must be. This had to be longest he'd ever been separated from Sage and me.

I waited until most of the other kids had shuffled off toward the dining room before waking Sage. *"C'mon."* I tugged him out of bed and dragged him, still more asleep than awake, toward the matron's office.

"What...?" He began, but once he caught a look at my face, he stopped, following me wordlessly through the door I didn't knock on before shoving open.

"Excuse me?" The woman behind the broad wooden desk was large. When she stood up, her eyes were level with mine, something which surprised me. Even at thirteen, I was used to my height being an advantage.

I pulled Sage around and held him in front of me.

"You want to tell me why we're here?" I asked, anger making my voice low and hoarse. "You want to tell me what we're supposed to be protected from?"

"What happened?" She came around the desk and stared at Sage's battered face.

"He had to go to the bathroom." I let the words fall to the floor, flat and hard. "He's never gotten a broken nose from doing that at home."

"No." Her face flushed and her hands fluttered helplessly around her throat. "I don't suppose so..."

"I want out," I said. "I want to take my brothers home. Clearly, they're safer there."

Mrs. ... Jude is silent for a moment after I tell her about the home.

"So, I'm guessing you got out?" she asks finally.

I nod. They didn't want to let us go, especially Wiley, but I kicked up such a stink... "I think they were embarrassed," I say.

"And so they should be," Jude says. "It's outrageous a child should be hurt in a shelter like that."

I shrug. I believe the facilities for older kids are even worse. I heard a girl died in one last year. It was one of those rumors I didn't question. You can't take a bunch of kids from terrible and often violent homes and throw them together without that kind of thing happening.

"It's inevitable," I say. "None of these kids know anything else. Behavior is learned, isn't it?"

She looks at me, the sadness returning to her eyes. "You're not like that, though. Neither are your brothers."

"How do you know?" I ask. And I mean it. I want to know. I've been terrified for years I'll end up like Mom. It's why I don't drink. The anger is there, burning inside me, a constant dull ache behind my heart. It takes strength and energy to keep it there. If I let myself lose control, even once, I'm afraid of what might happen.

"I've seen you with those kids." Jude nods toward my sleeping brothers. "You're so gentle with them. God, you were so gentle with me this afternoon. I can't imagine you hurting anyone."

I make a non-committal sound. She's right. I'd never hurt Sage or Wiley. Even when they infuriate me, I'd never lay a hand on either of them.

But it doesn't mean I wouldn't hurt someone else. It doesn't mean I haven't.

"You have hurt someone, haven't you?" Jude reaches up and touches the side of my face, forcing me to look directly at her.

I can't meet her eyes, but I nod. "One of Mom's 'boyfriends'."

It was two years ago, when I was fifteen.

Mom staggered in late one night, long after we'd gone to sleep.

I woke when the door slammed and lay there, listening to their voices, muffled through the door. The stereo went on, too loud for this late hour.

"Who..." Sage's voice was blurred with sleep.

"Mom," I whispered. "Go back to sleep."

But of course he didn't. The music and voices and rattling of glass on glass as she poured more drinks grew louder. Too loud to ignore.

The voices became even louder than the music. Mom was hollering at the top of her lungs. Her friend bellowed back.

And then, the unmistakable sound of a slap. It was a sound both Sage and I knew all too well.

I was at the door before I even knew I'd moved.

"Don't," Sage begged, but my hand was already turning the knob.

"I'll be fine," I promised as I stepped out into the hallway, closing the door carefully behind me. I wiped

my palms on the worn pajama pants I wore. My heart pounded in my chest, but I couldn't tell if it was with fear or excitement. Possibly a mixture of both. Because while I was scared to peek into the living room, I couldn't hide either.

Another slap sounded as I poked my head around the doorjamb.

A man's back was toward me. His black t-shirt strained over broad shoulders. Muscles rippled beneath it as he moved.

Mom said something, but I didn't catch what. Her voice was low and liquid, the way it got when she was drinking. Cigarette smoke hung in heavy wreathes around the ceiling, more drifting upward from a butt smoldering in an ashtray on the coffee table. I recognized the scarlet lipstick on the filter.

"Shut it, bitch," the man said, not angrily, but in a low, controlled voice. "You'll do what I say and you'll enjoy it."

He unbuckled his belt.

"Stop!" Jude shakes her head and presses a finger to my lips. "I get the picture. I don't need to hear any more."

So I stop. I don't tell her about hitting the guy, the satisfying crunch of his nose breaking under the weight of my fist. The way blood sprayed, then teeth, when I wound up and gave him another.

I don't tell her how he ran, not even bothering to re-zip his pants as he fled the house.

And I don't tell her about how Mom hit me after he was gone, screaming and shouting not about how I'd saved her, but about the mess I'd made on the rug. About how I'd ruined her good time yet again.

By the time I crawled back to my own room, even I wasn't sure anymore if what I'd seen was rape or

Mom's fucked up idea of intimacy.

"There is a difference," Jude says in a low, throaty voice.

"Yeah. I know."

"Do you?" She reaches up and touches me again, her fingertips warm and soft as they brush across my cheek. "What's this then?"

Chapter Twenty-Four

She leans toward me and I can smell the wine on her breath. It's not repulsive though, like the booze on Mom's breath tends to be. It's sweeter, fruitier.

When her lips touch mine, they're sweet too.

I pull away. "Are you…"

"Shh." Her hand reaches behind my head and cups my neck as she draws me closer to her. Her mouth moves toward mine again, and this time my lips meet hers.

She shifts her entire body toward me, our mouths never separating. Her legs find their way across mine and my arms creep around her waist, lifting her and drawing her closer. So close I can feel the movement of her ribs as she breathes in and out. So close I can feel her heartbeat thudding against my breastbone.

My own heartbeat speeds up as her tongue probes gently at my lips, forcing them open. The kiss deepens and I'm drowning in her. It's not terrible, the way I always imagined drowning would be. Quite the opposite, actually. I let her tongue dance across mine and try to catch it with my own.

She teases me, letting me catch up, only to dart away again. She tastes amazing, the hint of wine enhanced by a sweetness that can only be her own personal flavor. It's like summer-warmed strawberries or something.

Her hands explore my shoulders, caressing them through the fabric of my shirt. They move downward, tracing the map of my biceps, the inside of my elbows, and on toward my wrists. Her breasts are pressed against my chest, and they're warm and soft. Her belly is soft too; a small roll of flesh spills over the waistband of her jeans. My hands clasp her hips and I lift her up to straddle my lap. Her weight sends a jolt of pain through my ankle, and I flinch but ignore it.

One part of me marvels at her womanliness. These soft curves are unfamiliar. Apart from her booze-belly, Mom is all bones and sharp angles. The few girls from school I've been close enough to touch were lean and hard. This softness is luxury.

Another part of me screams for me to stop. This is my teacher I'm kissing. My brothers are inches away and could awaken at any moment.

But I don't stop. It feels too good to stop. Especially when she shifts her hips and grinds against me like that. When she captures one of my nipples between her fingertips and squeezes.

"Oh…" I groan.

She pulls back, stiffening. I let her go and she slides from my lap. My ankle gives a grateful throb when the pressure is lifted.

"I … I shouldn't have done that," she says. "I'm sorry, Blue."

I don't say anything. I probably should be sorry too, right? But I'm not.

"Intimacy is so important," she says finally, dropping back down onto the couch. "I never realized how much until Jeremy was gone. Sometimes I just need someone to hold me. Someone to touch."

She can keep touching me if it's what she wants. I'm happy to hold her if it will make her feel better. My voice is trapped somewhere at the base of my throat, and I don't know if it will ever get loose. I don't care. I'll never speak again if she'll kiss me again.

I move toward her, my lips and tongue itching to tangle with hers again. At the last minute, she shifts her head and my mouth collides with her neck instead. She smells even better than she tastes, that underlying sweetness mixed with the acidic scent of her shampoo and the faint muskiness of sweat.

I expect her to pull away, to stop me. She doesn't. She moves closer.

I lick a spot a little below her ear. I follow her jaw to the place her pulse throbs visibly beneath her skin. I kiss the spot, letting my lips and tongue absorb the vibration of her blood pumping around her body.

It's her turn to moan. She pulls herself back onto my lap, rubbing herself across me in a way that makes me almost lose my mind. I don't think I've ever been this hard. It's lucky I'm wearing sweats; if I was in jeans, the buttons on the fly would be exploding off. I giggle at the thought, imagining them pinging off the walls and ceiling as my dick strains against them and is finally freed.

"What?" Jude pulls away from me and studies my face.

"Nothing," I say. But it's not my voice. It's a low, throaty growl which doesn't sound anything like me.

A log shifts in the fireplace and falls with a dull thud against the metal grille.

Sage shifts in his sleep and rolls over so he's facing us on the couch. He's still asleep, his eyes firmly closed, but it's unnerving knowing they could open at any moment. Well, the one that isn't still swollen shut.

Jude follows my gaze, looking almost fondly at my sleeping brothers.

Wiley is nothing but a small hump of blankets, his head buried under a pillow.

"Does he always sleep like that?" Jude whispers, her breath tantalizingly hot against my ear.

I nod. While Sage and I have always kept one ear open for trouble, Wiley hides from it, blocking out any sound that might upset him.

"You don't mind … this?" Jude touches me again, setting off new fireworks across my skin and in my gut.

I shake my head. "I like it."

"Even with a tired old lady like me?" The words are teasing, but there's a serious note beneath them. I lean back and study her face, tracing her features with my eyes the way she traced mine earlier.

Her eyes are blue and slightly down-turned at the corners. It makes her look sad. Sage's eyes do the same thing, giving him an air of melancholy even when he's at his happiest. But in Sage's case, it's genetics. In Jude's, it's life taking its toll. Her eyes haven't always been this weighted and sad. The lines around them, and the ones bracketing her mouth like parentheses, paint a picture of her misery.

But she doesn't look old. Not like Mom looks old. And I bet Jude has a few years on Mom.

Gah! The thought washes over me like a tidal wave. I've been kissing a woman older than my mother.

I fight the thought away. I've been enjoying it too much to want to stop. "You're beautiful," I murmur, running my hand along the strong line of her jaw. I've never noticed that about her before. In class, she seemed remote even when she stood close enough I could smell her perfume. Yet now, this close, her hair tangled and wild, her lips red and a little swollen from the intensity of our kissing, she's beautiful. She's the most beautiful woman I've ever seen. Megan has nothing on this woman. Megan was a girl in comparison, her prettiness vague and unformed.

A loud snore breaks my reverie. I glance toward my brothers and see Sage has settled into his favorite sleeping position, sprawled on his back. He snores again, the noise like a chainsaw ripping through the air. At home, I'd poke him to get him to turn back onto his side, but he's too far away for me to even nudge with my toe.

Jude slides from my lap and moves to the other end of the couch. "I should go to bed."

I nod. I should too. I'm exhausted, my eyes gritty and sore with the need for sleep. But at the same time, I'm more awake, more alive than I've ever been before. My blood sings through my veins. My bones ache, not with cold this time, but with desire for this woman.

"Take the couch," I say finally, forcing myself to get up and move away from her. "I'll bunk with them." I gesture to my sleeping brothers. There are enough quilts and blankets for all of us.

"I have a bed upstairs," Jude says, but doesn't make any move to get up.

"It's cold up there," I point out. The wind hasn't quieted. It still howls around the house. "And dark."

She looks thoughtful for a second. "You're right." She gets up to pull a couple of blankets from the pile on the floor and drags them back to the couch. "Are you sure you'll be okay on the floor? With that ankle?"

I nod, leaning on the arm of the couch as I lower myself to the floor. She moves around the room, blowing out candles and throwing more wood onto the fire while I gather a quilt and some blankets to wrap around myself. I settle myself next to Wiley and lie down, facing the fire, watching the flames tango along the fresh logs Jude has just laid.

"Here," Jude appears next to me with a couple of pillows which she slides gently under my injured foot. She tucks the blankets more securely around me and rests a warm hand against my cheek for a second. "Sleep well."

"Mmm," I murmur, my eyes already dropping closed. "You too."

I wake once during the night. The fire has burned to glowing embers. Wiley has draped himself across my back, his arms hanging loosely over my shoulders. He's warm and heavy, and I can feel his ear pressed between my shoulder blades. I often find him sleeping against Sage like this, but it's been a long time since I've woken with him clinging to me. I smile and shift a little so he's positioned more securely against my spine and settle back into sleep.

Chapter Twenty-Five

I wake first the next morning. Wiley has turned over during the night and is now curled against Sage. I push myself into a sitting position, wincing when my ankle slides from the pillow it was resting on and protests. I'd hoped it would be less painful today, but that doesn't seem to be the case. It's still dark, but I can't tell if that's because it's early, or if it's the fault of the storm. The sound of wind in the trees tells me it's still pretty wild outside. I reach into my pocket and pull out the phone to check the time. 6:42 AM. The battery icon flashes red, telling me it has only six percent charge left. I'll have to find somewhere inconspicuous to plug it in. If the power has come back on.

As quietly as I can, I climb to my feet, using the arm of the couch to pull myself upright. Mrs. Applegarth—Jude—lies on the couch with her back to me under a mound of blankets. What happened between us last night doesn't feel real. Did I really kiss her? I touch my lips with my fingertips as if I'll be able to feel the imprint of her mouth against mine. She kissed me first, didn't she? I can't be sure anymore. The whole thing feels like an elusive fever dream, watery and unreal.

I test my ankle with a little weight and am pleased to discover it can take more pressure than it could yesterday. It still hurts though. Leaning on the couch, and then the wall, I limp to the windows and pull the curtain aside an inch or two. It's just beginning to get light, but even in the dimness I can see how much snow has fallen. It lies in drifts against the bases of the trees and against the window. It's thick, heavy, and white, unmarked by footprints. The lake shifts uneasily, tossing spumes of white foam this way and that. Dark clouds still blanket the sky, making the lake appear black rather than blue.

"Guess it's an indoor day," someone whispers behind me.

I turn and find Mrs. A at my shoulder. Her hair is tangled, her eyes puffy with sleep. Somehow, she looks both older and younger than she usually does.

"I didn't mean to wake you," I whisper back.

She shrugs. "I'm always up early."

I guess she is. School starts at eight-fifteen, and the teachers have to be there before the rest of us. I don't know where she lives, but unless she lives nearby—and I doubt she does, as Milton High isn't in the greatest neighborhood—she'd have a commute.

"What's your excuse?" She lifts the curtain again and peers out.

"I'm always up early too." I started forcing myself to wake early when I was still young enough to believe I could keep at least some of Mom's behavior a secret from Sage and Wiley. I'd get up before dawn to clean up whatever mess she'd left the night before, emptying ashtrays and dumping empty liquor bottles in the trash. Sometimes other things too. Things I didn't want to think too much about when I gingerly picked them up using a wad of toilet paper to protect my fingers. Things I didn't want my younger brothers to know existed, let alone find in their own home.

"How's the ankle?" Jude glances at my bandaged foot, frowning when she catches me standing on it, using my toes for balance.

"Better." I lift it from the floor and transfer my weight to the wall. "Still hurts some, but I'm okay."

She looks at me, the frown line between her eyes deepening. It's like she knows I'm telling her what I think she wants to hear, what I have to tell her to keep her from probing deeper and asking more questions I don't want to answer. She's already breached my defenses. She already knows too much.

"How's your head?" I change the subject, searching for the faint spread of bruise at her temple.

Her hand reaches up and touches the place Wiley hit her. "Fine. Not even much of a bump."

Not sure I believe her. She flinched when she touched it.

"Sit down," she says. "I'll make some coffee."

I ease myself around until I can drop down on the couch. "Is the power back on?"

She swears. "I forgot about that. I can deal with not having the lights, but there's no way I can face this morning without coffee."

I start pulling myself up, but she pushes me back into the cushions and tangled blankets still warm from her body. "Stay."

I stay.

The power comes back on some time mid-morning, but by then Jude has found an old camping stove and boiled water for coffee on that and made pancakes for breakfast. Wiley eats three before joining me on the couch, face and hands sticky with syrup.

"You need to take a shower, buddy," I tell him.

He licks at his fingers and a shiny patch on the back of his hand. Under the scent of maple—real, not flavored—he smells dirty, of sweat and fear and grime.

"Later," he says.

I shake my head. "Now, Wiley."

It's always been important to me that my brothers keep clean. You can show up at school in clothes with holes in them, that don't fit right, but if they smell, if *you* smell, you get noticed. By other kids and by teachers. So even if I had to wash our clothes in the bathroom sink, I made sure they didn't stink. And I made them both take showers or baths every day too.

Wiley pouts but slides off the couch.

"I'll find you a towel," Jude says, winking at me over Wiley's head.

I spend most of the day on the couch. Every time I make a move to get up, either Jude or Sage pushes me back, forcing me to rest my ankle.

"I was only going to put another log on the fire," I protest after Sage forces me to sit back down. "It's like two feet away."

"I can do it," he says, pitching a log into the fireplace. His face still looks horrible, but the swelling has gone down some. He's moving more easily too.

I beckon him to me and slide the phone out of my pocket. "Can you plug this in somewhere?"

He glances around, but Jude is nowhere to be seen.

"Where's the charger?" Sage fingers the buttons, starting when the screen suddenly springs to life.

"In her purse." I jut my chin toward the small table where Jude's purse sits, gaping open.

Sage gets up and moves toward the purse, only hesitating for a second before he reaches in and pulls out the neatly coiled charger.

"Somewhere she won't see it," I tell him as he searches the room for an outlet.

"Like here?" He kneels by the windows and shows me an outlet almost completely obscured by the drawn-back curtain.

"Perfect."

Sage plugs the phone in and arranges the curtain to cover it before coming back and sitting with me on the couch. "What's going on?"

"Huh?" I look at him, puzzled, unsure what he

means.

"Why'd you tell her?" he asks, searching my face with those familiar brown eyes.

I sigh. I've been asking myself the same question. What compelled me to tell Jude the truth about us? "I guess I'm just sick of lying."

"What happens to us now?" Sage toys with the fringe on one of the blankets, threading it through his fingers.

"We stay here," I tell him. "She said we could stay here."

He raises his eyebrows. "Forever?"

"For now." I glance at my bandaged ankle propped on the arm of the couch and at Sage's bruised cheek. "It's a good place for now."

And it is. It's not like we can go anywhere else. Not with the storm still whipping snow around the house. I'm grateful to have somewhere warm and safe to be right now. It gives me time to think. Time to recover. Time for Sage and I both to heal up before we have to go back out there and face the world. Time for me to figure out what to do next.

Sage looks like he wants to say something more, but Jude and Wiley enter the room and he clams up. He looks at the way Jude holds Wiley's hand and his eyes narrow.

"Wanna play a game, Wiles?" he asks, already off the couch and heading toward the shelves stacked with games and puzzles.

"Why don't we all play?" Jude says, following when Wiley lets go of her hand to join Sage. "How about Scrabble?"

The wind starts to drop late in the afternoon. We work our way through Scrabble and Clue before we settle into a Monopoly game which takes several hours and ends with Wiley bankrupting the rest of us.

"You've got a future as a property tycoon," Jude says as she hands over the cash she's raised by selling all the houses she'd managed to buy.

"I hope so." I reach out and rub at Wiley's hair. "Someone's going to need to take care of me in my old age."

Mrs. A snorts. "You've got a few years to go."

"Gives Wiley a few years to build his empire," I tell her.

"I'll go see what we can have for dinner," Sage says, unfolding himself from the floor. "I know when I'm beaten."

Wiley grins up at him and scoops up the remaining property cards and banknotes from Sage's place, adding them to his own considerable pile.

Jude climbs to her feet and stops Sage before he moves through to the kitchen. "You don't have to do all the cooking."

He looks down at the rug. "I don't mind. You made breakfast."

Jude considers this. "How about we do it together? Do you know how to make potato au gratin?"

They disappear through the kitchen door, leaving Wiley and me to gather up the pieces of the game and put them back in the box. It's when the box has been put back on the shelf and the room is momentarily silent that I realize the wind has dropped. It's quiet without the constant rustling of trees and whistling of wind as it pries its way at the windows looking for a way in.

With both Sage and Jude otherwise occupied, there's no one to stop me as I drag myself from the couch and limp to the windows. They're fogged with condensation, but I wipe it away, peering out at the gathering darkness.

"Is it still snowing?" Wiley asks, wriggling in beside me and wiping a lower patch of glass clear.

"It might be clearing," I say, peering up at the sky which no longer looks heavy and bruised. "Look, is that a star?"

Wiley looks where I'm pointing. "I think so."

I stare out at the snow-covered grass and the trees that are no longer tossing their limbs. Even the lake seems to have stilled. "Guess we can go now," I murmur to myself.

"We're leaving?" I'd almost forgotten Wiley was there.

I shake my head. "Not right now, no."

"But we will." It's not a question. Wiley's eyes are huge and trusting as he looks up at me.

"We'll have to," I say. "Eventually."

KATE LARKINDALE

Chapter Twenty-Six

After we eat dinner and the dishes are done, Sage goes to take a shower, leaving me to get Wiley ready for bed. He gets into his pajamas and curls up next to me on the couch with a book.

"Why don't you read to me?" I say.

He looks up at me. "You're supposed to read to me. Sage does."

"I know." I make no move to take the book though. "Let's switch things up. I'm sleepy and my leg hurts, but I bet I'd feel a lot better if you read to me."

Wiley gives me a skeptical look, but opens the book. "Me and Sage already read four chapters."

"That's okay." I wrap my arm around him and draw him closer to my side. "I'll catch up."

Wiley starts reading. He stumbles over the odd word, but mostly he manages, even if he has to sound them out. He even does different voices for each of the characters speaking. I used to do the same thing when I read to Sage. Maybe it's a family tradition—our first one.

Jude comes in with an armful of wood. Instinctively, I move to get up, to take the load from her, but she frowns and shakes her head, gesturing emphatically that I should stay where I am. She sets down the wood and goes back out, to get more I assume. It's a little frightening how much wood it takes to keep us warm. I know now why there is so much stacked up against the shed. And it won't be nearly enough if we decide to stay more than a week or two.

After dumping a second load of wood, Jude takes off her coat and gloves and sits down on Wiley's other side.

"Your brother is doing this all wrong," she says, taking the book out of Wiley's hand. "He's supposed to read to you."

"Told you!" Wiley gives me a triumphant look.

"Come with me." Jude takes Wiley's hand and pulls him off the couch with her. "I'll do it properly."

She leads Wiley to his nest on the floor. He finds Honey, his ratty old stuffed dog, and climbs under the pile of blankets and quilts. She tucks him and the toy in and sits by them, cross-legged, and starts reading where Wiley left off. Her voice is low and hypnotic as she reads, soothing. It takes only a few minutes for Wiley's eyelids to drop and only a few more before he's asleep.

Sage comes in wearing the sweats he sleeps in. He doesn't say anything when he sees Jude sitting by Wiley, the book open in her lap, but he does glance my way, eyebrows raised again.

I give him a small shrug, letting him know I'm as puzzled by all this as he is. Although when I consider it, maybe it isn't as weird as it initially seemed. Jude's a mom who lost her kids; Wiley's a kid with no mom.

It's not late, but Sage slips under the covers next to Wiley and closes his eyes. They snap open a second or two later when Jude leans across and tucks the quilts more tightly around him.

"Shh," she murmurs. "Go to sleep."

For a moment, he stares at her.

She reaches over and tugs the quilt higher on his shoulder, letting her hand rest there for a brief moment.

His face relaxes into a smile and he settles his head into the pillow, his eyes closing once more.

Jude stays on the floor with them until she's sure they're asleep, then she carefully places a couple of new logs on the fire and joins me on the couch. She sits close but doesn't touch me.

I can smell the woodsmoke on her clothes, her hair. The faint scent of citrus from the dishwashing soap she used. My nerves tingle with the proximity. I want to touch her. I want to feel her like I did last night. I need to know it was real.

"Jude?" I whisper, surprised at how strangled the word sounds as it escapes my throat.

"Hmmm?" She doesn't look at me, but I sense her hand shifting closer to my thigh. The muscles there jump with the need to be touched.

"Can I..." I don't wait to finish the question. I lean across and press my mouth to hers.

She freezes for a second, and I wonder if I've made a huge mistake. Her lips part and her tongue seeks mine out, her mouth moving hungrily against mine. My arms settle around her, drawing her closer.

"Blue..." She pulls away for a moment and stares into my face. "We really shouldn't..."

I kiss her again, silencing the words she was about to speak. This feels too good for shouldn't.

She gives a little sigh and settles herself into my lap, straddling my legs, her full breasts pressing into me as her hands cup my neck and draw my mouth to hers again. Her hands tangle in the hair at the nape of my neck.

My arms fall from her waist and my hands find her jeans-clad ass. I run my fingers across the taut denim. I trace the outline of first one pocket, then the other.

She groans and grinds herself against me.

I'm grateful again I'm wearing sweatpants, not jeans. The pressure would be unbearable.

One of her hands moves from my neck and drops to my lap, finding the hardness there.

It's my turn to moan. I never knew fingers could feel so good. Not even moving fingers. Just fingertips, resting there.

The rustle of covers comes to us from across the room and we both freeze. I don't know about her, but I'd almost forgotten my brothers are only a few feet away. Either one of them could open their eyes at any moment and see this.

Jude climbs from my lap and takes my hand. "Come with me," she whispers, pulling me up from the couch and leading me out of the warmth of the living room and into the cold darkness of the hallway beyond.

Moonlight streams through the marbled glass in the front door, creating weird bubbles of light across the carpet. It's cold out here, away from the fire. My skin prickles with goosebumps as I let Jude help me up the stairs. Walking is awkward, not only because of my hurt ankle, but because even my sweats are too tight around my crotch, digging into parts of me that don't like the pressure. I use my free hand to try and adjust things as I walk, but it doesn't really work.

At the top of the stairs, she hesitates a second before leading me into the master bedroom. She flicks on a small lamp at one end of the room, but doesn't touch the main switch or the bigger lamp on a low table by the bed.

The bed. It looked big in daylight, but now, with shadows swallowing most of the space, it's like an island in the center of the room. Beyond it, there is only darkness and our faint, watery reflections in the windows. I'm struck by how tiny she looks next to me, the top of her head not even reaching my shoulder when we stand side by side.

She lets go of my hand and crosses to the windows, drawing the curtains over the glass and extinguishing the reflection.

"Brrr…" She runs her hands up and down her

arms as she walks back toward me. "It's cold."

I nod and watch as she throws back the covers on the neatly made bed. The sheets look crisp, white, and new, the mattress beneath them firm.

"Jump in," she says in a low voice as she sits down and pulls off her shoes. "I'll keep you warm."

I stand there like my feet are encased in cement. I'm about to go to bed with my teacher. Well, I guess technically she's not my teacher anymore, but still...

I shake my head. I can't do this. Not in the bed where she and her husband would have slept. Where they would have made love. Where it's possible her children were conceived.

Not to mention, I've never done it before and I don't have the first idea where to start.

"Mrs..."

"Jude," she corrects firmly. "In here especially. It's Jude."

"Okay ... Jude. I'm not sure..."

"Blue." She crawls across the bed so she's closer to me. "We don't have to do anything you don't want to, okay?"

"Okay..." I still don't move. She's on her hands and knees on the bed, and her sweater gapes open at the top, revealing a dark, secretive pool of cleavage.

"Just get in here so we can get warm." This time it's an order. I recognize the tone from school and I can't fight it. Before I'm aware I've even moved, I'm sitting on the edge of the bed.

Jude shifts over to make room for me to swing my legs in, drawing the covers up over us as soon as I'm in.

"That's better," she says, wriggling closer to me.

I have to agree. Our two bodies quickly warm the sheets and create a small, tropical cocoon around us. Jude shifts a little, letting in a blast of cold air as she tugs her sweater and shirt off and tosses them carelessly on the floor.

For a brief second, I get a glimpse of her bra and the soft, fleshy stomach beneath it. She looks nothing like the models in the underwear catalogue one of the guys at school passed around last year. For one thing, her bra isn't made of skimpy lace, and the breasts the thick, heavy material hold up aren't tiny and pert.

I reach out and cup one of those breasts in my hand, feeling its weight and the way gravity tugs it downward. I roll my thumb across the fabric of the bra and am rewarded when her nipple springs to attention underneath.

She gasps and reaches for me. Her hands find their way beneath the hem of my shirt. They're cold against my stomach and I flinch away.

"Sorry," she says, not sounding sorry at all. "Bad circulation. My hands are always cold."

"S'okay," I say, through gritted teeth.

"You must work out," she murmurs. Her fingers, warming up now, run across my stomach muscles before climbing over the ridge of ribs to my pecs.

A snort of laughter escapes my mouth before I catch it.

"What?" She pulls away and looks at me curiously.

"Sorry." I pull her close again, my hand sinking into the soft fold of flesh at her waist. "Working out... It's funny."

"How?"

"I wouldn't have time."

"So..." She runs her fingers across my stomach again. It tickles and I squirm. "How'd you get these rock hard abs?"

I shrug. They're just there. "Probably from

working in the warehouse. I do a lot of heavy lifting."

She runs her hands along my arms and shoulders, her touch leaving behind a trail of sensation I can't describe. "I can tell," she says with a grin.

She doesn't say anything more. She kisses me again, and this time it's different, more intense, hungrier.

I kiss her back, allowing myself to focus only on the feelings her lips, fingers and body create in mine. It's the first time in... Well, I can't remember. Maybe the first time I've ever focused so entirely on myself and my own needs and desires. Needs and desires I've never even realized I have.

Her hand creeps lower, cupping me over my pants. She pulls them down and sets me free.

Gratefully, I shuck the pants. It's awkward with the heavy covers over us, her hands still exploring my body even as I struggle to untangle my legs. My ankle gives a vicious throb when I kick the offending garment away, but I pay it no attention. There are other things throbbing that need my focus.

"Is this okay?" she asks me as her fingers disappear beneath the waistband of my boxers.

I nod and she dives in.

****

Later, we lie side by side, breath quick and heavy, a sheen of sweat cooling on our skin.

"It was your first time," she says once the frantic panting has slowed.

"Yeah." I wish the light was off, but I'm not sure I have enough strength left to reach for the lamp. My entire body is as limp as a noodle, electric zings of pleasure still coursing along the length of my legs and coiling in my belly. This is why guys talk about nothing else. Or think about nothing else. I can't believe I've waited seventeen years before doing this. I mean, I've taken care of business myself, of course. All guys do. But what I can do to myself with my hand is nothing like what Jude did to me.

"Uh… Was I okay?" I heard her gasp and moan and hope my clumsy attempts to make her feel good actually did.

"You were fine," she says, running her fingers through the fine dusting of hair on my chest. "And practice makes perfect, right?"

Practice? Yes please. Now, if possible. I'll be a diligent student. I'll practice hours every day.

Eager to start, I lean over and kiss her again, sucking at her earlobe before making my way slowly back toward her lips.

"Not now," she says gently, pushing me away. "Later."

She climbs out of bed, pushing the covers aside just long enough to let in a gust of chilled air. Goosebumps scatter across my skin, only to be extinguished a second later when the heavy warmth of the covers settles over me again.

I raise myself onto my elbows and watch as she walks around the bed. She has a great ass. Big and soft and round. Under it, her thighs are thick and strong-looking, the flesh pebbled with cellulite.

"What?" she asks, turning before she reaches the door.

"You're gorgeous," I say. And I mean it. She's not pretty like a model is pretty. She's better. Not so polished and perfect. I'd be afraid to touch a girl who looked like a model; she might break.

She laughs. "Yeah. Right." Her breasts are heavy, the nipples large and dark against her pale skin. I can't help remembering how they felt against my tongue when she guided my mouth there, how the skin was hot and salty.

"I'll be back in a sec," she says, darting out the door without bothering to cover herself with the robe hanging on a hook on the back.

I flop back into the lemon-scented pillows. I should go back downstairs. If Sage or Wiley wakes up and finds me gone, they'll worry. And I don't want them to find me here if they come looking. How would I explain that one?

The soft patter of a shower running creeps through the half-open door. I roll over, planning to get out of bed. But before I do much more than remember where my clothes are scattered, I fall asleep.

KATE LARKINDALE

Chapter Twenty-Seven

It's still dark when I snap awake. For a second, I'm confused about where I am, but the heavy warmth of Jude's body next to me reminds me soon enough. She's no longer curled in my arms, but has shifted across the bed and now lies facing away from me, soft, snuffling snores drifting from her mouth.

I drag myself into a sitting position, trying hard not to disturb her. What woke me? A sound? I cock my head and listen to the darkness.

Nothing. Only Jude's breath as she sleeps. Yet I'm certain something woke me. I glance around the room, but it's so dark, it's difficult to make anything out. It's so different from the city where darkness is rarely actual darkness. For a second, I miss the garish glow of neon and streetlights filtered through the curtains in the apartment, making a mockery of night.

"Blue?"

My name comes as a whisper through the darkness and I know instantly it's Wiley.

"Wiley?" I climb out of bed, wincing when I put weight on my injured ankle and the pain flares. I feel my way to the door by trailing my fingertips along the wall. "What's up, buddy?"

I find the door and snag the robe, wrapping it around myself before I step out into the hallway where I find Wiley crouched beside the door.

"You were gone," he whispers. It's lighter out here. Moonlight streams through the window in the bedroom at the end of the hallway. The storm must have really cleared.

"Yeah, I'm sorry." I rub my hand across Wiley's

hair. "Jude and I were talking, and we didn't want to wake you and Sage. So we came up here and I fell asleep."

"Who's Jude?"

"Mrs. Applegarth. You know, the lady whose house this is?"

Wiley nods. "Her name's Jude?"

"Yeah. It's a little weird to keep calling someone 'Mrs. when we're living under the same roof. So she asked me to call her Jude. You can too."

"Okay." Wiley rubs sleepily at his eyes. I wonder what time it is, how long I was asleep.

"You want me to come back down with you?" I reach for the wall for support as my ankle gives another painful twinge.

Wiley peeks through the open door. "You were sleeping in the same bed as her?"

"Yeah."

Wiley makes a face. "Like Mom sleeps with…"

"No!" I'm grateful for the darkness now because it hides the blush I'm certain has risen to my cheeks. What I did is nothing like what Mom does. I know Jude's name for one thing. And I'll remember tonight, maybe forever. Not to mention, I'm not going anywhere. Mom's guys are rarely still there in the morning. I've smelled Mom's dragon breath when she wakes up. Seeing her in daylight with a hangover isn't a great experience either. Once the beer goggles wear off, being with Mom is less a dream come true than a nightmare. I don't blame them for sneaking out. More than once, I've run into a guy, unshaven, shoes in hand as he tiptoes across the apartment to make his escape. More than once, I've been tempted to ask him to take me with him.

Wiley nods, accepting this. He's too young to understand, yet I'm pretty sure he does and that's just depressing. An eight-year-old shouldn't. He yawns again and I start back downstairs, leaning heavily on the banister as I try limping without making too much noise. He follows me without a word, his feet nearly silent as we pad down the stairs. No surprise I didn't hear him come up.

The living room is warmer than the rest of the house despite the fire having burned down to smoldering embers. While Wiley resettles himself under the blankets, I poke at the glowing embers, blowing on them in the hope I can get them to ignite the fresh log I toss on. It takes a couple of minutes, but the dry strings of bark hanging from the log catch, and before long, the whole thing is blazing merrily. I throw on another log and sit back to enjoy the warmth.

"You okay there, Wiley?" I turn away from the flames.

"Mhhmm," he mumbles, already half asleep.

My eyes are dazzled by the firelight so I sit there for a moment, waiting for the weird smears of light and shadow to stop dancing in my field of vision. Once they have, I look down at my sleeping brothers. In the golden glow of the firelight, they both look very young. Sage especially. Wiley *is* young and I'm used to thinking of him as a child. I rarely think of Sage as being younger than me. I mean, he is, but's it's more an intellectual knowledge than something I actually consider. Sage and I are a team. We've had to be. For so long it was just the two of us.

But now, watching him sleep, his long, long eyelashes fluttering against his still-bruised cheeks, I realize he's still a child too. Or he should be. Maybe I've relied on him too much, asked him to take on too much responsibility. I know I have. But I've had to as well.

"What?" Sage asks sleepily. Was my gaze so

penetrating it woke him up?

I unfold my limbs from under me and leave the intense heat at my back behind. "Nothing," I say. "Go back to sleep."

Sage gives me a confused, puzzled look but soon lets his eyes drop closed again. I smile. He must be comfortable here. I don't believe he would have gone back to sleep at home. At least, not so easily.

I yawn. I'm tired too. I sink down on the couch which is still littered with pillows and blankets. A part of me wants to go back upstairs, back to Jude and her soft curves. But I'd wake her if I climbed into bed next to her again. And she may not even want me there.

I lie down and pull the covers over me, keeping my eyes on the fire and the weird shadows the flickering flames cast on the room. For the first time, I muse about Jude's reasons for what we did. My own are pretty simple. I'm a seventeen-year-old boy and as horny as all guys my age tend to be. I would never have initiated what we did, but I was never going to stop it once it had started. Not as long as she kept playing along.

But what was in it for her? I adjust the pillow under my head and try to figure it out. I was too clumsy and inexperienced for it to have been pleasurable for her. I mean, I'm pretty sure I made her come, but it may have been in spite of my efforts. Although, I remember, she was pretty good about showing me what she liked and what she didn't, how she wanted to be touched.

Was it loneliness? That need for intimacy she mentioned last night? The desire to be touched? She obviously misses her family. Her husband and her sons. But is that why? Do we remind her of the family she's lost?

Or is it this place? Her family clearly loved this place, so there must be a lot of memories here. Good memories. Maybe she came back here to get back in touch with those memories. I hope our presence here hasn't ruined this place for her. Bad enough that Wiley clocked her on the way in without us desecrating the memories of the people she loved.

But she appears to have forgiven Wiley for hitting her. And she can't be afraid of us. You don't sit down and eat dinner with people you're terrified of. You don't play board games with them. Or make pancakes from scratch for them. Or take one of them to bed and make him a man. So I'm just as confused as I was when I lay down here. My exhausted brain gives up, and as I drop off to sleep, the last thing I think about is the possibility of Stockholm Syndrome, something I remember reading about in history class last year. Maybe Jude has an extremely accelerated case?

****

The sound of voices and the scents of coffee and bacon drag me out of slumber long before I'm ready. I groan and roll over, taking my pillow with me and covering my head with it. It's too late though. I'm awake. And once I'm awake, I won't go back to sleep.

"There you are, sleepyhead." Jude must have been watching me because before I've even managed to scrape the sleep from my eyes, she's perched on the arm of the couch, a steaming mug held out toward me.

"Coffee?" I ask, sitting up and reaching for it.

"Of course," she says. "Do I look like someone who drinks tea in the mornings?"

I run my eyes across her. She's in a robe and slippers, the kind that are like little sheepskin boots. The robe is thick and soft looking, the belt tied loosely and carelessly around her waist. So loosely it's starting to fall open, revealing a glimpse of her large, fleshy breasts.

I look away. It's too early for me to be this

excited. Yet my eyes can't unsee them.

"Look how much it snowed!" Wiley jumps on the couch next to me and points toward the windows. The curtains are still drawn most of the way across, but a tiny slice of too-bright daylight dribbles through the small crack between them. "Blue! Come look."

I let Wiley drag me off the couch, only realizing once I'm standing in the middle of the floor that I'm still wearing the robe I pulled off Jude's door last night. In the dark, I couldn't see it properly and it's only now I realize how short it is. How short and how pink.

Sage, who is standing in the kitchen doorway, catches sight of me and bursts into a fit of giggles. "What are you wearing, dude?"

My face heats up. Does he know? Is the robe telling all the secrets I want to keep to myself?

"It's a robe," Jude says briskly. "An old one, I admit. But beggars can't be choosers, can they?"

"Blue! Come see." Wiley tugs at my hand. He doesn't care that I'm wearing a woman's pink robe. He doesn't even seem to care that it barely covers my bare ass.

But Jude does. She checks no one is looking, and rubs her hand across it as I hobble past. It takes every ounce of strength I possess not to react to her touch.

But I don't.

****

Wiley is still excited about the snow once we've eaten breakfast. It is pretty, I have to admit. It lies thick, soft, and white across the lawn. Beyond it, the lake sparkles in its various shades of blue.

"Do you want to go out there?" I ask Wiley after he's been to the window to stare out at the snow for the fifth or sixth time.

"Can I?" His face lights up at my suggestion.

I nod. "Just wrap up warmly."

He dashes away and comes back a minute or two later wearing a pair of too-small sweatpants over his jeans. He's shrugging on an extra sweater as he walks, his jacket dangling from one finger.

Jude, at the sink with Sage, both of them up to their elbows in soapsuds and hot water, glances over as Wiley zips his jacket.

"Oh, honey," Jude says. "Haven't you got any warm clothes? It's freezing out there."

Wiley looks down, clearly confused. "I put on my warm clothes."

Jude shakes her head. "You need snow pants. And a hat. Definitely a hat."

She dries her hands and leaves Sage's side. "Let's see if we can find some."

Less than five minutes later, she and Wiley are back, and Wiley's kitted out like he's going on an Arctic adventure. He has snow pants and a matching parka. Mittens cover his hands and a woolen hat perches on top of his thick dark hair, a pompom bobbing on top.

"You look like you could be in one of those outdoor clothing catalogues," Sage says, crossing the room to bat at the pompom.

"They're Caleb's," Jude says, straightening the hat Sage has knocked askew. "He'll be warm and dry."

"Can I go?" Wiley tugs down the hat and heads for the door. He shoves at it, but of course the snow has piled up against it, and he doesn't have the strength to push it away. I join him and add my weight, which is enough to shift the small drift enough for the door to slide ajar.

"You want me to come with you?" I ask as he slithers through the narrow space. "Can you clear the snow away from the door?"

He doesn't answer, simply slams the door behind him, leaving nothing but a gust of chilly air. But a moment later there's a scuffling sound from behind it and I know he's doing what I asked.

While Jude and Sage finish cleaning up the kitchen, I take a second cup of coffee and drift to the windows. I pull the curtains across, letting the bright winter sunshine pour into the room.

Wiley runs around the yard. He scoops snow into snowballs and piles them on the half-buried picnic table. When he's built a small pyramid of these missiles, he picks one up and hurls it at the trunk of an old gnarled tree. It explodes against the bark, leaving a satisfying smear of snow like a twisted smile across the trunk.

"He's having fun," Jude says, slipping behind me and wrapping her arms around my waist.

I whirl around, terrified Sage might catch this gesture of affection.

"Relax," she murmurs. "He's taking a shower."

I do as she says. If that's the case, we have a while.

"Where'd you go last night?" Her hand slips under the front of my robe.

I shrug. "Wiley came looking for me."

She nods, her fingers finding my nipple and giving it a tweak.

I gasp.

If she doesn't stop, I'll wind up tossing her down on the couch and then…

I force myself to stop thinking about what might happen next.

"I should get dressed," I say finally, looking down at the ridiculous pink robe.

Chapter Twenty-Eight

By the time Sage is out of the shower I'm dressed and Jude and I are tidying up the living room, putting the cushions back onto the couch and folding the bedding we've slept on. My ankle feels much better today, and although I'm still limping, I can move around without the pain being unbearable.

"There are plenty of beds upstairs," Jude says briskly. "No need to sleep down here."

"Are you sure?" I remember the children's room we found when we were exploring the house, the way it appeared to have been untouched since the children left it. It didn't feel sinister then, but it does now. Or maybe not sinister. Just sad.

Jude nods. "This place is like a museum. And it shouldn't be. I remember it full of light and laughter. I'd like it to be that way again."

So I gather our things and drag the backpack and Wiley's garbage bag upstairs.

"You want to bunk with Wiley, or take that room?" I ask Sage, pointing at the little study with its narrow daybed covered in colorful cushions.

He shrugs. "I don't mind. I can stay with Wiley."

I'm making assumptions, and I shouldn't, but I'm pretty sure wherever I put my stuff, I'm going to end up sleeping in that big double bed in the master bedroom. And it'll be easier to sneak out of the study than from next to a sleeping Wiley, but I want to give Sage the option. He's never had a room of his own.

As if it's already decided, Sage takes the backpack out of my hands and moves through the doorway to the room with the two beds, dropping it on the one closest to the door. I follow him, putting Wiley's bag on the other bed before heading into the study to stash my few things in there.

Sage follows me, and once we're in the narrow room he looks around and eases the door closed behind him.

"Did you…" His cheeks redden a little and he looks down at the floor. "Did you *sleep* with her?"

I whirl around. How did he know? Do I look different or something today? Is it obvious I've lost my virginity?

He shrugs, looking slightly embarrassed. "You were wearing her robe. And when I came up to take a shower, I saw your clothes on the floor of her room."

I sigh. I had hoped he wouldn't find out. At least, not so soon. "Yeah."

"Why, Blue?" Sage looks genuinely confused. "Did she make you?"

I shake my head. "It wasn't like that. We were talking and it just kind of happened."

"But she's so old!" Sage's face twists.

"She's not that old." But he's right. She has to be at least Mom's age. Maybe even a little older. Somehow it didn't seem to matter last night.

"Did you like it?" Sage sounds curious.

Now it's my turn to turn red. Heat blazes in my cheeks. "Yeah. I liked it a lot."

****

The next five days are among the best I've ever spent in my life. It remains cold, but it doesn't snow again and the sun shines brightly. The four of us bundle up in whatever warm clothes we can find and take walks around the lake or into the forest behind the houses. Short ones to begin with because of my ankle, but getting longer each day as it heals and strengthens.

Wiley runs and tumbles through the snow, his cheeks permanently glowing pink from a mixture of cold, sun, and wind. Sage is more reserved, but as the days go by and his bruises fade from purple to green to yellow, he joins Wiley and me in building a lopsided snowman, pelting it with snowballs until it collapses into a slumped pile of slush.

I leave Wiley and Sage to rebuild it and head back toward the house. I haven't managed to find any gloves that will fit my hands so my fingers are freezing.

"Here." Jude meets me at the door and hands me a steaming cup of coffee. "You look a little frostbitten."

I accept the coffee and set it down on the counter before it scalds my frozen fingers. "I'm okay."

"They look like they're having a good time." Jude gestures at the two boys who have now abandoned the snowman and are lying prone, making snow angels.

"Thanks to you." I sneak a glance out the window to make sure neither of them is looking my way and kiss Jude. She melts into me, sighing gently into my mouth. I've been sleeping with her every night and each time it gets better. I've learned the roadmap of her body and know where she likes to be touched, which parts make her turn to jelly. In turn, she's learned mine, taught me things about my own body I might never have become aware of otherwise.

We lie awake after, her head nestled into the place my shoulder meets my chest as if the spot was made for it. I like this part almost as much as I like the actual sex. The part where we lie here and talk, conversation slipping from topic to topic until one or the other of us drifts off to sleep. I've never talked to anyone other than Sage so much or so openly. It's like telling her about Mom opened a floodgate, and all kinds of other stuff is now free to spill out. Stuff I thought I'd buried or forgotten long ago.

"What about your dad?" Jude asks. "You never mention him."

"He's dead," I say. "And I never really knew him anyway. He and my mom split when I was about two."

"When did he die?"

It's not something I think about much. He was never a part of my life. I did still see him after he and Mom split, but not often. He was here and we were always on the road. "Maybe seven? Six or seven. Sage was around, I know."

When we were in town and Dad wanted to see me, Mom would always send Sage too, even though he had a different father. And if I remember right, Dad never spoke or acted differently with Sage than with me. Maybe it isn't so surprising Sage kept that photo of him. Rojan Patel was probably the only man who ever treated Sage like a son. Which goes to show what a classy guy he really was. I wouldn't be surprised if Mom was fooling around with Sage's dad even before they split. It's probably *why* they split, even if she didn't get pregnant with Sage until a few months later. Or at least, one of the reasons they split.

"What about Sage and Wiley's dad?" Jude traces circles across my stomach with her finger and it tickles.

"Dads," I tell her. "Plural. Can't you tell?" It has to be obvious that Sage is white while Wiley and I are different shades of brown.

"I didn't want to assume…"

"They're assholes. Sage's dad's in jail for drug dealing, and if I ever see Wiley's dad again I won't be responsible for what I do to him."

"Shh…." Jude rolls over and kisses the words off my lips. "You don't have to talk about them."

"Good," I murmur, kissing her back, hard enough

things start stirring again under the covers.

****

It's not all fun and games though. Jude, ever the teacher, makes sure we're learning too. She gets Wiley to help her bake cookies and turns it into a math class. A walk through the woods becomes a biology lesson. And of course, she gives us books to read and asks us about them, forcing even me to think harder about what I'm reading than I ever have before. Even in her classes.

"We're going to have to figure out a way to get you guys back in school," she says over dinner one night. "You're missing too much."

"It hasn't even been a week," I argue. But she's not saying anything I don't already know. I've already accepted being a dropout, but Wiley and Sage should be in school. My original plan would have kept them in school.

"A week is enough," Jude says. "You can miss a lot in a week."

I know that. I've missed a lot of school over the years, between all those years on the road, taking care of Mom when she was too wasted to be left alone, and taking care of one or the other of my brothers when they were hurt too badly to leave the house. Not to mention the days when I was too sore to get out of bed myself and had to let Sage take care of me. I always worked my ass off to catch up on what I missed, but there are still a couple of basic math concepts I never really got a handle on because I wasn't there the days they were taught.

We've been playing house up here, pretending we're a family. But I know it's pretend, and as soon as we leave, the illusion will fall away and Jude will realize we're a bunch of fucked up kids with nowhere to call home. We're living on borrowed time. One of these days Jude is going to come to her senses, and we'll get handed over to some social worker or organization. But while I'm here, I'm enjoying it.

Sage and Wiley are enjoying it too. I see it in the way Wiley curls up next to her on the couch to read without any hesitancy or caution. And in the way she and Sage move around the kitchen as they prepare meals, the gentle teasing between them that makes Sage laugh more than I've ever heard him laugh before.

Jude's enjoying it too, I think. The tense lines in her face have softened and the sadness in her eyes seems less. I watch her in unguarded moments when she's helping Wiley with a puzzle, or showing Sage how to separate eggs and catch something like joy in her expression. I like that we've helped her find this again. It makes me feel better about the way we've insinuated ourselves into her life.

"We're going to have to go to town," Jude says, opening the pantry and frowning at the contents. "We're almost out of food."

"Uh… Yeah." My face heats up. "I feel kind of responsible for that. You didn't shop knowing you'd be feeding three kids."

"Hungry kids," she says with a smile. "Two hungry kids. And one very hungry man." She closes the pantry and presses her back against it, eyes teasing as she looks up into my face, her hand finding my crotch and brushing across it.

I groan as my jeans tighten around me. Leaning forward, I let my arms fall on either side of her, my weight on the closed door as I lean down to kiss her.

Chapter Twenty-Nine

We don't talk a lot as we drive into town. Yet the quiet isn't uncomfortable. The radio is on low, and Jude occasionally hums along with a snatch of music, but mostly she's quiet too. Maybe she's enjoying the peace. Sage and Wiley had no interest in going back to town and stayed at the lake. I wish I could have stayed too, but least I could do after eating all her food was to help her shop for more.

"I usually shop in Warrington," she says after a long period of silence. "But it's a lot more expensive than the supermarkets in town, and with four of us, we'll need a lot more than I do on my own. So it makes sense to go back to Milton this time."

I don't argue. It's not my money, so I have no right to tell her how or where to spend it. I'm just grateful she's willing to keep us around, to keep feeding us.

"I don't mind," I say. I only hope I don't see anyone I know.

Almost as if she's read my mind, Jude pulls into a supermarket across town from the high school. I know this store well because it's the closest one to our apartment. I haven't been there in a while because it became easier for me to pick things up at the store near the warehouse on the way home, but Sage is a regular customer. I wonder if Jude chose to come here because it's not her regular store, if she thinks no one will recognize her here.

"Maybe..." I start, then bite my tongue. It's the middle of the day. A weekday. No one I know is likely to be at this store now. I'm being paranoid again.

The parking lot is crowded and we have to drive

almost three complete circuits before finding a space. I climb out of the vehicle, steeling myself for a crowd. After so many days isolated from the world, the hustle and bustle of this busy place is jarring.

"Let's do this," Jude says with a grim smile. "Every time I come back to the city I wonder why I don't give it up and live at the lake permanently."

We pass through the sliding glass doors and I grab a cart, hoping it doesn't have the wonky wheels most shopping carts seem to have. "You wouldn't miss anything about the city?" I ask.

Jude looks thoughtful for a moment, and I'm glad her mind is elsewhere. The cart appears to have a mind of its own, and it takes a fair bit of strength to keep it moving in an approximation of a straight line.

"Sure," she says finally. "I'd miss things. Theater and museums and certain people, but it's not like I'd be on the opposite side of the world. I could live at the lake and drive in to go to movies or to visit friends. It's only an hour away."

She's right of course. It feels like another country at the lake, so it's hard to remember it's actually not much farther from the central city than some of the outlying suburbs. Or maybe that's just me. If I came from a family who had a house up there and spent holidays and weekends there, would I feel the same way?

"Do the kids like eggplant?" Jude holds up one of the shiny, purple vegetables.

I smile at the way she calls them 'the kids', like we're their parents or something. It's how it's felt the past few days, but I thought it was only me who felt that way.

"No idea," I say, running my finger across the slightly waxy surface. "I don't know if they've ever had it. I don't know if I have either."

Jude drops it in the cart. "We shall have to remedy that! Eggplant parmigiana for dinner tonight."

We walk the aisles slowly, piling more and more food into the cart. Jude seems determined to both broaden our culinary horizons and make sure we have all our favorite comfort foods. Before we're halfway through the store I'm concerned about the amount of money she's about to spend on us.

"Don't we have enough?" I ask in the cereal aisle as she pulls box after box from the shelves. "We usually only get that one." I point to the generic store-brand cornflakes. Wiley has always wanted to try the other kinds, the ones in colorful boxes with cartoon animals. And now several of these boxes are piled in the cart in front of us.

"Please, Blue." Jude stops and looks right at me. "Stop being so responsible. Let me spoil them a little. It's been too long since I had anyone to spoil."

I grin and give up. She clearly wants to take care of us, and who am I to stop her? I even slip a package of my favorite cookies into the cart as we pass through the cookie aisle. At least, they used to be my favorite cookies. It's been so long since I had them, I'm curious if they'll taste as good as I remember them tasting.

"Blue?" A familiar, shrill voice calls my name and my stomach turns to ice.

I turn, my gaze flicking across the people standing in the freezer section.

I don't see her. Maybe I was imagining it. Maybe being in town again has me more on edge than I thought.

"Blue? Honey? Is that you?" Mom walks toward me, a little unsteady on her feet, but not too bad.

I look both ways, trying to figure out if there is a way to escape. Jude is a little way away from me, looking at plastic-wrapped packages of meat. She doesn't even appear to have heard Mom.

"Hi," I say quietly. There's nowhere to go, especially now she's here, so close she could grab hold of the cart if she needed to.

"Hi?" Her voice is too loud and all around us people stop what they're doing to turn and stare at us. "Is that all you have to say? Where have you been?"

I'm actually surprised she's even noticed we're gone. It's only been a few days. She's left us alone longer than that. Even when we were too young to be left.

"Away." I try to draw her farther down an aisle, away from Jude and all these strangers. She's going to make a scene, I know it.

"Away. Away where?" She follows me, stumbling once and grabbing the cart for balance. She looks pathetic. Worn and tired and pathetic. Her tights are laddered up one leg and her skirt hangs crookedly from her bony hips. She's wearing high-heeled boots, but the heels are worn and uneven. Her jacket is unzipped and has slipped off one shoulder. Lipstick smears across her mouth and dark eye makeup smudges around her eyes.

"Away from you," I say. "I had to."

"You had to?" Now she looks outraged. "Why did you have to, Blue? I'm their mother. I'm your mother."

Jude chooses that moment to find me. She hears Mom's words and freezes at the top of the aisle. Her hands are full of packages, and I know they must be cold.

"Excuse me." I shove the cart past Mom and take the meat out of Jude's hands. Hopefully we can just leave. Keep pushing the cart up the aisle and vanish into the vast, crowded supermarket.

But, of course, the cart decides to have a mind of its own. Instead of heading straight up through the mouth of the aisle, the wheels twist and send the heavy cart to the left. It glances off the metal railing at the end of the row of shelves, making the entire unit rock.

It's not a huge crash, and only a single package falls from the shelf, but it's long enough for Mom to catch up to us.

"Who is this, Blue?" she asks, staring at Jude with daggers in her eyes.

"I'm sorry." Jude wipes her hands on her pants and holds one out for Mom to shake. "Jude Applegarth. I'm a teacher at Milton High. Blue was one of my students."

Mom takes her hand and gives it a single limp shake. "Tabitha Lannigan."

Jude withdraws her hand and it looks like she wants to wipe it again. She doesn't. She smiles nervously at Mom. "So nice to meet you."

"Is it?" Mom narrows her eyes. "Why is it nice? What has Blue told you about me? What have those other kids said?"

Jude takes a step back, clearly surprised by the venom in Mom's voice. "Uh ... nothing. Nothing bad, anyway." She's a terrible liar.

"Oh, I bet." Mom's slurring worse now. She probably downed something before she came in here, and it's only just hitting her system now. "I bet he didn't. This one's had it in for me for years. Been telling the same story to anyone who'll listen. Gets better every time he tells it."

I close my eyes against her voice. I've heard this before. Any time she feels like she's being cornered, she'll accuse me of lying. She did it to the social workers too, when we got taken away from her and put into that place. That time I agreed with her and told them I lied. But it was because I was so desperate to get out of there. Desperate enough to want to go back to this woman who beats us. This time, I'm ready to tell anyone who wants to listen the truth. It's like telling Jude broke a spell I've been imprisoned by for years and now I'm free.

"Um … no." Jude looks desperately in my direction. She wants out of there as much as I do. People are watching us. Small knots of them cluster around the end of the aisles.

"Oh, you can tell me." Mom leans in and takes Jude's arm, drawing her in like a conspirator. "You know what kids are like. If you're a teacher, you do."

"I do," Jude agrees reluctantly, turning her head like she smells something bad. Mom's breath, probably. "And you have three wonderful sons. You should be very proud of them."

Mom snorts but says nothing. I'm grateful for that. But it's time to take charge here. She's not going to leave on her own, so it's up to me to get us out of this situation. Again.

"Mom." I let go of the cart and take her by the arm. "Let's go home, huh? I'll take you home."

"I'm not done yet," Mom says, pulling away from me and pointing at the shopping basket she's holding. It has three lemons, two bottles of tonic water, and three frozen pizzas in it. Mom's idea of a balanced diet. I imagine she has gin at home, hence the tonic and lemons.

"Well, what else do you need?" I do my best to draw Mom toward the front of the store. She's made her scene now. It's time to get her home before she gets louder and messier and someone calls the cops.

"I need you and those brothers of yours to come home." She's shouting now, and more people are beginning to drift our way to see what's going on. "You don't get to walk out on me like that. You're not eighteen yet."

I grit my teeth against the fury surging into my throat. How dare she. After all the nights she's left Sage and me alone? The days on end we had to deal with Wiley as a baby because she decided to run off with a boyfriend for a dirty weekend? Or go off somewhere to get drunk or high?

"Maybe I'm not," I say. I keep my voice low because I want so much to scream at her and talking quietly is the only way I can keep from it. "But I'm ten times more responsible than you. Not to mention more mature. When are you going to grow up, Mom? I've been waiting seventeen years. Isn't it about time?"

A circle has formed around us.

Jude stands at my elbow, a look of utter helplessness on her face. She doesn't know what to do, I realize. She's embarrassed to be the center of attention, but she doesn't have any way to deescalate this situation. She doesn't have the tools or the experience to do it.

I do, but my own anger has reared its ugly head, and in the fiery blaze which fills my skull and turns my vision red, I don't have the presence of mind to use them.

KATE LARKINDALE

Chapter Thirty

"Don't you speak to me like that." Mom steps forward, her face a mask of anger. Her fingers are wrapped around the neck of a soda bottle with such force the knuckles are white.

I'm glad it's a plastic bottle. It'll hurt when she hits me, but she doesn't have the height or the strength to do any real damage with plastic. If it was glass... Well, that's a whole different story.

"Blue, please..." Jude reaches for me, her fingers brushing the back of my hand as she tries to draw me away. I should go with her. Forget the groceries. I should just take her hand and let her take me out of the store. There are other places we can buy food. Why the hell did we pick this store anyway?

"I'll talk to you how I like," I say, shaking off Jude's hand and stepping toward Mom. I don't know why I think my size will intimidate her. It never has before. Probably because I've never hit back before. I've wanted to. God knows I've wanted to. But something has always stopped me.

This time, I don't feel the need to stop. In fact, my hands itch to hurt her. I want to slap her face the way she's so often slapped mine, the burn across each cheek more humiliating than really painful. I want to punch her ribs until they're black and blue and each intake of breath is a painful reminder of the beating. I want her stomach to ache, her hips, her knees, her wrists. I want her to feel the pain of every injury she's ever inflicted on me or my brothers.

Maybe then she'll understand.

"You're weak," she sneers as she looks up at me.

"You always were. You're all weak. You never fight back. A real man fights back."

"I guess you'd know. The guys you drag home are such gentlemen."

"Don't you go calling me a whore, Blue. Don't you go there."

"Why not?" I'm close enough now I can smell the booze on her, the sharp tang of gin. So I was right about that. "It's the truth."

And that's when she flies at me. Considering the way she's swaying on her feet and how mushy her words sound, she's surprisingly quick. She barrels right at me, one sharp, bony elbow plowing directly into my solar plexus.

I grunt and stagger backward at the force of her body colliding with mine.

"Blue!" Jude cries from somewhere to the left.

I turn to make sure she's well out of the way. I don't want her to get hurt too.

Mom uses this tiny moment of distraction and swings the bottle at me. I clock the blur of motion, but it's too late. The heavy plastic connects with my jaw as I turn, my feet still unsteady from her first blow.

I go down, managing to catch myself on my elbows before my head hits the floor. My jaw throbs and I taste blood in my mouth. I don't have time to check my teeth are all still there because she swings again, more wildly this time, the bottle glancing off my collarbone.

"I'm calling the police," someone says from behind me.

"No…" I try to see who's talking. They can't call the cops. They'll take the boys away from me. They'll split us up or send us back to that place. I need to take Mom home. She'll pass out before too long anyway. "Please…"

Mom's already moving in to take another swing at me, and I won't let her. She had surprise on her side when she nailed me, so let's see how she handles it when it's my turn.

I let her come toward me, all bendy legs and flailing arms. I'm on my hands and knees, head bowed as if in too much pain to stand up. I hope she thinks that. Believes it. When she's only a foot or so away, I make my move. I lunge forward and catch her around the legs, slinging her over my shoulder in a fireman's lift.

"I'm taking you home," I say as I haul myself to my feet.

She squeals and shrieks. She pounds on my back with her fists, but I ignore it.

"Meet you at the car," I say to Jude. "Okay? I might be a little while."

"But, Blue..." She's pale, her lips trembling so much she can barely form words. I guess it looks bad to someone who hasn't seen it before.

"I'm okay," I say, my voice vibrating weirdly from the way Mom hammers on my back. "I'll take her home."

"You don't want me..."

"No." I cut her off. I don't want her seeing where we lived. Her house is so comfortable, so clean, orderly, and warm. The chaos and squalor of our apartment would horrify her.

Mom squirms so much I almost lose my grip on her as I head for the sliding doors at the front of the store. I tighten my arms around her legs. People stare as I pass, but no one tries to stop me. I don't know if that surprises me or not.

I'm halfway across the parking lot when the first police car arrives. Its lights are flashing, but there's no siren to announce its presence. A second follows, also gliding along in stealth mode.

I set my jaw and keep walking, faster now, my feet eating up the distance between the store and the street. If I can get there, I'm free. There's an alley behind the deli on the corner which cuts through to the street where our building is. If I can slip into the alley before the cops find me, I'll be okay.

"Over there," someone shouts from behind me. I risk a quick, awkward glance behind me and see the crowd from inside the store is now outside it, watching me go. Watching us go.

Mom has gone silent now. Limp. Her body is dead weight against my shoulder.

Good. This way I won't have to fight to get her into bed. I can dump her on the sofa and leave again. And this time, I'm not coming back. Not ever.

"Freeze!" The voice is loud, hard, and deadly serious.

I freeze.

"Now turn around."

I turn, but not before marveling about how this is playing out exactly like a cop movie. Yet I'm the hero in this movie, and I'm being treated like a criminal.

Big surprise. Mom's a little white woman. I'm 6"5 and brown.

There are four policemen in front of me, three with guns drawn. I sigh. Talk about overdramatic. Yet my heart pounds in my chest and sweat trickles a line down my back. I could get killed for this. I'd laugh if it wasn't so surreal. If I wasn't so scared.

"Put her down." The cop without a gun in his hands walks slowly toward me. "C'mon, son. Let her go."

"With pleasure." I swing Mom off my shoulder and set her on the ground. The snow here has turned to slush and lies across the parking lot in puddles and browning drifts.

I'm just straightening up after setting Mom down when two cops rush at me. Before I know what's happened, I'm on the ground too, my nose inches from the damp, gritty asphalt. My arms are twisted behind me and I feel the cold metal cuffs being snapped around my wrists.

They're cuffing me? I'm the victim here. Didn't anyone in there see the way she clocked me with that bottle? Didn't Jude tell them…

Jude! Her name explodes through my head. Where is she? I whip my head around, hoping for a glimpse of her, but all I see is dirty snow and blue uniforms as the cops drag me to my feet.

"Why…"

The cops walk me toward the nearest of the two cars. The lights flash red, white, and blue in my eyes.

"Jude?" I search for her over my shoulder, but the damn lights have left dark spots dancing over my vision and if she's there, I can't recognize her. "Jude!"

"Duck." The cops push down on the top of my head as they bundle me into the back of the police car. There's a lump there, and it hurts, but I don't duck away. I don't fight them at all. This is bad, but fighting will only make it worse. I need to go with it, get to the police station, and tell my story. I'm certain once I've explained everything, they'll let me go. I wish I'd thought to leave the damn cell phone at the cabin. I'm pretty sure I'll be allowed a phone call at some point, and I need to call Sage and Wiley to let them know what's happened. But the phone is here, digging into my hip from the pocket of my jeans. Sage and Wiley are alone up there, and when Jude and I don't return, they'll think the worst. They'll worry. And what will happen to them if something happens to me?

****

The drive to the police station is short, just a few blocks. No one talks to me so I listen to the faint hiss and spit of the radio hanging on the dash. Occasionally, single words are clear through the fuzz, but for the most part, they're garbled approximations of speech.

I lean my head back against the seat. The cuffs are too tight and having my bodyweight pressed against them makes my hands ache painfully. I focus on other hurts to try and keep my mind off the fact I'm in shackles. The one in my belly, for instance, from where Mom's elbow jabbed into me. My jaw which throbs steadily. I run my tongue across my teeth, grateful when I discover they are all still there and none are loose. The blood must have come from the inside of my lip. I find a raw, painful spot there and probe it with my tongue. The metallic taste of blood is still there, only faint now.

What is going to happen to me? I stare out at the street flashing by. It's still daylight and the people outside the window walk around chatting, shopping, and carrying on with their lives. I wish I could be there with them. No, I wish I was at the lake with Wiley and Sage, building snowmen or punching holes in the thickening ice with well-aimed stones.

Or in bed with Jude, her limbs wrapped around mine, our bodies creating the delicious friction that warms both our insides and outsides.

Where is Jude now? Have they hauled her in too? I hope not. She had nothing to do with this. It's unfortunate she was there and had to see it, but at the same time, I'm almost glad she did. Now she knows I wasn't lying or exaggerating our situation. We weren't being overdramatic teenagers who had a little spat with our parent.

I don't believe she ever thought that, but if she did...

The car slows and swings into a narrow parking lot alongside the main police station. I can't move my arms to reach the door handle, so I have to sit there like a lump until one of the cops deigns to release me. And they take their time. The driver rounds the car and joins the other guy. They talk for a moment, too low for me to hear anything through the glass.

My hands tingle with pins and needles, and I try to wriggle my fingers. They move, but not enough to stop the painful numbness creeping over them. I shift my weight so I'm leaning forward over my knees. It takes the weight off my hands, but strains my shoulders so much I'm forced to lean back again after only a few minutes. When will they let me out?

KATE LARKINDALE

Chapter Thirty-One

Inside the police station I'm taken into a small room and left there. It has a table in it, four chairs, and a door that locks behind anyone who comes in. I tried it. At least they took the cuffs off. A single fluorescent tube over the table provides the only light. There are no windows, no clock, and they took the phone and my watch so I have no idea how much time passes before the first guy comes in to question me. Or the second.

I'm guessing both Jude and Mom have been dragged down here too, because the cops who question me seem to have a couple of different theories about what's actually going on.

One, Jude kidnapped us and is holding us hostage up at the lake house, and two, we ran away and Jude is hiding us away up there. The second is closer to the truth, but the way they're talking, it sounds like we planned it together, that Jude and I have been in some kinky, illicit relationship for a long time. And I never even mentioned that part of it. It somehow felt like I shouldn't.

The door rattles for a third time and I leap to my feet. It feels like I've been in here several hours, and I can't begin to imagine how frantic Sage will be by now. He'll be trying to hide it, keeping Wiley busy so he doesn't pick up on how concerned he is. But even Wiley will have realized it doesn't take this long to go grocery shopping.

A tall, thin guy in an ugly brown suit steps into the room. He has slumped shoulders and needs a shave. Dark rings hang under his eyes like polluted moons.

"I sure as hell hope you can make some sense of all this," he says finally, dropping down into a chair at one end of the table. "I have three people here, all telling me different stories and none of them make sense. You gonna tell me the truth, Blue?"

He gestures for me to sit again, but I don't. I stand there, leaning back against the wall, my fists jammed deep into the pockets of my jeans. "Don't I get a phone call? My brothers are on their own up there. They're going to be worried. Can I let them know I'm okay? Then I'll tell you anything you want to know."

I'm not lying either. I'll say anything to get out of here. To get back to them.

"Your brothers are fine," the cop says. "We sent someone up to get them a while ago. They'll be with a social worker by now."

"What?" I step away from the wall and tear my hands from my pockets to rake through my hair. "A social worker?"

He nods wearily. "After that little scene at the MegaMart, we weren't gonna send them home to Mommy. She whale on you like that in public a lot?"

"Not in public," I say wryly. "Do you know where they'll be taken?"

"Most likely a temporary foster home. They'll be taken care of. So will you, when we're done here. You don't need to worry about that." He pulls out a notebook just like the ones all the other people who've been in to speak to me carried. "Now, can you tell me what the actual hell is going on here?"

I don't want to, but I want to get out. I want to see my brothers, to make sure they really are being taken care of. That they haven't been dumped back at Dunstan or another place like it, as bad, or worse. So I tell him.

I tell him everything.

Almost.

He says nothing when I'm done. Just sits there

looking at me, his face blank and unreadable. I hate it and it takes every bit of self-control I possess not to start squirming in my seat.

Finally, he glances down at the notebook on the table in front of him. "You've told this story before. About your mom."

I nod. It's not a story, but yeah. He's right. I have told on her before.

"Then the next day you said you lied, that you had a fight with her and wanted to get her in trouble." His eyes remain steady, fixed on mine. "Doesn't exactly make your story credible."

Crap. Everything always comes back to bite you on the ass. I nod, keeping my own gaze as steady as his. "Yeah. I lied. But it was the second part that was a lie. Not the first."

He runs his hand across his forehead, closing his eyes for a second like he's tired. He probably is. I am.

"Explain this to me. I'm not sure I'm getting it."

I shrug, impatient now. It was years ago. I'm not sure why it's suddenly so important again now. "I got tired of Mom slapping my brothers and me around all the time. So I told. And they took us away from her, but the place they took us was terrible. They took Wiley away from Sage and me, and Sage got beaten up the first night. It was worse than being at home with Mom. So I lied and told them I'd made it all up. I'd do it again, too."

And I would. Everything I've done the past week or so proves I'll do about anything to keep those kids safe.

The cop nods. I hope it means he gets it.

"So tell me about Jude Applegarth."

"What?" The change in subject is so sudden, my head spins.

"Jude Applegarth. What's going on there?"

"I told you." I'm uncomfortable now. "She let us stay at her lake house while we figured out what to do next."

"And she just happened to take a leave of absence from school the same day you dropped out?" The cop raises a single eyebrow.

"I … I … didn't know that." And I didn't. Although it should have crossed my mind. I mean, we've been up there almost a week. She should have been at school.

"You want to tell me what's going on with you two? How long have you been sleeping with her?"

My face heats up. I didn't tell him that. Which means Jude did. Or he's a way better detective than he seems. "I'm seventeen," I say finally. "Over the age of consent."

"That's not what I asked you."

I press my lips together and cross my arms in front of me. This is personal. I don't have to discuss my sex life with this stranger. My very new sex life.

"She force you into it?"

"No!" I shake my head. "I mean, I wouldn't have initiated it, but…" I trail off. He got me.

Things get confused. The questions start coming too quickly, and my brain isn't working fast enough to answer them. Especially since a big part of it is taken up with worrying about Wiley and Sage and where they might be right now.

About an hour later, I feel like we've been around in circles three times and haven't moved. He's still asking me about Jude, and no matter what I tell him, how honest I am, he doesn't seem to get that what happened up there was innocent. We didn't plan to run away together. She didn't kidnap us. She wasn't holding me, and therefore my brothers, hostage. God, the reverse is actually closer to the truth, but I'm not going to tell the cops that.

Yet, somehow, everything that comes out my mouth seems to make this cop more certain of Jude's guilt. And the more I try to defend her, the more it sounds like he's right. I'm not even sure myself anymore what happened up there. It's starting to feel like some weird, long-ago dream.

"Are we done?" I rest my elbows on the table and drop my head into my hands.

"For now." The cop stands, scooping up his notebook as he does. "We may have more questions, but we'll be in touch."

"How?" I ask, but it's too late. He's already gone and I'm alone again.

****

When I'm finally released, a woman is waiting for me by the sliding glass doors.

"Blue?" She steps forward and I know instantly she's a social worker. Her blue blazer and low-heeled shoes scream her profession.

"Yeah?"

"I'm Andrea King. I'm going to be your caseworker. Let's get you somewhere to stay tonight."

I regard her suspiciously. "Just tonight?"

She smiles. "One step at a time, okay?"

I sigh, but follow her out of the police station, looking around as I do to see if I can get a glimpse of Jude or her car or any sign she's been released too. I can't believe I got her tangled up in our mess. But tangled she is. I hope now I've told the cops everything, she's free to go.

"Do you know where they took my brothers?" I ask Andrea when we get to her car, a dented hatchback that has to be a least fifteen years old. "Sage and Wiley?"

She unlocks the vehicle and gestures for me to get

in before sliding into the driver's seat.

"Do you?" I ask again.

"I don't," she says finally. "But we can find out. Let's get you settled for tonight. Tomorrow we can find out where your brothers were taken, okay?"

It isn't okay, but I grunt something she takes as acquiescence. I stare out at the street as we drive, not paying attention to where we're going. My fingernails dig crescents into the worn fabric of my jeans and bite into my thighs. I focus on those small pinches of pain while I try to figure out what to do next. But I can't think of anything. I'm powerless here. I have no control over anything that's happening to me. I hate it, yet I have no choice.

****

Around twenty minutes later we pull up in front of a closed gate. I'm unsurprised when I glance at the sign to left of the gate and it says Carlisle House. It's not Dunstan, but it's the same kind of place. It feels almost inevitable I'd end up back at a place like this.

"Are my brothers here too?" I ask Andrea after she's spoken into the intercom and had the gates opened to admit us. "Did they get brought here too?"

"I really don't know, Blue," Andrea says in a voice that's irritatingly calm. "They must have been assigned a different caseworker. But like I said, we'll find out in the morning. It's after eleven now, so even if they are here, they'll be asleep."

I run my hand through my hair again, trying to think. If they're here, at least I'll find them and we'll be together. But here is the last place in the world I want them to be. I promised them we'd never come back to a place like this. But if they're somewhere else... I tug at my hair savagely. I hope they're safe, wherever they are. I hope they're together. Wiley will be okay with Sage.

Sage will take care of him. They'll take care of each other. If they were separated…

"This way." Andrea has parked in front of the low brick buildings. A few lights glimmer behind the windows, but most of them are in darkness. I climb slowly out of the car, a sick feeling of dread layering the pit of my stomach. I don't want to go in there. It takes an enormous act of will to force my feet to move when Andrea leads the way toward the heavy front doors. My knees tremble a little when she presses a buzzer and announces our arrival to a tiny intercom in the frame. When the door opens, the scent of the place hits me immediately, bringing with it a bolt of terror.

I can't stay here. I'll go nuts. I've had nightmares about places like this for too long, and now those nightmares have come true. I close my eyes for a second and force myself to calm down. I'm tough. I can survive anything. God knows, if I can survive seventeen years with Mom, I can manage one night here. I don't have to like it. I just have to get through it.

KATE LARKINDALE

Chapter Thirty-Two

After what feels like endless paperwork in an overheated office, Andrea leaves me with the night manager, a gruff, bearded guy who introduces himself as Gus. He hasn't been any more help than Andrea in terms of helping me find out where my brothers are. He doesn't know and doesn't have access to the files which would tell him. Or so he says. So I take Andrea's card when she offers it and follow Gus a short distance down the hall.

"It's too late to get you into a dorm," he says, opening a door and leaning inside to flick on the light. "So you can sleep here tonight. In the morning, we'll get you assigned somewhere more permanent."

It sounds like a punishment. I don't want to be here permanently. I want to be with Sage and Wiley, wherever they are. I want to be back at the lake with Jude. I want to be anywhere but here.

"Thanks," I say as I step into the cell-like room, taking in the narrow cot against the wall, the single window with its tangle of wire covering it from the outside. A small pile of items sits in the center of the bed. A towel. A toothbrush and toothpaste. A washcloth. Soap. A cheap razor. I realize suddenly I have nothing but the clothes on my back. I wonder if Sage and Wiley were given any time to pack before they were taken … wherever they were taken.

"Get some sleep," Gus says kindly. "Bathrooms are across the hall. Breakfast is at seven in the dining hall to the left. You won't be able to miss it. If you head to the office we were just in after breakfast, we'll find you a room."

"You mean I'm going to have to stay here?" I run

my fingers through my hair again. My scalp is starting to feel like a well-plowed field, but I can't seem to stop myself.

Gus looks steadily at me. "It's not as easy to find foster homes for older kids. Especially since you're so close to eighteen. I'm not saying it's not possible, but it's more likely you'll stay here."

"And my brothers? Does that mean if they've been fostered somewhere, I don't get to go with them?" Panic rises in my throat, hot and bitter tasting. They can't separate us. Not now. Not after everything I've done to keep us together.

"Look," Gus says. "We can't do anything to find them now. Best thing to do is to get some sleep and we can figure it out in the morning. Is there anything else you need?"

I drop down on the bed which sags dangerously under my weight. "No. I guess not. Thanks."

"Okay. Sleep well. I'm down the hall if you need me." Gus smiles and closes the door behind him.

Once he's gone, I get up and check to make sure it isn't locked. This place feels like a prison, but thankfully the door handle turns easily.

****

I didn't believe I'd sleep in the tiny, sagging cot, but I wake to find the first traces of dawn painting colors on the wall of my cell. Room. It's not a prison, I remind myself. It could have been. I told the cops about breaking into Jude's house. They could easily have chosen to arrest me. It's just good luck they didn't. Either that or Jude asked them not to.

I get up and pull my jeans and boots back on. I slept in my t-shirt and underwear, and they smell sourly of my unwashed body. I wonder if I'll be given some clean clothes later. I hope so, even though I bet anything they give me will be too small.

The light trickling through the window tells me it's still early so I grab the stuff that was left on the bed last night and head out in search of a bathroom. A shower might make me feel more human. I find a door with the words 'boys' bathroom' written on it and hesitate a second before pushing it open. I can't help remembering what happened to Sage when he went into a bathroom at Dunstan alone. God, I hope he's okay.

The bathroom is empty. It's small too, unlike the huge, cavernous ones I remember from the dorms at Dunstan. This must be an admin area or something. That's why I had a room to myself last night.

When I leave the bathroom, feeling better despite having to put my dirty, smelly clothes back on, voices echo down the hallway from somewhere in the opposite direction to the office I was taken to last night. The dining hall, maybe. My stomach growls at the thought of food, and I remember I haven't eaten anything since lunch at the lake yesterday. So after dumping my towel and stuff back into the room I slept in, I head toward the voices.

The dining hall is large. Kids sit around tables and line up at the counter to be served. It's kind of like our school cafeteria, but about half the size. At Dunstan, I remember there being kids of all ages and sizes lining up for food. Here, everyone looks older. Teenagers. But maybe the younger ones haven't been sent down from their dorms yet. I scan the room anyway, searching for Sage's blond head and Wiley's dark one. They don't seem to be here, but more kids keep trickling in, yawning or chattering with their friends.

I grab a tray and join the food queue. I accept oatmeal and toast and a spoonful of pale, limp scrambled eggs. I take a glass of juice and an apple too, then search out a place to sit. A couple of kids give me curious glances, but most of them ignore me. I guess they're used to new kids showing up all the time. I give the ones who look at me a cursory nod but don't smile. I'm not interested in making friends with anyone here. I don't plan on being here long enough to need them. So I take a seat at a small table near the door. That way I can keep an eye out for Sage and Wiley if they come in.

They don't.

I linger over my tasteless breakfast as long as I can, until the servers start cleaning up and the room is practically empty. I'm not sure if I'm relieved or disappointed Sage and Wiley aren't here. Or don't seem to be. I guess there's a chance I could have missed them. But it's a pretty small chance. So I get up and head for the office like Gus told me to, fingering Andrea's card in my pocket. It's not too early to call her now, is it? I really need to find my brothers.

****

The office and the area around it are busier this morning. Kids wander through the hallways and head out the front door. I wonder how hard it would be to join them, but I bet there's some kind of system to it. A place like this wouldn't let people walk out without accounting for them. And besides, where would I go? They have me trapped here now. I'm not going anywhere until I find my brothers.

So instead of leaving, I knock on the office door.

"Come in," a woman calls.

I do and find a broad-shouldered woman with a lot of thick red hair gathered into a messy knot on top of her head. She shuffles through a pile of papers and manila files on her desk, gnawing on a pencil.

She looks up and jams the pencil into the middle of that chaotic mess of hair. It disappears. "Can I help you?"

"Uh, yeah. I'm Blue Lannigan. I got here late last night. Gus said for me to come here in the morning?"

She frowns. "Right. Yeah. I saw the file somewhere here. Latham?"

"Lannigan."

"Ah. Yes." She pulls a file out from somewhere near the top of a tower of other files and flicks it open. Her eyes move rapidly across it. "You're seventeen?"

I nod. "I'll be eighteen in October."

She looks up at me and realizes I'm still standing. "Sit. Please. Sit down. I'm Mrs. Hunt, but you can call me Bonnie."

I sit and watch as she keeps reading. I wish I could take a look too. I'd like to know what these people have on me.

Finally, she finishes and sits back, studying me. "You're at Milton High?"

"I was. I dropped out."

"Wanna go back?" She has a blunt, challenging way of speaking.

I shake my head. "I have a job. Or at least, I had one. I should probably call to find out if I still do. I haven't been in for over a week."

"You can use the phone when we're done here."

"I have two brothers. Do you know if they were brought here too? We were separated yesterday, and no one seems to be able to tell me where they are." I try to keep my voice low and measured, but it's hard. The more time goes by, the farther away Sage and Wiley feel and the more panicked my stomach gets.

"What are their names?" Bonnie starts flicking through the pile of files again.

"Sage and Wiley. Sage is fourteen and Wiley's eight."

"They wouldn't have been brought here. Carlisle is for kids fifteen and older. If they were taken to a home, they'd be at Dunstan Hall."

Great. Exactly what I wanted to hear. "Can you see if they were taken there?"

She sets the files aside and turns to the computer sitting on her desk, her fingers hammering the keys as she types.

"Doesn't look like any other Lannigans were brought to group homes," she says, turning back to me. "Just you."

"They might be under different last names." We all use Lannigan, but it's Mom's name. On my birth certificate I'm Blue Akshy Patel. "Sage could be under Curtis…" I doubt it though. If they were asked, they'd have said their name is Lannigan. It's only if these people looked up their birth certificates that they'd know we all legally have different last names. Although, to be honest, I bet Mom never put Wiley's dad's name on his birth certificate. By the time he was born, that asshole was long gone, taking his name and most of Mom's money with him.

Bonnie turns back to the computer. "Sorry. Nothing here."

I slump over and rest my elbow on my knees for a moment, digging my fingernails into my scalp again. "Okay, so they're not there. How do I find out where they are?"

I'm in the office an hour and by the end of it, I'm no closer to finding my brothers. We've called Andrea King, and she promised to look into it for me, to call me once she has some news. I'm not holding my breath. If the files in her office are as messed up as Bonnie's, it could take months for her to figure it out.

I guess I should be happy they're not in a home

like this, but I'm not. I'm worried. I'm frightened. And, increasingly, frustrated. I keep my hands jammed into my pockets to keep from punching something. Or someone. The last thing I need is to get myself in trouble the first day I'm here.

So I keep my mouth shut when a young guy with a beard shows up to take me to the dorm.

"I'm Harry," he says. "Let me show you your room, and go through the rules and stuff."

"Blue," I growl as I follow him through a maze of hallways, doorways, and courtyards to a squat brick building behind the one the dining hall and office are in. We climb two flights of stairs and push through a door painted yellow.

"So, this is the yellow wing," Harry says. "A bed just opened up here this morning, so you're in luck."

Yeah, I feel really lucky right now. How am I supposed to stay here? Live here?

"This is the common room," Harry says, leading me through a brightly-lit room with a TV, a couple of small tables, and a few worn couches scattered around. "Study room is over there." He points through an open door to a room with two long tables and a bunch of mismatched chairs in it. "Bathrooms are at the end of each of the hallways."

I don't listen fully to everything he says as he shows me around. Just enough to know this side of the yellow wing is for boys, and the other is for girls. The common room and study area are shared. There are no big dorms here, not like the one Sage and I were in at Dunstan. Instead, there are rooms, each with three sets of bunks lining the walls.

Harry shows me into one with Y4 painted next to the door and points to a top bunk that isn't made up with sheets or blankets yet. "That's yours. We'll find you some linen and anything else you need. You bring anything with you from home?"

I shake my head. I wonder where the stuff I took to the lake is now. Still in Jude's bedroom? It wasn't much, but I still kind of want it back. And whatever happened to Jude? To Mom? I've been so worried about my brothers I haven't given much thought to them. And without having found Sage and Wiley, I can't really give much attention to them now either.

Chapter Thirty-Three

Life settles into something resembling a holding pattern.

Mr. Carter hasn't kept my job at the warehouse open for me. It kind of surprises me—I was only gone a little over a week—but I guess I never called to explain my absence, so I can't blame him. It does piss me off though. I was good at that job. And apart from that one week, I've been one hundred percent reliable.

Bonnie, the lady in charge of Carlisle, tries to use my unemployment to coerce me into going back to school. But I can't do it. I feel too old for school. Too worn down. So I spend a few days looking for a new job, applying for every piece of grunt work I find advertised. Within a week, I have a new job moving furniture. The pay's better than at the warehouse, and there's weekend work too, which means I get a day off during the week. A good thing, because the people and agencies that might be able to help me find my brothers are pretty strictly nine-to-five.

I haunt every social worker's office in town. And I call when I can't make it in. I call daily. I even spend some of my first paycheck on a cell phone so I have a number I can be reached on.

But no one ever calls.

No one can tell me anything. They all try to calm me with platitudes, assuring me my brothers are well taken care of, that they're safe.

But they won't tell me where they are.

I spend one of my days off haunting the streets outside Dunstan, watching kids stream out on their way to school in the morning, then trickle back in after school and into the evening. No sign of Sage or Wiley. A part of me is relieved, but at the same time, it feels like yet another dead end.

Another day off I spend loitering outside Milton High, hoping to catch a glimpse of Sage. But I don't.

After spending a day feeling like some kind of creep hanging around Wiley's old elementary school, I have to come to the conclusion they're not back at their old schools. Which leads me to call every other public school in town. But they either won't give out their pupils' names over the phone, or Sage and Wiley aren't at any of the public schools in the city.

So I go back to badgering the social workers, frustration growing in me with every brick wall I face, every bored yet gentle, "I'm sorry. I can't help you."

****

I'm near the social worker's office when it's time for my lunch break, so while the other guys on my truck head down to the diner on the corner to eat, I turn the other way and walk the three blocks to the now-familiar building on the corner of Marshall and Dunne. The receptionist looks up when I walk in.

"You again," she says with a sigh. "Who do you want to see this time?"

I shrug. I've been here enough times now I've seen pretty much every one of the social workers based here. None of them have been able to help me so far, so it doesn't really matter which one I meet. I only want to make sure no one forgets about me and my brothers. "Anyone who'll talk to me."

"Take a seat." She gestures to the worn, lumpy couch.

I haven't even been sitting there long enough to pick up one of the tattered magazines from the coffee table before someone walks out from an office at the back.

She starts striding toward the door, but catches sight of me and stops.

"Blue, right?" She frowns.

I stand, nodding, trying not to look too eager. I'm pretty sure this woman is in charge here. I've only spoken to her once before, and only briefly, but she seemed even then to be the one who might actually be able to make something happen.

"Come with me," she says, turning on a spiked heel and heading into the area behind the reception desk. She leads me into an office, rather than to the open plan area where the bulk of the social workers have their desks.

"You've been bugging my staff," she says lightly as she closes the door behind me.

"Your staff haven't been helping me."

"Have you ever considered that maybe they can't?" She gestures for me to sit down, before sitting next to me, rather than moving around the desk to sit opposite.

I have to turn to look at her.

"Your brothers are in foster care," she begins.

"Together?" I interrupt.

She nods. "Yes. They're together."

Thank goodness. Thank god. Thank Allah. Thank whatever higher power might be working for us. I'm so grateful I almost burst into tears. If they're together, they'll be okay.

"Can I see them?"

She gives me a sad smile. "No. Not right now."

"What?" I leap to my feet. A second ago they felt so close. I was sure by tonight we'd be together again. "Why not?"

"Sit down, Blue." She says this softly, but there's

something about her voice which makes me not want to argue. So I sit.

"I've spoken to the parents," she says slowly. "And I've explained the situation. I've told them you want contact. The boys are settling in, and the parents would rather you didn't see them until they're settled."

I swallow hard. Suddenly my brothers are out of reach again. Anger surges through me. How dare they keep my brothers from me? We're family. I'm the only real family either of them have ever known. Clenching my fists in my lap, I fight the rage. I have to stay in control. If I lose it now, I could jeopardize any chance I might have to ever see them again.

"Okay." I nod even though this situation is anything but okay. "How long's that going to be?"

She gives me a sad smile. "I don't know. But we have your number. We know where to find you. As soon as the parents are ready, we'll organize a visit."

"A visit?"

"A visit," she confirms.

I close my eyes briefly while I swallow this. Of course it will be a visit. Whoever this family is, they're not going to take me in as well. And I can't swoop in and take them away with me. Not without getting myself into a whole pile of trouble.

"Okay," I say finally. There isn't anything else I can say. This is as good as it gets right now. I still don't know where they are, but at least I now know someone does.

"They're being well looked after," the social worker says. "I promise you."

I don't say anything to that. I bet their idea of well looked after is different to mine. But as long as they're not being slugged every time they turn around, it has to be better than home.

"How about you, Blue? How are you doing?"

I shrug. "Fine, I guess."

"Carlisle treating you okay?"

Something in the way she asks makes me look up from my hands which I've been focused on throughout most of this conversation.

"Yeah. It's okay." And it actually is. I mean, it's not where I'd choose to live, but it's warm, and dry, and I get fed. Plus, I don't have to pay anything to live there. I've saved quite a bit of money, am well on my way to having enough to rent a place of my own once I turn eighteen and get out of the system.

But after this conversation, I'm beginning to think I might need to save a whole lot more. I suspect I'm going to need a lawyer to get guardianship of my brothers. I also suspect it's going to be a whole lot harder than I could ever have imagined.

I get up and start to leave the office.

"You're leaving?" the social worker asks, sounding slightly surprised.

Did she think I was going to kick up some kind of fuss? I know better. That kind of behavior gets you nowhere. So despite wanting to kick, scream, and tear the stupid inspirational posters off the walls, I walk toward the door.

"Why not? You can't help me. So thanks for nothing."

I walk out of the office and head toward the front door. I'm not going to have time to get anything to eat now. But I don't have much of an appetite now either.

"You know," she calls after me. "I'm just doing my job."

I stop and turn back to look at her. "Yeah? Anyone ever tell you your job sucks?"

She kind of crumples, her body sagging, her face

falling in a way that makes her look suddenly much older. "Every day," she says, sounding like she's close to tears. "I tell myself every day. It's not fun, Blue. But it's worth it. Every time we get a kid out of a place where they're being hurt or neglected and put them somewhere else, it's worth it. Even if you kids don't seem to understand that."

I stare at her. "I get that," I say finally. "What I don't get is why you're keeping me and my brothers apart. We've always been together. We've always taken care of each other."

I become aware of how quiet the room has become and look around, finding all the people at their desks staring at me. Was I shouting? I didn't mean to, if I was.

"I'm sorry," the social worker says finally. "Sometimes things don't work out the way we want them to. I'll do what I can to get the foster family to agree to a visit. At this stage, it's about all I can do."

There isn't anything else I can do or say either, so I nod. "Thanks," I mutter, and then I leave.

****

I'm lying on my bunk with a book after another lonely, barely edible meal in the dining hall. Jude and Sage spoiled me up at the lake with all their good cooking. Before, I was grateful for anything to fill my belly. Now, I want stuff that tastes good too. Not that I have much of an appetite anyway. Every time I sit down at one of the sticky, chipped Formica tables alone, I miss Sage and Wiley more and whatever appetite I might have had dwindles to nothing. I've even had to cinch my belt two holes tighter. But that might also have to do with the work I'm doing, too. I thought working at the warehouse was physical. It was nothing compared with lugging couches and refrigerators five days a week. By the time I get back to Carlisle each night, I'm too exhausted to do much more than shower, eat, and fall into bed.

"Blue?" One of the college kids who acts as a warden sticks his head around the door. Sorry, not a warden. A supervisor. That's what they call themselves. They just act like wardens and treat us like inmates.

"Yeah?" I don't bother to look up from the page I'm reading.

"You got a visitor. Down in the cafeteria."

That makes me look up. "A visitor? Who?" My heart is suddenly beating way too fast and hard. It's a cool night and the heating in this part of the building only works on alternate Tuesdays, yet sweat springs to the back of my neck and tickles its sluggish way down my spine.

The kid shrugs. "I don't know. They called me from the office and told me."

Before he's finished speaking, I've swung myself down from my bunk, tossing the book carelessly aside. My stomach swarms with something that feels like bees buzzing, but I can't tell if it's excitement or fear. I don't want to dare believe it might be my brothers. Yet my heart aches for it to be them.

I hurry toward the cafeteria, dodging around knots of people hanging out in the hallways.

A couple of skinny, long-haired boys skateboard toward me, navigating around me with an easy shift of their hips. They'll be in trouble if they get caught.

"Nice," I call over my shoulder as they disappear.

At the door to the cafeteria, I stop to take a deep breath. I need a moment to prepare myself. "It's not going to be them," I whisper, but even saying it aloud doesn't stop me wishing for it to be true.

Chapter Thirty-Four

The cafeteria is almost empty. The lights are mostly turned off, leaving the room dim and shadowy. It still smells like tonight's sloppy joes. On the far side of the room a bunch of kids sit around a big table playing cards under one of the long fluorescent lights hanging from the ceiling.

At another table, two farther over, a single figure sits.

I cross the room toward that table, stopping just before I reach it when I recognize who it is. "Jude?"

My voice makes her head snap up, and sure enough, it's her.

"Blue." She stands and comes around the table to stand before me.

"What are you doing here?" I can't quite believe my eyes, can't take in she's actually here.

She smiles, but it's a nervous smile. "I should have come sooner. It's taken me a while to find you. And... Well, I was away for a while."

I follow her back to the table and sit down across from her. She looks better. More like the teacher I remember from school. Less fragile and worn. Less broken.

"What happened to you?" I ask finally. "No one would tell me." I'm ashamed suddenly that I didn't ask more often about her. For all I know, she could've been in jail because of me. And I've been too consumed with trying to find my brothers to give her more than a few cursory thoughts.

"Sounds like a common theme. No one would tell me anything about you either." She gives a soft laugh. "I had to lie to get in here today. If anyone asks, I'm your aunt."

I raise an eyebrow. "Okay…"

"It won't stand up to any interrogation, of course, but it did get me in to see you." She tosses me a wicked grin, but it doesn't stay there. Her face turns serious. "I'm sorry, Blue."

I stare at her. "You're sorry? I should be apologizing to you. I dragged you into our shit. You shouldn't have had to deal with any of this."

"And I dragged you into mine. Plus, I took something from you I shouldn't have." She looks right at me, her blue eyes meeting mine with a frankness that's almost confrontational.

"Are you talking about … sex?" My face heats up and I glance around to make sure no one is listening in to the conversation. Privacy is an illusion in a place like this. Everyone is always in everyone else's business.

She nods. "I shouldn't have done that with you. I was lonely and messed up and needed something. But it's no excuse for what I did."

"I didn't mind," I say finally. "I liked it. I told the cops too. They tried to make it sound like something else, and I couldn't seem to convince them. I'm sorry. If you got in trouble for that."

She shakes her head. "It was a mess, but in a way it did me a huge favor. I figured out how screwed up I really was and I got some help. That's why I didn't come sooner. I was away, getting help. That and the fact the social workers weren't exactly helpful when it came to telling me where you were."

I can't help the wry grin twisting my lips. I know all about how unhelpful those people can be.

"You're better now?" I study her face. She looks stronger. The old determination I remember from the classroom is back in the set of her shoulders, the way she holds her jaw. She looks like Mrs. Applegarth again.

"I am." She nods slowly, her gaze settling somewhere far beyond me. "I still have bad days, but I have ways to cope with them now. And someone to turn to when I can't cope. It's not a quick and easy process."

"I bet." I know nothing about therapy, can't even imagine how hard it must be to learn to accept losing the people you love most. But if anyone can do it, it'll be Jude. Maybe she can teach me something about it. She's a teacher, after all.

"I lost my job," she says, as if she's read my thoughts. "And my teaching registration."

So, not a teacher anymore. I should have known. But it's not fair. Jude didn't do anything wrong. It's not like we screwed on her desk in the English faculty office or in the copy room behind the library. I wasn't even a student at the time. Yet she's lost her job, one she was really good at, one she loved.

"I'm sorry," I say, even though it's not enough. "What are you going to do now?"

She gives a wan smile and a small shrug. "I'm not sure. I never wanted to be anything except a teacher. But I'll figure it out. It's kind of nice to have some time and space to think about what I want. It's been a long time since I had that."

Jude looks down at the table in front of her for a second, then back up, her gaze traveling around the room. "I'm so sorry, Blue. I know this is the last place you wanted to wind up."

I shrug. I've grown used to it. I don't love it, but in many ways it's easier than living anywhere else. I have to follow their rules and I get a bed to sleep in and food to eat. I don't have to find enough money to keep the electricity and heat on or to buy groceries. I don't have to sleep with one eye open to keep myself and my brothers safe. I have to do my share of the chores and be back by ten every night.

"It's not so bad," I tell Jude.

"And how are the boys?"

My chest seizes up and my throat thickens. "They're not here."

"What?" She sits up straighter in her chair. "What do you mean they're not here?"

"This place is for older kids. They'd be in Dunstan, if they were in one of these homes. But they're not. I don't know where they are."

"You don't know?" She leans forward, concern painted across her face. "How do you not know?"

I can't look at her. The concern and pity in her expression makes me want to cry. This is someone I barely know. Not really. Not on any real, human level. Yet she cares more about me and my brothers than even my own mother does. Certainly more than the social workers who are supposedly responsible for our wellbeing.

"They won't tell me," I manage finally. "I've talked to about a hundred social workers, plus a lawyer, but no one can help me. They're in a foster home somewhere. But no one will tell me where."

"Are they together?"

I nod. "That's what the social worker told me. So that's a relief. But apparently the family doesn't want them to see me until they're 'settled', whatever that means."

"Oh, Blue." Jude reaches across the table and takes my hand. "I'm so sorry."

That's when I finally let go. The control I've managed to keep over my emotions all these months crumbles at the warmth in her fingers around mine. I drop my head to the table as the first sob rolls through me. And once I start crying, I can't stop. All these months of pain and frustration, worry and despair overwhelm me.

Jude lets me cry. She squeezes my hand in hers but doesn't offer any other comfort. She waits until my sobs quiet into hitching hiccups and passes me a wad of napkins from the dispenser in the center of the table. I take them without looking at her, disentangling my hand from hers to wipe at my face and blow my nose.

"I fucked everything up," I say finally. "I should have stuck with the original plan. I survived seventeen years with Mom. We could have made it through another ten months."

Jude passes me some more napkins. "Maybe. But who's to say your mother wouldn't have really hurt one of you in those ten months? Maybe even killed one of you."

"I know." The tears well up in my eyes again. "And even if it wasn't physical, she was destroying them. Wiley was scared of everything, and Sage was getting bitter. And Sage isn't like that. I couldn't stand watching them get warped from living like that."

Jude doesn't say anything for a long time. She waits for me to get myself under control again. But I'm not sure how to do that. My entire life has spun so far out of my control I feel like I should allow myself the luxury of this tantrum or breakdown. I should revel in its messiness, the rawness of the emotions I'm finally letting out into the open, finally allowing myself to feel after choking them down inside me for so long.

"Well," Jude says after what feels like hours. "You did get them out. Wherever they are now, at least they're not with your mom. They're safe."

"But are they?" I swipe at my eyes with a napkin. They burn from crying and feel like they're bulging out of my head. I probably look like crap, but I don't really care. "How do I know they're safe? I don't know anything about the people they're with. And I've heard some pretty awful stories from kids here about foster parents too…"

Jude gives a helpless shrug. "I don't know, Blue. I guess you have to trust they are."

Trust, huh? I've never had anyone I could trust before. Only Sage and Wiley, the three of us locked together into keeping our shitty little secrets.

"I miss them," I say quietly.

She takes my hand again. "I know you do."

And then we're silent. I wish I knew what she was thinking.

That they're gone is like a toothache. A constant, steady pain that's almost manageable most of the time. Yet it flares up every now and again, always unexpectedly, and when it does, it destroys me.

"I need to see them," I tell her. "If I saw them, I'd know if they were okay."

I'm certain of it. What's ruining me is the uncertainty. I have no idea who the people are who they're living with. I don't know if they're being treated well or with the same cruelty Mom brought us up with. If I could see them, even for only a minute or two, I'd be sure.

"You're not going to rest until you find them, are you?"

"I can't."

"I want you to be happy. You're smart and talented and have the biggest heart of any man I've ever met. You have so much to offer the world. I know you love those kids. But maybe now it's time to think about you for a while. I don't think you've ever done that."

I'm confused. What is she talking about? "What?"

"You've been taking care of them for years, Blue. You've put their needs ahead of your own. Maybe this has all happened so you get the chance to give some thought to what you want for once."

"I know what I want." The words come out like pebbles, hard and smooth. "I want them back."

Jude takes my hand and rubs her thumb across the soft part at the base of my thumb. "Really? Is that really what you want?"

I look up and find her studying me. She must see the answer in my eyes because she looks away. Her hand leaves mine and she stands up. "I'll see what I can do."

"They won't tell you anything." I know. I've tried.

She doesn't say anything for a moment, then looks back at me. "Are you still working at the warehouse?"

Surprised at the change in subject, and that she remembers where I worked, I shake my head. "Nah. They wouldn't take me back. I'm working for a moving company now. The pay's better and I get more hours."

Jude sighs and starts gathering her things, slipping into her coat and picking up her purse from beside her chair. "Don't you want something more?"

"Another job?" I wouldn't mind. A second job would mean more money coming in. More savings for when I get out of here and get my brothers back.

"No. Not another job. School. Haven't you ever thought about college?"

College? Of course I've thought about college. It's just not something that's ever been on the cards for me. Even if I could have wrangled a scholarship or work-study arrangement, I could never leave the kids. Besides, my grades weren't fantastic, even before I dropped out. It's hard to stay at the top of the class when you're forced to miss school on a regular basis to keep your mother from dying or to look after a kid whose been bashed within an inch of his life.

"Sure, I've thought about it," I say. "I've thought about going to the moon too."

Jude laughs, but I can tell it's forced. "A smart kid like you should go to college."

I shrug. "Probably. But that's not going to make it happen."

Jude sighs again. "You're too smart to be working such a menial job."

"I'll tell my boss. Maybe he'll move me into management."

Jude starts walking away, heading toward the doors to the cafeteria. I feel shitty again now. She's been nothing but kind to me. It's not her fault I can't find my brothers. None of this is her fault.

I run after her, catching her before she pushes through to the hallway. I take her hand, stopping her from leaving the room. "Thank you," I say. "Thank you for everything."

Jude smiles and clasps my hand so it's sandwiched between hers. "You're worth it, Blue. I'm going to do what I can to help you find those kids, okay?"

I nod. I'm not sure if she'll be able to do anything more than I've already done, but knowing there's someone else on my side helps. It's been hard, this being alone. I didn't realize quite how hard until now.

"Thank you," I say again. It's not enough, but there aren't any other words, so they'll have to do.

"You're welcome."

She lets go of my hand and sweeps out of the room.

Chapter Thirty-Five

Andrea drives down a long, suburban street. I peer out the windows, admiring the large houses with their neatly mowed lawns and smooth, pristine driveways. Even the trees lining the street seem to have been put there on purpose. They're all the same size, their branches arcing over the blacktop so it's like driving through a green, leafy tunnel.

The cars parked on the street and in front of garages are all recent models, their paint still gleaming and sparkling in the sunlight. A couple of kids ride past us on bikes, and my heart leaps into my throat for a second. Wiley and Sage? But no... The bikes fly past and I catch a glimpse of red hair blowing out from beneath the pair of helmets. Definitely not my brothers.

"It's this one." The social worker pulls up in front of a house painted in three shades of gray. It might look dull or severe except the front door and the door to the garage are a deep, wine color which looks striking against the bright green of the grass in front of the house.

I glance at the mailbox which is painted the same burgundy color. "Yeah. This is it." Heavy iron numbers announce this is 83 Tarradale Road.

"It's a nice neighborhood," Andrea says as she climbs out of the car, waiting for me on the sidewalk when I don't follow straight away.

This neighborhood is nice. Too nice for me. I feel as out of place as a snowdrift in a desert as I step out onto the smooth, uncracked sidewalk.

I turn back to the house. It looks even bigger from where I stand. I take a deep breath and follow Andrea up the flagstone path from the sidewalk to the front door.

While she rings the bell, I run my hand through my hair. I look down at my jeans and wonder why the hell I didn't think to put on a pair without holes in the knees. My boots look heavy and dirty under the frayed cuffs and I wish I'd changed them too.

Too late now though.

Footsteps come from inside. Running footsteps.

The door flies open and Wiley's there.

"Blue!" he cries, looking up at me with those huge brown eyes I know so well.

"Wiley." My throat is tight and I can feel tears welling behind my eyes. He looks good. Taller than I remember him, and not so skinny. His hair has been cut shorter than he's ever had it before, and it doesn't hang in his eyes. "Oh, Wiley. I've missed you so much."

"I've missed you too." Wiley steps forward and I reach for him, drawing him close and wrapping him in my arms as I've done so many times before. He still smells like Wiley. Like cinnamon and rain. But those familiar scents hide beneath other, unfamiliar ones. His hair smells different, and his clothes.

But when his arms snake around my waist and he squeezes me, it's like coming home.

"You must be Blue." The woman's voice startles me and I jump, letting Wiley go.

"Yes." Andrea clears her throat. "Blue, this is Mrs. Banks. Mrs. Banks, Blue."

"Nice to meet you, Mrs. Banks." I try keeping my voice steady, calm, not as if I'm about to burst into stupid baby sobs.

She nods. "Call me Melissa. And please. Come in."

"Would you like me to stay?" Andrea hangs back on the doorstep, and I'm not sure if she's speaking to me or to Mrs. Banks.

I glance up at her. I don't want this to be uncomfortable. If Mrs. Banks feel safer with the social worker there, I'm happy for Andrea to stay. But I don't need her. I don't need another stranger between myself and my brothers. Not after all this time.

Mrs. Banks shakes her head. "I think it'll be fine. Blue, please come in."

"Where's Sage?" I ask as I follow her into the house, pausing to kick my boots off in the entryway. The carpeting is beige, and thick, and looks new. I don't want to track anything across it.

"He's at hockey," Wiley says. "He had a game today."

I smile, happy Sage is playing the game he loves so much. I hope this team appreciates his talents more than the one at the downtown rec center. But, I bet he's not missing every second practice and game here.

"He wanted to skip the game today," Mrs. Banks says quietly. "So he'd be here when you arrived. But he made a commitment to the team, and it's important he sticks with it. My husband is picking him up now."

I nod. We've walked into a huge open plan room that appears to be a combined kitchen, living, and dining room. Floor to ceiling windows at one end look out over a huge back yard with a swing set and a trampoline.

"Coffee, Blue?" Mrs. Banks reaches into a cabinet and pulls out a couple of mugs.

"Uh … yes, please." I feel as big, clumsy, and out of place here as I did outside.

"Come and see my room." Wiley tugs my hand and pulls me in the opposite direction to the kitchen. "I have my own room."

"Wiley," Mrs. Banks says in a low voice. "Maybe in a minute. Let's sit down and have a little chat first."

Wiley pouts but doesn't argue. He plops himself

down on one of the big, squishy couches surrounding a glass coffee table.

"Please. Sit." Mrs. Banks sets the two steaming mugs onto the table and perches next to Wiley on the couch. I look around for another chair, one maybe not covered in some pale colored, expensive-looking fabric. But there isn't anything. And Wiley is bouncing up and down with excitement, his eyes never leaving my face.

So I sit next to him, liking the way my weight makes the cushions dip and slide him closer to my side.

"You have a lovely home," I say finally.

"Thank you." Mrs. Banks smiles and lifts her coffee cup to her lips.

The silence is suffocating. I have no idea what to say, even though my head spins with all the questions I want to ask.

"You working hard at school?" I look down at Wiley so I don't have to maintain eye contact with the stranger across from me.

"Yes. I got moved to the best reading group this week." Wiley sounds proud of himself.

"Good work." I grin at him. "How about math?"

Wiley squirms. "I'm not in the best math group."

"I'll let you in on a secret." I lean down closer to Wiley's ear. "I never was either."

"Wiley's very musical," Mrs. Banks adds. "He's been taking piano lessons, and he's really very good."

"Well, our mom's a musician," I say. "I guess it makes sense."

"I didn't know." Mrs. Banks glances at Wiley, and I wonder how much he and Sage have told her about our past, about Mom.

The front door slams and footsteps move in our direction.

My breath catches in my throat and I'm on my

feet, halfway to the doorway before I'm even aware I've moved.

"Blue?" Sage freezes in the hallway, a million thoughts and emotions flashing across his face as he looks at me.

"Sage." I take a step toward him then stop, taking a moment to check out how he looks. Like Wiley, his hair has been cut short. And like Wiley, he's grown. He's filled out some too, looks less like the little boy I remember.

I look into his eyes, hoping to find the answers to all my questions there. But he looks away, something that looks almost like fear darting across his expression as he moves closer and finally allows me to embrace him.

"Missed you," he whispers as he rests his head briefly on my shoulder.

"Yeah, me too." I hold him tightly, trying to get used to this new, larger Sage. "You good?"

Before Sage can answer, Wiley grabs at my hand. "Come on! I want to show you my room."

I let go of Sage, laughing. "Soon, Wiley."

"Hello, Blue." A man I hadn't even registered steps forward and stretches out his hand. "I'm Gabe. It's really nice to meet you."

I shake his hand. "Nice to meet you too."

But it isn't really. It's awkward and strange. And I don't think it's only me. Sage looks uncomfortable too, shuffling from foot to foot as he glances from me to Mr. Banks; from Wiley to Mrs. Banks and back again.

"You wanted to show me your room?" I look down at Wiley before glancing back up at the two Bankses. "If it's okay?"

Mrs. Banks gives a quick nod. "Yes. All right."

Wiley grabs my hand and pulls me toward the stairs. "This is it." He pushes open a door with a giant

'W 'painted across it in purple paint. I follow him in, taking in the clean white walls and the colorful posters of planes and trucks framed on them. A huge plastic tub of Lego bricks sits in one corner. A red-painted toy chest sits in the other, its lid half open to reveal a clutter of games, puzzles, and toy vehicles. Along one wall a bookcase is filled with books. I run my fingers across the spines—Roald Dahl, Narnia, Diary of a Wimpy Kid.

"You read all these?" I ask.

"Most of 'em." Wiley scrambles up the ladder to his loft bed. A desk sits underneath, a tiny lamp sitting on it. And a laptop computer. "This is my bed."

I don't even need to stand on the bottom rung of the ladder to admire his pillowcases and comforter, emblazoned with characters from a cartoon movie. Nestled amongst the pillows I catch sight of the worn, old stuffed dog and smile. Some things never change.

"Pretty nice, huh?" Sage leans in the doorway watching me.

I nod. "It sure is."

And it is. It's everything I ever wanted when I was a kid. More, even. I wouldn't have had the capacity to even imagine a room like this.

"You want to show me yours?" I turn to Sage, who hesitates a second before giving me a reluctant nod.

I follow him down the hallway to an unmarked door. Inside, the room is neat and tidy, the single bed made neatly with a plain blue comforter. A desk against the wall is stacked with books and papers in neat piles, pens and pencils organized in jars. A laptop sits on this one too. A blazer hangs across the back of the desk chair, and I recognize it as being part of the uniform kids at St. Ignatius wear. Guess that's why I couldn't find them when I was scoping out public schools.

"So … do you like it here?" I ask finally,

jamming my hands in the pockets of my jeans.

Sage regards me cautiously before offering a quick nod. "Are you going to take us away?"

I bite my lip. "Do you want me to?"

Sage looks down, the toe of his brand-new sneaker gouging a divot into the thick pile of the carpet. "No."

The word hits me like a bullet to the chest. I move to the desk and sit heavily in the chair before it. My head spins wildly. This isn't how I pictured this visit. I'm not sure what I pictured. Maybe the two of them throwing themselves at me, begging me to take them home with me.

I look up and Sage is staring at me, his eyes huge. "I'm sorry," he says.

I force a smile. "What for? Because you're happy?"

He gives an awkward shrug. "Maybe?"

"Well, quit it. You deserve to be happy."

"Are you?" Sage's gaze burns through me.

It's my turn to shrug. "I think I will be."

The silence between us is charged. Sage and I have never been uncomfortable with quiet between us, but this quiet is different. It seethes with questions and accusations, years of shared history and shared pain. I look up from my hands, which I have been staring at, and find Sage studying me.

"What happened to you?" he asks.

"Huh?"

"Where did they put you?" Sage perches on the very edge of his bed, his eyes huge and dark in the lamplight.

"Who?" I try to buy some time, knowing even as I do Sage won't let me stall too long.

"The social workers. No one would tell us where

you were."

I nod. "Yeah. Me too. I've been trying to find you guys for months. No one would tell me anything."

"So where'd you end up? With another foster family?" He studies me, taking in my torn jeans and worn boots. The same torn jeans and worn boots I've had for at least two years. It has to be obvious to him I didn't get taken in by a family like this.

"I'm okay," I tell him. "I have a place to live. You don't need to worry about me."

"But where?" His voice rises a little. "You're not back at … that home?"

I look away, not wanting him to find the truth in my eyes. I didn't want them to know. Knowing isn't going to do them any good.

"You are, aren't you?" Sage's voice is low, but that doesn't mask the crack in it.

"Not Dunstan, but another place like it" I say finally. "But it's okay, Sage. It's only for a few more months. Just until I turn eighteen."

He looks at me, his face a mask of misery and disbelief.

"Honestly. It's fine. I'm older now. Bigger. It's basically just a place to sleep. And they feed me a couple of times a day. It could be worse."

"Yeah? How?" Sage keeps studying me, his eyes begging me for something I can't give him.

"I don't lie to you, Sage," I say quietly. "You know that. I could be in jail, you know. So a group home isn't the worst."

He gives me a sad smile. "Way to look on the bright side, dude."

I get up and sit by him on the bed, pulling him into a hug. "Sometimes it's all you can do."

He hugs me back, his arms too tight around me

for a moment. "You won't disappear again?"

"No. I'm here for you. Anytime you need me." I scribble my cell phone number onto a scrap of paper and hand it to him. "You can call me whenever."

He looks down at the numbers, nodding.

KATE LARKINDALE

Chapter Thirty-Six

Later, after we eat dinner around the big, round table in the kitchen, Mrs. Banks draws me into the living room.

"Let the boys do the dishes," she says, including her husband in the term 'boys'.

"You sure you don't need me to help?"

She shakes her head. "You're our guest. And besides, I want to talk to you."

I nod and follow her to the couch, sitting down on one end while she takes the other, her eyes never leaving me.

"We adore having the boys," she says finally. "They've completely changed our lives, but in the best possible way."

I don't know what to say in response to this and look down at my hands, picking at my cuticles to avoid having to look back at her face.

"They're happy here. They're settled. They're doing well in school." It sounds like she's pleading with me. "Gabe and I can give them everything they need."

"More than they need, I think." I glance around the room, taking in the artwork, the bookcases jammed with books, the stereo, and the giant flat-screen TV.

"We'll give them a good life."

I run my hand through my hair and nod. I can't argue with her. I can't offer the kids even a quarter what they can offer. My life is going to be all scrabbling and scraping just to get by. It'll be compromise after compromise. Sage and Wiley deserve more than that. They shouldn't have to choose between paying the electric bill and eating.

"I know," I manage. And I do. When I came here, I was so sure they'd be unhappy, that they'd beg me to take them away from here. I thought I would have to tell them to be patient, that they'd only have to wait another six months or so before I was eighteen and could petition to be their guardian.

But everything has changed.

"I know you've been worried about them," she says. "The social workers told us you'd been calling every day. I'm sorry. We thought they needed to settle in before they saw you."

For a moment, I'm furious. For months, I've been living in a state of barely controlled panic and despair. I've felt helpless and bullied as I've struggled against one faceless institution after another. And all along it was her. Her and her husband. With one phone call they could have put me out of my misery.

My thoughts must show on my face because Mrs. Banks looks down, something like shame in her eyes. "I hope you'll forgive us."

I don't have much choice. If I want to remain part of Sage and Wiley's lives, I have to be nice to these people. And they seem like good people. I don't want to admit it, but they do.

"Thank you," I say finally. "Thank you for giving them all this."

"They've missed you," she adds, almost reluctantly, like she doesn't want to even give me that much.

"I've missed them." The words seem too small for what I've felt. It's been more than missing them. It's been like the center of my life was torn away, leaving nothing but an empty void somewhere right in the middle of me.

The dishes must be finished because the others come into the living room not long after.

"It's almost bedtime," Mr. Banks says to Wiley. "It's time we said goodbye to Blue."

Wiley looks up at me, a look of confusion on his face. "You're not staying?"

I force a smile I don't feel. "No, Wiley. I can't. I don't live here, remember?"

Wiley frowns. "Where do you live? With Jude?"

I laugh softly and shake my head. "No. Not with Jude. She did come and see me though."

"She did?" Sage looks surprised. "Is she okay?"

"Yeah. She's doing better." I'm pleased I can tell them that, pleased she's managing to get her life back together. One of us should. "She says hi."

"I liked her," Wiley says.

"Me too." I rub the top of Wiley's head, marveling at how soft and shiny his hair is now.

"But if you don't live with Jude, where do you live? Do you have new parents too?" Wiley wriggles out from under my hand so he can look up at me.

I can't meet his eyes. New parents. Is that what these people have told him? Or is it what he wants? I turn to Sage. Does he consider these people his new parents too?

"Blue lives with a bunch of other kids," Sage says, coming to my rescue. "He's almost a grown-up, remember?"

I throw him a grateful look. I guess Wiley has asked why I'm not living here too. That I'm practically grown up seems like as good an answer as any, even if it isn't true.

He pouts. "I thought…"

Mrs. Banks comes over and draws Wiley toward her. "We talked about this, remember, Wiley? Blue came for a visit. He came to see you. But he can't stay."

"Will he come again?" Wiley doesn't ask me this,

he asks Mrs. Banks. In fact, he doesn't even look at me. Sage does though. His eyes are fixed on me, studying me as if he's not sure what I might do next.

We haven't talked about this. I gave both Sage and Wiley my number and told them they could call me whenever they wanted to, whenever they need me. But the more I see them here, in this place they now call home, the more certain I am they won't call. What can I give them that these people can't? What can I offer apart from memories of things which probably should be forgotten?

"I should go." I get up and move toward the hallway and the front door. "I have curfew."

"Curfew." Sage chuckles, but it isn't humorous. "Can't believe you have a curfew."

"You and me both, kiddo." I laugh. "But that's how it is right now."

I have to get out of here. I'm suffocating. I'm choking. I can't breathe through all the emotions swirling through me, all the thoughts spiraling through my brain. I thought finding them would solve everything. That once I knew where they were, the sucking emptiness inside me would fill again. But if anything, the vacuum is growing larger, the emptiness more all-encompassing.

Mrs. Banks gets up too, passes me as she leads me toward the front door. "It's been lovely to meet you," she says.

"Yeah. You too." And I'm not lying. Even though I feel hollowed out, knowing they are here, with good people who care about them, reassures me. "I'll … umm … I'll keep in touch? And … you have my number, right?"

She nods, her face and lips tight. "Yes. We'll be in touch."

Mr. Banks follows her to the door, the boys

trailing him. It's dark outside now and he flicks a switch by the door, illuminating the garden and the pathway to the street.

"Good to meet you, Blue," he says gruffly.

I nod at him, my eyes fixed on my brothers who stand a little behind him, so familiar, yet like strangers in this place. Sage has his hand resting gently on Wiley's head.

"Guess I'll see you around," I say casually, as if I'll be back tomorrow or the next day. "Call me if you need me."

Wiley ducks out from under Sage's hand. "Bye, Blue."

I crouch down on the doormat and let him wrap his arms around my neck, enfolding him in my own. His heart beats very hard and fast against my chest. "I love you, Wiley."

I don't want to let him go, but I do, taking my time standing back up so I have a moment to compose myself before facing anyone else.

When I straighten, Sage is the first person I see. He steps toward me and throws his arms around my neck. "Thank you," he murmurs.

I hold him for a moment, not wanting to let him go. Sage and I... We've been a team for almost as long as I can remember. We've shared so much. So many decisions. "Love you," I say finally. It seems important to say the words even though I know he already knows this.

"Yeah," he whispers back. "Me too."

There's nothing more to say. I manage to hold it together long enough to say goodbye to Mr. and Mrs. Banks, to thank them for dinner and their hospitality, to listen to their promises that they'll contact me about the kids. I stumble down the neat flagstone path, hearing the heavy front door click shut before I've even reached the street.

I glance back once, watching their shadows moving past the lighted windows. Sage's cowlick silhouetted against the closed blinds. Wiley's little upturned nose.

I turn away, my throat choked with emotion, and walk quickly down the block toward the bus stop.

The streets I walk along are wide and silent. Large trees arch over them, shadowing the streetlights which stand sentry at regular intervals. The houses are set back from the street, so their lighted windows do little to brighten the night.

I'm not used to this kind of contented, privileged silence. No cars glide by. No one is out walking a dog. If it weren't for shadows passing by lighted windows, I might imagine the neighborhood was deserted. This is decidedly not my part of town. I'm not sure I've ever been here before tonight. I was so excited when I was on my way, I didn't pay attention to how we got here.

Excited.

The tears that have been threatening to fall since I left the Banks's house burn my eyes. How could I have been so wrong?

I grit my teeth and force the tears back. I should be happy Sage and Wiley have this chance. They're not going to end up moving furniture or packing boxes for the rest of their lives. At least, not if they get to stay there long-term. And it looks to me like the Bankes are expecting them to stay. They wouldn't be investing in private schools or new laptops or decorating bedrooms if they weren't. At least, I don't think they would.

I sigh and jam my hands into the pockets of my jeans. I turn a corner, hoping to find lights and people and traffic. I don't want to be alone with my thoughts. I don't want to be alone. For the first time, I wish I'd taken the time to get to know some kids at Carlisle. It would be good to have a friend to talk to right now. But I've never had time for friends.

The wind gusts around me. It's cold and I feel as if it's blowing right through me, like I have a gaping void at my center. For almost as long as I can remember, my brothers have been my center. And now they're gone.

I trudge up a hill and from the top I can see lights and movement. It's a few blocks away, but at least I'm heading toward something. The houses get smaller and closer together as I move toward the larger road I saw from up there. The trees become smaller and sparser until they disappear altogether.

The houses disappear too, replaced by shuttered stores, gas stations, and warehouses. I walk faster. I know where I am now, and this isn't the kind of neighborhood where it's a good idea to walk alone at night. I also know I'm a long way from Carlisle, and a glance at my watch tells me curfew is less than half an hour away. How is it I haven't seen a bus stop? Surely even those swanky suburbs have a bus service to the city.

My phone rings in my pocket, startling me so much with its vibration I jump. I don't believe it's ever rung before, and its volume startles me.

I fumble as I answer it, almost dropping the damn thing in the process. "Hello?"

"It's me."

"Sage?" I pull the phone from my ear and stare at it for a second before replacing it.

"Yeah."

I can hear his breathing, heavy and slightly ragged. "What's up?"

"I … I wanted to say sorry," he blurts out. "I wanted to see you so much. All those months. And I was an asshole to you. I'm sorry, Blue."

"I already told you," I say roughly. "You don't need to apologize for being happy. I'm glad you're in a good place with people who treat you well. Make the most of it."

"But I'm not happy." Sage's voice cracks. "I miss you. So does Wiley."

The hole at my center widens and those hot tears sear my eyes again. I brush them away savagely. "Well, I miss you too, Sage. Both of you. But don't fuck this up."

"I won't." His voice is almost a whisper. "When can we see you again?"

My muscles resign and I sag against a building, feeling dampness seeping through my clothes almost as soon as they hit the wall. My heart aches in a way I never thought possible and the emptiness inside echoes with misery.

"I need some time, Sage. To … you know. Get used to this."

"I knew it." Sage's voice is low and strained. "I knew you'd hate us."

His words are like a nail through my heart. A blunt nail, ripping and tearing its way through. "No. I could never hate you. Remember that. Always remember that. I just need to get a handle on things, the way they are now. But like I said, I'm here for you. Anytime you or Wiley needs me, I'm here."

There's a long silence. I listen to Sage's snuffling and breathing through the phone. In my head, I can see the way his fingers will be tugging at that tuft of hair at the front, which, by now, is no doubt sticking up like a flagpole.

"Promise?" he says finally.

"Promise. I don't lie to you, remember?"

Sage sighs. "There's a first time for everything."

"Not that."

There's silence again, but this time it's not uncomfortable. It's the way Sage and I are sometimes. We don't need to talk. Not after everything we've been through together.

"Look, I'll see you soon, okay?" I peel myself away from the wall.

He sighs again. "Yeah. Okay."

He hangs up. It's irrational, but in the part of me that knows these things, I feel like I'll never see him again.

KATE LARKINDALE

Chapter Thirty-Seven

I start walking again, simply because I don't know what else to do. It's getting late. There's no way I'm going to get back to Carlisle before curfew. I've never missed it before, but they're serious about not letting us in if we're late. I've heard it from enough people. Not to mention seen the empty bunks in my own dorm when someone miscalculates the time. It seems unfair in some ways. I mean, this is a home for kids with nowhere else to go. Locking us out if we get back more than five minutes after ten seems counterproductive.

The street I'm on ends, so I turn a corner. The warehouse I worked in is a block or two away from here, so I know where I am now. I've walked these streets at night before. And the bus stop I used to use every time I did a late shift is not far away.

The flashing of colored lights catches my eye, and I pause to look up at a window strung with a single strand of Christmas lights. The glass is steamed up so the people moving around inside are nothing more than blurry shapes. I shiver as a finger of cold wind slips its way under my collar and inches its way down my spine. Or maybe it's the memory of this place making me shiver. I remember my discomfort when Megan brought me here. It feels so long ago. I was a child then.

Before I've even thought about it, I find myself pushing open the bar door. A blast of warm air hits me, scented with a mixture of ancient cigarette smoke and fresh beer. There's music playing, some old song from the eighties I remember Mom singing along to when it came on the radio. It's too loud and grates on my nerves, frayed to breaking point as they are. I almost turn and walk back out, but the warmth beckons me in.

The bouncer barely glances up from his phone as I pass by. I head into the bar and look around. It's not as busy as the last time I was here, and the small stage where Megan sang her karaoke is dark. Figures. It was early evening when I was here before. By now, the after-work crowd will have gone home, leaving only the more serious drinkers.

"Coke, please." I settle myself on one of the high stools at the bar. I'd rather have coffee, but I'm not sure you can even get coffee at a place like this. I rub my hands together to warm them while I wait for my drink. I have to think. I have to figure out a few things. Firstly, where I'm going to go tonight. Secondly, what the hell I'm going to do now that my brothers don't seem to need me anymore.

My throat thickens and I drop my forehead to the sticky surface of the bar in front of me.

"Blue?" Someone sidles in next to me at the bar, startling me so much I almost fall off the stool. "Is that you, Blue?"

"Yeah?" I raise my head and find myself looking at Megan.

Her eyes widen and I wonder what the hell I look like. I feel like I've aged twenty years since I last saw her. But it's only been a few months.

"Hi, Megan," I say.

"Don't 'hi, Megan' me," she says. "What the hell happened to you? It's like you vanished into thin air."

I sigh. "It's a long story. And I really don't want to talk about it."

She studies me for a moment, her head cocked to one side. "You do look kind of like a truck hit you."

My lips curl upward in something that might resemble a smile. "Sounds about right."

Megan glances across the room and I follow her gaze to one of the booths against the wall. A bunch of the guys from the warehouse sit at a table littered with empty glasses and a few half-full ones.

"You want to join us?" she asks.

I shake my head. "Not feeling real social right now."

I sip at my Coke. It's too sweet and too cold, and it makes my teeth ache. I push it away. Coming here was a mistake. I guess some part of me was hoping Megan was here, but now that she is, I have no idea what to say to her. The guy she flirted with a few months ago is gone, and I don't know who the hell he is now. He's more experienced. Has fewer responsibilities. But other than that, I'm not sure.

"You look like you need someone to talk to," Megan says finally. "You want to go somewhere and talk?"

I look up at her, recognizing the concern in her expression. "I don't want to take you away from your friends…"

She laughs and waves away my comment. "I see those guys every day. I'll see them in the morning. Let me go grab my stuff and I'll meet you outside."

And just like that, I'm caught up in her whirlwind again. I throw some money on the bar, slide from the stool, and am outside the door before I've even had time to consider what I'm doing. But maybe that's a good thing. Thinking hurts. Whenever I let myself start thinking, I remember my brothers are gone, and now I know it's for good.

Megan finds me in the parking lot. She's put on a hat and her long dark hair spills out from under it like a glossy waterfall down her back.

"Catch!" She tosses something in my direction.

I grab at it out of instinct and find myself holding a set of keys.

"I might've had one or two drinks too many to drive," she says, looking slightly sheepish. "But I trust you." She walks toward the little blue car I remember and waits by the passenger door for me to unlock it.

I join her and drop the keys back into her hand. I can't drive," I say "I don't have a license. And I never learned how."

She raises her eyebrows but doesn't say anything. I'm grateful for that. Most people think it's some kind of big deal I don't drive, like I'm somehow deficient because of it. I plan to learn, but right now, it's not one of my top priorities. It's not like I'm going to be able to afford a car any time soon.

"Guess we're walking." She takes my hand and starts striding away from the bar, her heels shattering the quiet of the night with their chatter. "I don't live far."

"We're going to your place?" I stop walking and drop her hand.

"Sure. Why not? My roommate's away until Tuesday, so we'll have the place to ourselves. Or do you need to get home?"

I shake my head slowly. "No. I don't need to be anywhere until tomorrow morning."

"So, there's no problem, is there?" She starts walking again, not even looking back to see if I'm following her. I guess she's the kind of woman who's used to being followed without question. I hesitate a moment though, a thousand thoughts streaming through my head. But in the end, going with her makes sense. I have nowhere else to go tonight and if she lets me stay, I'll be off the street for the night.

"Wait up!" I call and hurry to catch up with her.

We walk for quite a while, moving quickly out of

the industrial area the bar sits on the edge of and into a part of town that was once run down and kind of funky, but has become nicer over the last few years as people moved in and did up some of the old houses and bowled the others to make room for condos and low-level apartment buildings. There are cafes, delis, and boutiques on almost every corner, most of them closed at this time of night.

"It's around the corner," Megan says, gesturing to the next block.

The street is quiet and lined with trees that look like they've been recently planted—nothing like the huge, arching ones on the street my brothers now live on. They're scrawny and struggling in their tiny patches of dirt. I feel sorry for them.

Megan turns and leads me down a short driveway. Three low buildings surround a parking lot almost completely filled with cars. It looks a lot like the motels we used to stay at when we were touring with Mom.

"I'm on the first floor," Megan says, stepping off the slick asphalt of the parking lot and following a cement path around the side of one of the buildings.

"Are you sure this is okay?" I ask her before I follow her up the stairs. She doesn't seem real drunk or anything, but I'd hate this to be something she might regret tomorrow.

"It's fine, Blue," she says. "We're just going to talk, right?"

Oh yeah. That's what the offer was. I'm going to have to tell her something. And I have no clue what that might be. I'm not sure if I can talk about it. I'm still too confused about everything that happened today. Too raw. It's like someone took a cheese grater to my skin.

We stop in front of a door painted green. A light burns above it, illuminating the number 14 screwed into it.

"This is it," Megan says, fumbling in her purse for her keys. "Home sweet home."

"Nice place," I say.

"Well, not really," she says, unlocking the door and flicking on a light as she steps in. "But it's convenient and affordable, so…"

I step inside and close the door behind me. We're in a large room with windows on two sides. Megan drops her bag on an over-stuffed sofa and walks around the room, drawing the curtains closed over these windows.

"Throw your stuff wherever," she calls over her shoulder.

I slide my coat off and drape it over the back of one of the chairs around a small, square dining table on one side of the room.

"Want a drink?" Megan is in the kitchen now, which is separated from the rest of the room by a long breakfast bar. "Tea, maybe?"

I cross the room and drop down on one of the bar stools on the opposite side of the breakfast bar. "Tea would be nice," I say.

She opens a pantry and pulls out several colorful boxes. "Take your pick."

I glance at all of them, but I've never tried any of these flavors. "Give me whatever you like the best."

She raises an eyebrow but doesn't say anything, just opens one of the boxes and pulls out two tea bags, dropping them into the two mugs she's pulled from the cabinet over the sink. I can't help noticing they match, each of them featuring a movie poster from a classic film. After pouring hot water over the tea bags, Megan pushes the one with the poster from *Double Indemnity* my way, keeping the *North by Northwest* one for herself.

"I like your mugs," I say finally.

She laughs and looks at her own. "These? My mom gave me a whole set of them for Christmas a couple of years back. She loves old movies. Me, not so much. The only one of these I've actually seen is *Casablanca*, and I fell asleep partway through. Are you into old movies?"

I shrug. "I've seen a lot of them." Late nights in motel rooms, waiting for Mom to come back, never certain she actually would, Sage and I would keep the TV on for company. And a lot of times, the only thing on worth watching was old movies. Sage usually fell asleep pretty quickly, but I never let myself sleep until I was sure she was back. And on the nights she didn't come back, I'd stay up all night watching movies, trying to lose myself in those other lives so I wouldn't have to think about the chaos that was my own.

Megan switches the light off in the kitchen and moves over to the sofa, kicking off her shoes before curling up in a corner of it, cupping her hands around her tea. When I don't join her right away, she pats the cushion next her.

"I don't bite," she says. "And you'll be more comfortable down here."

I cross the room slowly, savoring the sweet, herbal scent of the steam climbing from the tea. I sit down at the opposite end of the sofa and set the mug down on the coffee table sitting in front of it.

"So," Megan says, squinting at me through the steam drifting from her own mug. "Are you going to tell me what the hell happened to you?"

KATE LARKINDALE

Chapter Thirty-Eight

I rub at a spot over my eye where the beginnings of a headache are starting to drill into my skull. I'm exhausted, but also wired to the point where I know I'd never sleep, even if I did have somewhere warm and dark to lie down. My head spins with too many thoughts and emotions—probably why it's starting to ache—while my stomach and chest feel as if they've been hollowed out. I don't even know who I am anymore. If I'm not Sage and Wiley's older brother, or Tabby Lannigan's son, then who the hell am I?

"Do you need to call someone?" Megan asks suddenly. "Do your parents know where you are?"

I look up at her, feeling my lips twisting into a bitter smile. "My parents? No. But it's okay. I'm not going to get into trouble or anything."

But that's not entirely true. Carlisle has a whole system for punishing kids who break the rules. Not only am I locked out tonight for missing curfew, but when I get back, I'll have some privileges revoked. Not that I really care if I get banned from the TV room for a week or two, or if I get extra chores over the weekend.

"Well, good. I'd hate to get you into trouble. We can pick up my car in the morning and I'll drop you home before I go into work."

"You don't have to do that. I have to be at work at seven-thirty, so I can go from here."

Megan cocks her head. "So you got a new job?"

"Had to. Mr. Carter wouldn't take me back when I got back from..." I trail off, realizing I'm about to talk about the lake.

"Where did you go? You never called or

anything. I was worried about you. I even drove down to your apartment building to see if I could find you." She shivers. "That place is kind of scary."

"Yeah. I know. I'm not living there anymore."

"I'm glad. I can't really picture you in a place like that. You're too sweet."

Sweet? I raise my eyebrows. "You don't know me that well, Megan."

"Maybe not, but I'm an excellent judge of character."

Not if she's hanging out with me. Can't she see the way trouble follows me around like a shadow or a bad smell? Doesn't she sense the failure oozing from every pore? If she was any judge of character she'd be running as far from me as she possibly can.

"Blue." She shuffles over on the sofa and reaches for my hand, covering it with her own which is warm, soft, and far too gentle. "Tell me what's going on with you."

There's so much going on, I don't have the first clue where to start. I struggle to piece together everything that's happened since I last saw her, since she dropped me off in front of the apartment building that night. It swirls together in an incomprehensible blur. Mom. Jude. The lake. The police. Carlisle. Sage and Wiley. Wiley and Sage.

"I lost my brothers," I choke, the pain hitting me in a fresh wave as I say the words aloud. "I think I lost them for good."

Megan doesn't say anything for a moment. She studies me as I fight the tears threatening to fall again. I scrub at my eyes with my fists, hard enough fireworks explode behind my lids. It doesn't help. Hot tears burn there and eventually spill out across my cheeks.

"Here." Megan hands me a box of tissues. I take a

handful and blow my nose. I shouldn't be crying now. It's too late for crying. Besides, I *don't* cry. It never did me any good, so I gave it up. Or I thought I had. I've cried more in the last few months than I have since I was three.

"What do you mean you lost them?" Megan asks when I've controlled myself as much as I can right now. "Did they... Did they die?"

I shake my head. "No. They're alive. They're living with a foster family. They're happy there. Those people can give them everything they need." I feel like I'm saying these words more to convince myself than anything. They're all true. Yet everything still feels so wrong.

"Okay?" Megan looks curiously at me. "That sounds good. Isn't it?"

I bite my lip. "It is good," I admit. "It's just not what I planned. And now I don't know what to do."

"And what had you planned?" Megan pushes the tissues back toward me. I hadn't realized I was crying again. Or still crying. I'm not sure I ever stopped.

I tell her everything. About dropping out of school to work so I could afford to move us out of Mom's apartment. About Mom and her drunken rages. About my own anger and how it led to us running away. About the lake house. About Jude—although I leave out the part about sleeping with her. About the police and ending up in Carlisle. About the months I've spent badgering social workers in an attempt to find my brothers. And finally, about tonight, about seeing them again, about realizing they're far better off with people like the Bankses than with me.

When I'm done, I'm drained. I'm no longer a guy, only a husk. An empty shell of the person I've been up until now. I feel like I could blow away in the faintest of breezes, crumble at the lightest touch. I curl up in the corner of Megan's couch as if I'm trying to disappear into it.

"That's quite a story," Megan says, handing me a fresh cup of tea. "You really love those kids, don't you?"

I nod, accepting the cup but unable to meet her eye. I feel naked and exposed even though I'm fully clothed. "They're all I have," I say finally. "I'm all they have. I promised I'd take care of them."

Megan is calm as she raises her mug to her lips and takes a long, thoughtful sip. "It sounds to me like they are taken care of. You said yourself they're happy with the foster family."

"But they're not with me," I say. "We've always been together. They're supposed to be with me."

"You're not their father, Blue," Megan says. "They're not supposed to be your responsibility. You're supposed to grow up and move out and build a life of your own. That's what kids do. It doesn't mean you can't stay close to your family if it's what you want, but it's not your job to take care of them."

"But I promised…"

"Maybe you did. It's still not your job." Megan's eyes drill into me, making me feel even more exposed than before. It's like she can read my most innermost thoughts through my skin. I fight to piece myself back together. I hate feeling this way, like my guts are hanging out for her to study, like my sins are painted across my flesh.

"So, what is my job?" I ask. She seems to have all the answers. Maybe she can help me figure out what I'm supposed to do from here.

Megan moves a little closer and touches me for the first time since my tears started falling, her hand closing around mine. "Your job is looking after yourself.

You've been living for your brothers, Blue. It's time you started living for you."

She gets up and gathers up the empty mugs and the wadded-up tissues littering the table. I should help, but I'm so exhausted I can't force myself to move. My muscles have resigned their responsibilities. I don't even stir when Megan drapes a blanket over me and slides my boots from my feet.

"Thank you," I whisper as she tiptoes from the room, leaving a single lamp burning in the corner but turning off the rest.

****

I wake to the scent of coffee brewing. Digging salty sleep from my eyes, I sit up, disorientated for a moment before I remember I'm on Megan's couch. Then I remember everything and it's all I can do to keep from collapsing back into the blanket. My stomach hollows again and I fight against the lump swelling in my throat. What a fucking crybaby I turned out to be.

"Morning," Megan says, appearing in front of me with a steaming cup of coffee, her hair wrapped in a soft-looking yellow towel. "You take it black, right?"

I nod, accepting the cup. I've always drunk it black, probably because that's how Mom does. Plus, it's easier. Especially when you never know how old the milk in the fridge might be.

"Thanks," I say, running my fingers through my hair and wincing at how greasy and tangled it feels. "For everything. I appreciate you letting me stay here last night. And for listening to me like that."

Megan shrugs. "It was nothing. You give any thought to what you're going to do now?"

I glance at my watch. It's after six-thirty. I need to be at the depot by seven-thirty to get my assignments for the day. And the depot is across town. "I gotta go to work now if I'm going to make it on time."

"I'll give you a ride," she says. "I have to go pick up my car from the bar anyway."

"You don't have to do that," I say, kicking off the blanket covering me and pulling on my boots. "You're practically at work once you pick up your car. I have to go to the other side of town."

"We'd better get going," she says. "Bathroom's down the hall. The green towel's yours."

She disappears through a doorway to the side of the room, and a moment later, a hair-dryer starts up. I get up, gulping coffee as I search out the bathroom. I splash cold water on my face, trying to wake myself up. I'd love to take a shower, but I don't have time for that, so I reach under my clothes and scrub at my underarms with some soap. Hopefully it will be enough to keep the rest of the guys in the truck from complaining.

Back in the other room, I put my jacket on and look around to make sure I haven't left anything behind. But I didn't have anything with me except the wallet and phone in my pockets.

"Ready?" Megan emerges from her bedroom in her skinny jeans and a crimson sweater which clings to every curve. Her hair is loose around her shoulders and her lips are the same color as the sweater. I can't believe she managed to make herself look this good in the time it took me to piss and give myself a sponge bath.

"Sure." I walk toward the front door and open it, letting her, still shrugging into her coat, exit ahead of me.

It's still mostly dark outside, the sunrise little more than a faint glow on the horizon. We walk in silence through the parking lot and back up to the street. The stores and cafes we passed last night are still shuttered apart from one on the corner which blazes with light, the door wide open to let out the delicious scents of coffee and baking bread. My stomach growls. I hope I get to work early enough to grab a donut or something before we head out to our first job. It's going to be a long morning otherwise.

"Are you going to be in trouble for staying out last night?" Megan asks as we leave the cluster of boutiques and cafes and head back toward the bar.

I shrug. "Probably. I'll call later and let them know I'm not dead in a gutter or in jail or something."

"Do you want me to call them?" Megan looks up at me. "I can explain…"

I shake my head. Nothing they do to me is going to hurt me. And it's not like they're going to kick me out for being late once. One of the guys in my room misses curfew at least once or twice a week and he's still there. "It's fine," I say. "I'll probably have to do extra kitchen chores or something. I don't care."

"Well, if you're sure…"

"I am," I assure her.

We reach the car and she makes me get in. "If I get to work now, I'll be stupidly early," she says. "And who wants to work more hours than they have to? Let me drive you to work."

I don't tell her I want to work as many hours as are available, always. Working helps keep my mind off all the things I can't fix. "Are you sure?"

"I'm sure," she says firmly. "I want to talk to you some more, anyway. In case you vanish again after this."

"You know where I live," I tell her. "Kind of hard to vanish."

She doesn't respond to that, just gets into the car and waits for me to join her.

"So," she says once we're on our way, driving past the street the warehouse is on and heading toward the center of the city. "Where do you work now?"

"I move furniture," I say. "The depot's in one of those old warehouses by the wharf. Opposite the stadium."

She nods. "I know it. And I guess that explains why you're looking so buff too."

My face heats up. She noticed? It didn't occur to me it was obvious with my clothes on. "I guess. Even more heavy lifting than at the warehouse."

She sighs. "I can't say it doesn't suit you, but don't you want something more, Blue? What happens when you get an injury or something? What are you going to do then? Or when you get too old to lift sofas?"

She sounds like Jude and that surprises me. I can't think of any two women who are more different. "I guess I'll find something else," I say.

We pull up at a light and Megan turns to look at me, an expression on her face that's way too serious for this early hour. The sun's rising now and the light shining across her is a riot of pink, yellow, and gold. It makes her look like she's glowing. "But what do you want, Blue? Surely there's something? What are your dreams?"

I stopped wanting things when I was about six, knowing that dreaming, wanting, was an exercise in disappointment. It didn't matter what I wanted. No one cared. So it was easier to not want things, to be grateful for anything that came my way that didn't hurt or make my life worse in some way.

"I don't know," I say as the car starts moving again. "I've never really had the chance to think about it."

She looks fierce as she changes gears, shoving the stick harder than is strictly necessary. "Well, you need to think about it now, Blue. You're seventeen. You have a whole life ahead of you, but if you fuck things up now, it's going to be a pretty shitty life."

I've never heard her swear before and it surprises

me. So do her words, to be honest. "You work in a warehouse, Megan," I say. "Is that what you want? Is it the best you can do?"

"It's a job," she says. "And it's temporary. You know what I want to do. I told you that the first night we were in the bar. The warehouse is a way to support myself while I figure out how to live my dream. Besides, I'm not the one doing grunt work for minimum wage. I have a degree, Blue. I'm not just Mr. Carter's ditzy assistant. I do the accounts for the entire business as well as being the receptionist and PA. I have choices. Right now, you don't."

I glance over at her. She looks so earnest. I didn't know she does the accounts. I didn't know she has a degree. It never occurred to me you'd need one to work in a place like that. The thought depresses me. She's spent all those years in school, and this is the best she can do? What hope is there for me?

"How's the singing going?" I ask finally, wanting to change the subject, to get the conversation away from me and my shitty life choices.

She throws me a look that tells me she recognizes what I'm doing. I don't care if she does. I want her to quit asking questions I can't answer.

"It's going okay," she says. "I'm auditioning to sing with a band this weekend. They're pretty good. You want to hear?"

"Sure." I lean back in the seat and watch as she flips the stereo on, filling the car with a blaze of electric guitars. She reaches out to turn the volume down, but I stop her, turning it up even louder so there's no chance of any more conversation.

KATE LARKINDALE

Chapter Thirty-Nine

Back at Carlisle, I lie on my bunk, staring up at the ceiling. What do I want? That's what Megan asked me. That's what I couldn't answer. I've spent all day with those words circling my head as I lifted wardrobes and dressers and shifted refrigerators and other appliances.

I wasn't lying when I said I'd never thought about it. I've never had the luxury. Until now, my life has been an exercise in survival. All that's mattered was keeping myself and my brothers alive. If I could provide them with a little happiness or joy, all the better. There hasn't been any room for wanting things for myself in there.

Now there is and I don't know how to think that way. I don't know how to want things.

But deep down, I'm lying. Maybe I never admitted it to myself, but I suppose I've always wanted things. I just never let myself think about it too much. Now that I'm allowing myself, I realize there are millions of things I want. More than I know how to deal with. Or how to get.

I should go to sleep. It was a grueling day at work and I'm on again tomorrow too. Saturdays are always busy; people like to move house over the weekend. Plus, I was up way too late last night with Megan.

But my head is too busy for sleep. I'm too wired. There's something I need to do.

I pull out my phone and select the number Mrs. Banks gave me last night, punching it before I have a chance to change my mind.

"Hello?"

"Hi, it's Blue," I say and for once I'm grateful my

name is so distinctive I don't need to say anything more for her to know who I am. "I wanted to call to say thanks for last night. It was a lovely meal, and it was so nice to meet you and your husband."

There's a pause. She gives a nervous laugh. "Blue. How funny. I was just thinking I should call you."

"You were? Why? What's wrong?" My heart speeds up. Has something happened to Sage? To Wiley?

She laughs again, but this time it's real. "Nothing's wrong, Blue. I only wanted to say how nice it was to meet you last night. It meant so much to the boys. Wiley's been talking about nothing else since."

I bet. He's been reminded and now he's probably driving Mrs. Banks crazy talking about me. She probably wishes she never let me visit at all.

"I'm sorry," I say.

She laughs again. "You have nothing to be sorry about. I'm the one who's sorry. I should have recognized how much they missed you. They're so much happier today, having seen you."

I'm unsure what to say to this. My throat aches, but not with panic this time. "I'm glad I saw them too," I manage.

"Gabe and I talked about it," she goes on. "And we believe it's important you remain a part of their lives. We didn't appreciate how close you all are until we saw you together last night. Sage tried to tell us, but..."

"What does that mean?" I ask. I can't quite believe what I'm hearing. It's so different to the feeling I got from them when I left their house last night. So different to the feeling I got when Sage called.

"I'm not exactly sure," she says. "But we'll figure it out. You're welcome to visit whenever you like, Blue."

"Thank you," I say. "Thank you, so much."

"So, would you want to come for dinner on

Sunday?"

"Yeah. I'd like that a lot."

****

I have to wait until my next weekday off, Wednesday, to do the other thing I need to do.

I take an unfamiliar bus out to the suburbs, peering out the window anxiously so I don't miss the stop I need to get off at. There. Glover Place. I buzz the driver and climb out of my seat, heading to the door. The bus slows and I step onto the sidewalk outside a small cluster of stores—a dry cleaner, a drugstore, and a Chinese restaurant that looks like it might not have been open for a while. I take note of these landmarks so I know where to come later, when I need to head back into the city.

It takes only a few minutes for me to walk back to Glover Place. It's a fine day and I tilt my face up to the sun as I turn down the narrower street lined with neat little houses. Each is set back from the road a little, with driveways and patches of mown lawn at the front. At first, I think all the houses are the same, but I start noticing the little differences. That one has a bay window in the front, the one across the street has a garage, this one has added a second story and a verandah encircles the entire thing.

I walk for about five minutes before I find the house I'm looking for, number 58. It's painted pale green with darker green trim. Window-boxes sit below each of the sills in the front and a riot of colored flowers spill from them. A familiar blue car sits in the driveway.

I take a deep breath, wipe my hands on my jeans, and head for the front door.

There's a bell, but I knock instead.

"Coming," says someone from inside.

A moment later, I hear footsteps hurrying toward the door. It swings open and Jude stands there, her hair in a messy knot on top of her head.

"Blue?" A confused look crosses her face. "What are you doing here?"

"I need to talk to you."

She hesitates a moment and I wonder if I've made a huge mistake in coming here. Maybe I should have called first. The last thing I want to do is get her in more trouble. I already feel responsible for her losing her job. Partly, anyway.

"Well, okay…" She moves aside and opens the door wider, gesturing for me to come in. "I'm cleaning, so the house is a pigsty. I wasn't expecting guests."

I look at her. After everything, does she really think a messy house is going to bother me?

"However did you find me?" she asks as she leads me down a short hallway to the kitchen. A sliding door opens off it to a deck and the backyard beyond.

"There's this thing called the phone book."

"Didn't think anyone under the age of about forty even knew what one was." She gives a little laugh. "What can I do for you, Blue?"

"I'm hoping you can help me."

She moves toward a small table sitting in a puddle of sunshine by the sliding doors and gestures for me to sit.

I do, first moving a small pile of books from the chair.

"Dump those on the counter," Jude says. "I'm trying to declutter and those need to go to the second-hand store."

I do as she says, adding the books to a pile of tattered magazines already on the counter. I can't help noticing they're children's books. Some of the same ones I saw on the shelves in Wiley's new bedroom. Guess the rooms she's cleaning are her kids'.

"I guess the fact you're here at eleven AM on a Wednesday means you're not back in school."

I shake my head. I have thought about it, but I can't imagine being back at Milton High again. And I like working. I like having my own money. "No. But I'm hoping you can help me."

She frowns, clearly disappointed, but I'm pretty sure she understands. I'm not the same kid who dropped out in November. I'm not the same kid she fucked at the lake even. I'm not sure I'm even a kid anymore, despite what the social workers seem to believe.

I drop down into the chair across from her, pushing it to one side so I can stretch out my legs. "I want to go to college," I say. "I know there are tests and things I can do to graduate without having to go back to school. I was hoping you'd be able to help me with that."

She nods slowly, studying me. "What are you thinking about studying in college?"

My face heats up. I'm a seventeen-year-old dropout. Talking about going to college feels preposterous enough without specifying what I want to do there. "Architecture?" I say. It's not meant to be a question, but it comes out that way. "Maybe?"

She smiles. "You'd make an excellent architect. You're observant and you pay attention to details. Not to mention you're sensitive to everything around you."

"Thanks, Mrs. A." I duck my head to hide the blush I'm certain is staining my cheeks. She knows way too much about me. But somehow, I don't mind.

"You look a lot happier than you did the last time I saw you," she says.

I nod. "I am. I got to see my brothers. If you had anything to do with…"

"I didn't," she says. "But I'm glad you saw them. Are they all right?"

I nod again. "Yeah. They're with good people. They're happy."

And so am I, now that I know I can see them whenever I want to, that they can call me whenever they want without being afraid their foster parents will find out and be angry. I'm invited for dinner every Sunday and for now, it feels like enough. It's not what I imagined for us, but it's okay. Maybe I didn't have a big enough imagination.

"I'm so pleased." She does look pleased. She's smiling and it's a real smile, not a fake one pasted on over her sadness.

"How about you?" I ask. "Are you doing okay?"

"I am," she says, sounding almost surprised by it. "I actually am."

"Good." I say. "So, you can help me with the tests?"

"Yes. I'll find out what you need to do. You might need a tutor…"

I grin. "Are you volunteering?"

She shrugs and picks up an apple from the fruit bowl in the center of the table. "Depends what subjects you need help with. We'll see. I'm not a teacher anymore, remember."

"I know…" But I also know she'll always be a teacher. She may not be getting paid for it, or heading to a school building every morning, but she's still a teacher.

"Give me your phone number," she says. "I'll call you once I've found out the details."

I scribble my number on the notepad she pushes in my direction. "Can I help you with anything?"

She starts to shake her head, then stops. "You move furniture for a living, right?"

I nod, a grin already spreading across my face. "It's my day off today."

"Not anymore." She returns my grin as she gets up from her chair.

"It's the least I can do," I say, following her down the hallway.

KATE LARKINDALE

Epilogue

Smoke from the barbecue drifts skyward, the scent of grilled meat filling the air. It's still hot, but as the sun falls lower in the sky a faint chill touches the air. Wiley, bouncing on the trampoline in nothing but the bathing suit he put on to go swimming this afternoon, doesn't seem to notice.

"School again tomorrow," Sage groans, throwing himself down onto the bench next to me. He smells of barbecue smoke, sunscreen, and chlorine from the pool. "How can summer be over already?"

I shrug, smiling. At home, we always looked forward to school going back after summer vacation. School got us out of the house and away from Mom. Summers were always tough for us, finding places to go and be so we weren't constantly in her line of sight. There's only so much time you can spend at the park and the library.

"You looking forward to college?" Sage elbows me to get my attention.

"It's not exactly college..." Jude helped me get my high-school equivalency and got me enrolled in some classes at an adult education center. It's not college, but the classes give me credits toward a degree and at the end of the year, or the semester, I can transfer to a real college if I want to. It felt like a good first step, rather than plunging right into a full course load, and it means I can still work part-time. I'm still seventeen for another couple of months, so it's not like I'm going to be a whole lot older than anyone else when I actually make it to college. Especially since a lot of kids take a year out after high school to figure out what they want to do.

"School then," Sage says, rolling his eyes. "Are you looking forward to it?"

I think about it for a moment. "Yeah," I say finally. "But I'm kind of nervous too." Just getting the high school equivalency was hard enough. College is going to be challenging, but I'm up for the challenge.

"You'll be great," Sage says and I hope he's right. It would suck to have done all that work only to flunk out after a single semester. "Where's Megan?"

"London, I think. Or maybe Paris." I try to remember the dates of the European tour her band is doing. They're on a poster above my bed at Carlisle. I know she's done Prague and Warsaw, and she called me from Berlin last week. Sounds like she's having a ball, despite the small venues they're playing not filling up every night. She's living her dream.

"We're going to Paris at spring break," Sage says. "Melissa and Gabe want us to practice our French."

"That'll be fun," I say, choking down the peppery taste of jealousy that spills across my tongue. I'm not sure I'll ever get used to Wiley and Sage having so much more than me. Experiences, opportunities, stuff. I'm happy for them of course, but that doesn't stop me from envying them every now and then.

"Wiley's more excited about getting to go on a plane," Sage says with a laugh and a fond glance at Wiley on the trampoline.

I look that way too, watching as Wiley bounces and flips, seemingly tireless on that thing. All the caution which used to be so much a part of him is gone. He moves easily, his movements sure and confident now instead of quick and cringing. I sigh and look back at Sage who has his face turned up to the late afternoon sun, his eyes closed. He looks relaxed and happy. Comfortable.

"Sage?"

He turns back to me and opens his eyes. "Yeah?"

I hesitate a moment before I speak. "My social worker called me yesterday. Mom wants to see us."

Sage's posture changes. He sits up, leaning toward me, every muscle suddenly thrumming with tension. "What did you say?"

"I said I needed to talk to you." I hate the fear that has reappeared in Sage's eyes, the way he seems to have curled back in on himself, suddenly smaller than he seemed a minute ago.

"Do we have to?" He glances back toward Wiley who still bounces happily, blissfully unaware of what we're talking about over here.

"No," I say. "But she is our mom. She's been in rehab and clean for almost six months. At least, that's what they told me."

Sage snorts. I admit, I had a similar reaction. Mom's tried to quit before. It never lasted though. It only ever took one disappointment, one piece of bad news, and she'd be on another bender. If we refuse to see her, I wonder how long it will be before it's the excuse to hit the booze again.

"Are you going to see her?" Sage looks at me, his eyes wide and unbelieving.

I shrug. "I haven't decided. I wanted to talk to you first. She wants to see all of us."

Sage slumps in his seat, a horrible resignation splashed across his features again. "Can she make us come back?"

I look away from him, unable to look at that expression. Guilt slices through me. I made him look like this. "I don't think so," I say. "Not now, anyway. She'll need to prove she can stay straight and hold down a job that pays enough to support us before she can make any move to get us out of the system. And the fact she used to hit us isn't going to do her any favors."

He nods slowly, staring over at Wiley on the trampoline again. Melissa has come outside and is talking to him through the net surrounding the bouncy surface. Probably negotiating with him to put some clothes on to eat dinner. He unzips the net and climbs down, taking Melissa's hand and letting her lead him into the house.

"He ever talk about her?" I ask, turning back to Sage.

He starts. "Huh?"

"Wiley," I say. "Does he ever talk about Mom?"

Sage sighs and tugs at that tuft of hair he always goes for when he's anxious or thinking hard about something. "No."

I raise my eyebrows. "Not at all?"

He shakes his head, still toying with his hair. "I don't think so. Not to me, anyway."

I wonder if Wiley's young enough to forget all about her. I remember a lot about being eight, but maybe I've hung onto it because I wanted to remember. If I'd wanted to forget, would I have been able to?

"Do you think he could handle seeing her?" I reach up and pull Sage's hand away from his hair.

"You're asking me?" He doesn't look at me.

"You're with him more than I am. You know him better."

Now he looks at me, his expression pained. "That's… That's not right."

I shrug. It's the way it is. Sage lives with Wiley and sees him every day. I see the two of them once a week, at most. I'm not part of their day-to-day existence anymore. So I don't know them the way I used to. Especially Wiley who has changed so much more than Sage has. "Right or not, it's the truth."

Sage looks like he might cry. He turns his head and when he speaks, it's so quiet I can barely catch the words. "I don't know if *I* can handle seeing her."

"Okay." I nod. "You don't have to. Nobody's going to force you to."

"But you're going to?"

I bite my lip. Andrea's call took me by surprise. Mom wanting to see us wasn't something that had ever crossed my mind. I was more concerned about running into her on the street than her ever asking to see us. It hadn't occurred to me she'd want to. She'd spent so many years blaming the three of us for everything she saw as wrong in her life, I'd thought she'd be glad to have finally gotten rid of us.

"Are you?" Sage elbows me.

"I don't know yet. I need to think about it some more." I'm not sure how I feel about seeing her. A part of me is still angry with her for not being a better mother to us, for hurting us for so many years. But another part of me remembers what she was like before the drugs and alcohol got their hooks in her. That's the mom I want. If she really has cleaned herself up, maybe she can get back to that person. The one who used to read to Sage and me, sing to us, take us places.

"If you do..." Sage taps my arm to get my attention this time. "Will you let me know how she is?"

I smile at him and sling my arm across his shoulders, drawing him in against me. "Of course I will, silly."

Wiley runs out of the house, clothed now, his hair combed. "Dinner's ready," he says. "We're eating on the deck."

I give Sage a final squeeze and let him go as I stand up. "We'd better go," I say, scooping Wiley up and tossing him over my shoulder. "Wouldn't want to miss out on those barbecued burgers, would we?"

He giggles, drumming on my shoulder blades with his soft, little fists. "I like hot dogs better."

****

Andrea and I walk through the gates of the park and follow the main path to the duck pond. It's a warm, sunny Sunday afternoon and the park is full of people. Kids run around the fountain, squealing as they spray themselves and each other by putting their fingers over the mouths of the frogs which spew endless streams of water into the pool. People have blankets spread out on the grassy areas between the beds of flowers and lie there, reading, eating, chattering, or just staring up at the clear blue sky.

"This is a supervised visit," Andrea says as we near the open-air theater where she's arranged for Mom and I to meet. "So I'll be there the whole time. I can observe from a distance, if that's what you want, or I can be with you the whole time. It's up to you."

I nod. I can't focus on her words. My stomach is tangled up in knots and the parts that aren't knotted are churning around faster than a washing machine. I take a deep breath and try to keep from puking up my breakfast. In a few minutes, I'm going to see my mother for the first time since she attacked me at the supermarket in November.

I wipe my hands on my jeans. I wish Sage was here. I get why he didn't want to, but I'd be much more confident if he were here with me.

No. I'm lying to myself. I wouldn't *be* more confident, I'd pretend to be so he wouldn't see how scared I really am. Without him or Wiley to protect, I'm on my own with my emotions.

"Blue?" Andrea taps my arm. "Do you want me to stay with you?"

We're at the theater already. The broad lawn is crowded with people despite the fact the stage is bare and stripped for the season. I search the crowd for Mom. Will she have come alone? Will she have come at all? It's a valid question. Mom has never been great at keeping appointments.

Then I see her.

She's sitting at one of the picnic tables lining one side of the grassy area. She hasn't seen Andrea and me yet, so I take a moment to study her.

Her hair is shorter than I remember it ever being, just brushing her shoulders. She wears oversized sunglasses and her trademark red lipstick. Her sweater is red too, an old one I remember her wearing back when Wiley was a baby. Her jeans are new, though, not skin-tight, but loose and comfortable-looking. She doesn't look like Tabby Lannigan the singer; she looks like a mom.

"I'll be okay," I tell Andrea as I wipe my palms on my jeans for what feels like the tenth time. "You can watch from a distance."

She nods. "Okay. I'll be over there." She gestures at the low bank facing the stage. "If you need me, wave. And if she does anything inappropriate, I'll be right over."

"Thanks." I barely glance at her before I'm heading across the lawn, my feet moving quickly as I walk toward my mother.

"Blue!" She sees me coming and leaps to her feet. She runs toward me and I freeze in my tracks.

"Oh, Blue," she says when she nears me. "I've missed you, baby."

She reaches for me as if she's about to touch me and I flinch away, taking a step backward. "Hi, Mom."

She drops her hand and stops moving closer,

317

keeping a good foot or two between us. I wonder if she was told to do that and forgot in her excitement at seeing me again.

"You look good, Blue," she says after a moment. "They treating you okay?"

I can't speak. My throat is thick and I feel like I've swallowed a grapefruit or something. So I nod.

"And your brothers?" She looks around as if they might be here, hanging back the way they always used to, letting me test the waters before moving cautiously closer to her orbit.

"They're fine," I say, the words hoarse as I force them past the obstacle lodged in my throat. "They're with good people who care about them."

She keeps searching the crowd before finally turning back to me. "But they're not here with you?"

I shake my head, hating that the gesture feels apologetic. I don't owe her any apologies and neither do Sage or Wiley. If anything, she should be apologizing to us.

"We should sit down," she says, gesturing at the table she got up from when she saw me. "I brought a picnic."

My eyebrows raise as I trail her toward the table. Mom made a picnic? My mom?

"There's too much food," she says as I slide onto the bench across the table from her. I feel safer with this sturdy wooden barrier between us. "I thought you would all be here, so I brought enough for four."

She unpacks paper bags and Tupperware containers, spreading the table with bread, cheese, salad, and meat. It looks good, but my stomach still churns so much I'll never manage to keep anything down.

"Go on," she says finally. "Eat."

I take a slice of bread and nibble on the crust,

more for something to do with my hands than anything else. I can't think of anything to say to her. This woman with her plastic containers of ham and potato salad isn't my mom. I don't know who this is.

"So, how's school?" Mom asks, layering a piece of bread with lettuce, tomato, ham, and cheese.

"I work," I tell her. "I quit school." I'm not going into the whole college thing with her. That's something I did for myself.

She frowns. "Why'd you do a stupid thing like that? School's important, Blue."

"I know it's important. But back in November when I quit, getting Sage and Wiley away from you was more important."

Her head snaps up and for a brief second, I catch a glimpse of the familiar fury in her eyes. Her features harden, become the ones I recognize again. Then it's gone and she appears to crumple. She sets down her sandwich and rests her forehead in her hand.

"Was it that bad?" she asks. "Was *I* that bad?"

The lump swells in my throat again and I swallow hard to dislodge it. "Yeah, Mom. It was."

She looks up, studying my face for a moment. Her eyes linger in certain places and I realize she's searching out the scars she gave me. The thick one above my left eye, a finer one tracing a jagged line beneath my cheekbone; the crescent-shaped one curling under my chin and the one which slices through my upper lip. They're not obvious anymore, but they're there if you know where to look.

"I guess it was," she says quietly.

I nod. I like that she isn't trying to apologize for it. Nothing she can say now is going to change the past. Nothing she does now is going to make up for all those years of pain and terror.

"I'm doing better now," she says finally, picking up her sandwich again. "I've been through rehab, I'm seeing a therapist, and I'm working."

My eyebrows shoot up again. "Yeah? Where are you working?" A strip joint again? Or is she back bagging groceries?

"As a receptionist," she says, a note of pride in her voice. "I've been there three months."

I guess she really has turned things around. Or she wants me to believe she has. "Good for you."

"Where do you work, Blue?"

"I move furniture."

"And you like the place you're living?" She sounds so hopeful when she asks that.

I shrug. "It's okay. I'm only there another month or so. Then I turn eighteen."

"And after that?"

I shrug again. I haven't decided yet. Carlisle has a program for kids who age out of the system and I could get a room in one of their houses if I wanted one. And Megan's asked if I want to move in with her. As friends. We haven't defined our relationship, and with her being away so much, it seems unlikely we'll be anything other than friends. Especially if I do decide to go to college next semester. But it's okay. I need some friends.

"You can come home," Mom says. "You're always welcome. So are your brothers. Will you tell them?"

I shake my head. "I know it's hard, Mom, but you have to trust me. They're better off where they are. It took me a while to accept it too, but they really are. You need to leave them alone."

Tears fill her eyes and she nods. "I guess I was just hoping… What about you? Have I lost you too?"

I bite my lip. I don't know how to answer her. She

lost me a long time ago. The first time she hit Sage instead of me. Yet I'm here today and that has to mean something. What, I'm not sure. It could be curiosity, or maybe I want some closure, a neat little ending to the first chapters of my life.

Or maybe I miss my mom.

I stand up and untangle myself from the bench. I round the table so I'm standing over her. She's so small. It's hard for me to believe I was once so scared of her I'd lock myself in my room rather than face her.

She stands too, keeping space between us, but holding onto me with those eyes that so perfectly match my own.

I can't think of anything to say, so I bend and give her a quick kiss on the cheek, breathing in her scent, unrecognizable untainted by tobacco or alcohol.

"Bye, Mom," I say quietly. "It was good to see you."

She reaches up and cups her hand around the back of my neck. A shock of recognition pulses through me. She's always done that; the sensation as warm and familiar as a hug.

"It was," she says and pulls away, dropping her hand to start repacking her barely-touched picnic.

I walk away, slowly at first, expecting, I think, she'll call me back or run after me. When she doesn't, I speed up, barging through the crowd like a runaway train. Tears burn behind my eyes, but I fight them. I'm not going to cry. Not again. Not now.

For the first time, I realize I'm proud of myself. I promised to keep my brothers safe and I kept that promise. It doesn't matter that reality doesn't fit the neat little picture I had in my head. It doesn't matter that I couldn't do it all on my own the way I wanted. Asking for help doesn't make me weak and accepting it doesn't take anything away from me.

I slow my steps so I don't feel like I'm running from the past. I push my shoulders back and lift my head as I stride out of the park and toward my future.

The End

Evernight Teen ®

www.evernightteen.com